A STUDENT'S COMPANION FOR
Successful College Writing

A STUDENT'S COMPANION FOR
Successful College Writing

Carolyn Lengel

Rubrics by Andrew B. Preslar
Lamar State College—Orange

bedford/st.martin's
Macmillan Learning
Boston | New York

Copyright © 2018 by Bedford/St. Martin's

For information, write: Bedford/St. Martin's, 75 Arlington Street, Boston, MA 02116   (617-399-4000)

ISBN 978-1-319-13029-9

PREFACE

A Student's Companion for Successful College Writing reinforces the most foundational elements in academic writing. While recognizing and respecting students' abilities, this supplement breaks down the steps necessary to excel in college writing, build confidence, tackle time management, and write ethically; it provides additional activities to help students draft, revise, and edit successful college-level essays; and it provides sentence guides for academic writing, editing practice, and writing self-assessments to help students take control of their learning. This companion, meant to supplement the coverage in *Successful College Writing*, gives students the additional support they need to get or stay on level in the composition classroom. It is an ideal solution for accelerated learning programs or co-requisite courses, while the deep integration with *Successful College Writing* makes it an ideal resource for any instructor who wants students to build a strong foundation in academic writing.

Part 1: Succeeding in College

Part 1 addresses topics that are critical to student success: confidence building, time management, and ethical and responsible writing. This coverage can be a useful way to begin the term, or act as a handy reference for students outside of class.

Part 2: Writing Activities

Part 2 begins with an overview of the nine patterns of development covered in *Successful College Writing*:

- Narration
- Description
- Illustration
- Process analysis
- Comparison and contrast
- Classification and division
- Definition
- Cause and effect
- Argument

Chapter 4 offers activities students can use to craft paragraphs in each of these modes, so they can get a sense of how each pattern works.

Since students learn best by doing, subsequent chapters in Part 2 offer step-by-step activities, with loads of sentence guides. Each of these activities is designed to help students devise a topic, assess their audience, craft a thesis, develop their ideas fully, and revise and edit their drafts. Also included in each of these chapters is a rubric that instructors and students can use to make the expectations of college writing clear for assignments in each of these modes. The activities and rubrics in Part 2 effectively supplement the Guided Writing Assignments in Parts 3 and 4 of *Successful College Writing* and can be used in a workshop-oriented class or be assigned as homework to encourage students to think, write, and revise critically and deeply.

Part 3: Additional Tools and Practice

Part 3 begins with sentence guides that help budding academic writers learn to present information and ideas to others, present their own views, and then put the pieces together to write an effective academic essay. Students who need additional help can also get practice with editing sentences and paragraphs, reviewing the parts of speech, writing correct sentences, managing punctuation, mechanics, and spelling, and more.

LaunchPad

A Student's Companion for Successful College Writing can be used in conjunction with LaunchPad for *Successful College Writing* to provide a complete writing course (an interactive e-Book, auto-graded reading comprehension quizzes and summary activities with a sample summary as feedback, and LearningCurve, Bedford/St. Martin's adaptive quizzing program). To order *A Student's Companion for Successful College Writing* with the textbook and LaunchPad, use one of these ISBNs:

- *Successful College Writing*, Seventh Edition (with handbook) + LaunchPad + *A Student's Companion*: 978-1-319-16734-9
- *Successful College Writing*, Brief Seventh Edition (without handbook) + LaunchPad + *A Student's Companion*: 978-1-319-16738-7

Acknowledgments

I extend my gratitude to the instructors who took the time to review the plan for this text: Matthew Holrah, University of Central Oklahoma; Dorothy (Dottie) Miller, Harford College; Kimberly Murphy, Montgomery College; Andrew Preslar, Lamar State College; Melissa Reddish, Wor-Wic Community College; Mary Seel, Broome Community College; and Nicole Williams, Bridgewater State University. I especially thank Andrew Preslar, Lamar State College, for his terrific work on the assessment rubrics included in Part 2.

Carolyn Lengel

CONTENTS

*Supplements the Guided Writing Assignments in Parts 3 and 4 of *Successful College Writing*, Seventh Edition, by Kathleen T. McWhorter

A STUDENT'S COMPANION FOR

Successful College Writing

Succeeding in College

Building Your Confidence

Confidence can help drive and shape your experiences as a student, performer, athlete, employee, parent, and the many other roles you play in your life. True confidence is often defined as having a positive and realistic belief about yourself and your talents and traits. *Assertive, optimistic, eager, proud, independent, trustworthy,* and *mature* are some of the many terms associated with someone who has true confidence. Conversely, a lack of confidence can result in a poor performance in those same roles.

Here are just a few reasons to develop confidence:

- **Confidence helps sell who you are.** Knowledge, skills, and experience are necessary and important. If you do not possess and project an air of confidence, others may not realize you have these qualities.

- **Confidence reassures others.** It can create trust in the people in your life, whether they are your peers, classmates, coworkers, or loved ones.

This guide explores the role that confidence plays in everyday success and offers strategies on building your confidence levels around all of the roles you play in your life.

Not Feeling Confident

Have you had any trouble maintaining your confidence since you started college? It may surprise you to learn that you are not the only first-year student who feels this way. Many students who enter college for the first time feel just like you do: not very certain of all that lies ahead and unsure how to deal with a number of challenges, both in and out of the classroom. Below are just a few steps you can take to help to develop more confidence:

- **Take a strengths inventory.** Make a list of what you're good at.

- **Set measurable, attainable goals.** Ask yourself what you want to accomplish in the next week, month, or year, and then break those goals up into smaller, short-term goals.

- **Take responsibility for your actions.** Make a consistent effort to learn from your experiences (the good and the bad) and own your choices.

- **Dare to take intellectual risks.** Question assumptions, and ask yourself if the things you believe to be true actually are.

- **Examine and acknowledge feelings.** When something bothers you, ask why.

- **Take charge and be persistent.** Remember, luck is 99% perseverance.

- **Assert yourself.** When you want something, you've got to ask.

- **Remember, you're not alone.** Identify individuals who exhibit confidence and make a strong effort to model the types of behavior that make the greatest impression on you.

- **Believe in yourself.**

Identifying Strengths and Setting Goals

Why not start building your confidence by reminding yourself what you are good at? You can start with this simple, yet effective, activity:

Make a list of what you believe are your strongest skills and qualities. Take the time to think deeply and honestly about this exercise before you start. Another way to do this is to ask yourself: "When I feel like I am at my best, what am I doing?" Continue performing those activities to create an increased sense of confidence.

Long-term goals vs. short-term goals: How do they differ? A crucial part of developing, building, and maintaining your confidence is to set long- and short-term goals that you can reach and that are able to meet your expectations. Think of long-term goals as the final product and short-term goals as the steps along the way. For example, if you were to write a ten-chapter novel, you'd have ten short-term goals (write a chapter) and one long-term goal (write a novel).

 THE CONFIDENCE CHECKLIST

Before examining a series of meaningful steps you can take to build confidence, let's start with the following confidence checklist. How would you respond to the following statements? Be as completely truthful and objective as you can be.

	Yes	No
I believe I know what is best for me.	❑	❑
I feel I am a genuine person.	❑	❑
I am extremely tolerant of others in my life.	❑	❑
I am consistent — I do as I say.	❑	❑
I avoid procrastinating.	❑	❑
I take an active role in classroom discussions.	❑	❑

	Yes	No
I have an inner voice that guides my decisions.	❏	❏
I maintain good eye contact and tone of voice when speaking.	❏	❏
I often doubt myself.	❏	❏
I am able to handle constructive criticism.	❏	❏
I have difficulty trusting others.	❏	❏
I prefer being alone than being with groups of people.	❏	❏
I would describe myself as an outgoing and assertive individual.	❏	❏
I feel I am capable of assessing my true capabilities.	❏	❏
I am an optimistic person by nature.	❏	❏

If you answered "no" to more than half of the statements, your level of confidence is likely not where you want it to be — and you're probably not alone! Keep reading for some proven strategies to boost your confidence.

Now it's your turn.

- Select one goal you would like to achieve in the next month. Be specific about what that goal is.
- Now identify two to three effective actions you will take to obtain this goal. Once again, be specific and include a time frame for performing these actions.
- Think of one possible barrier that might prevent you from reaching this goal.
- Now consider one action you will take to overcome this barrier. Be sure to detail what this action will be.
- Last, predict what you honestly believe will be your degree of success in eventually achieving this goal.

> **TIP**
>
> So how does setting goals help build confidence? Think about it this way: If you set up a series of short-term goals you know you can achieve, aren't you going to feel more confident each time you check off one of those goals? Even better, aren't you going to feel like a rock star by the time you achieve your ultimate long-term goal? There is nothing that builds more confidence than seeing hard work pay off.

Learning from Your Experiences and Choices

Wisdom can often be gained through both good and bad experiences, and through the outcomes of the choices we make. If you can accept that you are ultimately the one responsible — not others — for your actions, this is the first important step to practicing this philosophy while in college.

One strategy for maintaining this belief is to not play the blame game; for example, if you received a bad grade, be honest with yourself and ask what role you played in earning the grade. Admitting you are the one responsible for your actions and then responding (and learning) from that outcome will help strengthen your self-esteem and confidence.

Taking Risks

Has anyone ever said, "Nothing ventured, nothing gained" to you? To take a risk can be an unsettling challenge—you can't be sure it will be worth it, you may question whether you have the ability and the desire to attempt something, and you might think about the consequences of that risk if you are unsuccessful.

Now that's the negative approach. What if you turned this around and, instead, took a chance on something daunting? What if you decided that no matter what obstacles got in your way or what doubts crept into your mind, you would continue to pursue whatever you set out to accomplish? Imagine how you will feel when the results turn out to be positive ones.

Another way of thinking about this is "If you remain in your comfort zone you will not go any further." While taking a risk can seem difficult at first, it almost always pays off in the end—especially in the classroom.

Taking Risks in the Classroom

Your instructors have probably urged you to question rather than to simply accept everything you read or hear. If you follow this advice, you'll take risks in the classroom all the time—intellectual risks, otherwise known as critical thinking. You do this when you speak up in class, when you write an essay, and whenever you carefully rethink long-held beliefs.

Speaking Up in Class

The reward for intellectual risk-taking is that you come away with a better understanding of yourself and the world around you. But what if you are terrified of speaking up in class and of saying something dumb? What if you simply don't know where to start? Below are two case studies to help you start thinking about how to better approach intellectual risks.

Student A read the class material twice and completed all the assignments. She came to class prepared to take notes and was ready and willing to listen to what the instructor had to say on the topic being presented. As an adult student, she was used to participating in meetings at work, and she didn't feel nervous about speaking up, so she didn't think that she needed to prepare any additional material.

Student B also completed the assigned homework and believed he knew the material but also knew he would be reluctant to share his thoughts or respond to questions posed to the class. As a strategy, he wrote down several questions and responses to what he assumed would be a part of the class discussion. When he attended class, he referred to his questions and answers when those areas of discussion came up.

What were some strategies that each student employed that would help them take intellectual risks? Who do you think came to class better prepared? For each case study, what would you recommend the student do differently next time?

Exercise: Questions and Answers

What do you do to prepare for class discussions? Both Student A and Student B are good students. They read the material and did their assignments. Student B, however, uses higher-level thinking questions to help stimulate critical thinking. As you prepare for class, try to use the following generic question stems to ask questions about the material covered. Then take a few minutes to jot down your answers.

What would happen if _____?

What is the difference between _____ and _____?

What are the implications of _____?

Why is _____ important?

What is another way to look at _____?

Examining Emotions

Daniel Goleman, author and creator of the theory of emotional intelligence (EQ), stresses the vital role EQ plays in building self-confidence. One of his key components is Emotional Self-Management, or the ability to make sensible decisions even when your emotions tell you to do otherwise. For example, if you received a failing grade on a quiz, your first impulse might be to get angry. Even worse, you might consider dropping the class. A better strategy would be to take the time to examine why you earned the grade that you did and to allow yourself the time needed to learn how to succeed in the course. Examining your feelings and how you react to certain situations can keep you from giving up too early on something that is challenging.

Exercise: What Makes a Success?

Make a list of the qualities you see in people you think of as confident. Share the list with someone else in your class and discuss which of these qualities have to do with feelings and interactions with other people. How many of these qualities do you see in yourself?

Being Persistent

One of the simplest ways to gain confidence is to be persistent. *Persistence* simply means the ability to stick with something through completion, even if you don't always want to. If a task or challenge seems difficult at times and the outcome may be uncertain, persistence helps you keep at it. Let's look at an example:

Imagine that you are frustrated with the teaching style of one of your instructors. She presents the material in a way that doesn't work for you (but it seems to do so for your classmates). You can elect to drop the class early in the semester and perhaps have a different teacher next time, or you could take steps that will allow you to persist in the course, such as working with a tutor, forming a study group, or meeting with your professor for clarification. In the end, you will not have given up and your outcome could likely be a favorable one.

Ultimately, it is *your* responsibility to take charge of your success and persist — even if you have some setbacks at first. When you feel like you may be about to give up, remind yourself of your long-term goals and how persisting at the current task will help you attain those goals.

ASSERTIVENESS CHECK-UP

Answer the following questions as honestly as you can:

- Do you express your point of view even when it is not the same as others'?
- Will you actually say "no" to a request made by friends or coworkers that you feel is unreasonable?
- How easily do you accept constructive criticism?
- Are you willing to ask for help?
- Do you make decisions or judgments with confidence?
- How open are you to another person's suggestions or advice?
- When you state your thoughts or feelings, do you do so in a direct and sincere manner?
- Are you likely to cooperate with others to achieve a worthwhile goal?

Being Assertive

One of the best ways to build confidence is to let people know what you want and don't want, how you feel, and when you need help. The more skilled you are at letting people know these things, the more assertive you'll become. The more you *successfully* assert yourself, the more confident you'll become. So how do you become more assertive? Let's start by assessing where you are right now.

If you answered "yes" to less than half of the questions in the "Assertiveness Check-up" box above, the strategies below can help you feel more confident when you are attempting to be assertive.

- Use suitable facial expressions.
- Always maintain good eye contact.
- Watch your tone of voice. Your voice should be firm, audible, and pleasant.
- Be aware of your body language—how you stand, sit, and gesture.
- Actively listen to others so that you can accurately confirm what they have said.
- Ask reasoned questions when something is unclear to you.
- Take a win-win approach to solving problems: How can what you're asking for benefit both you and the person you're asking?

Developing a Network

When you create a supportive network of individuals, you are being interdependent, and this is a key to fostering self-confidence. By building mutually helpful relationships you are more likely to achieve your goals and dreams. Here are some strategies for developing this interdependence:

- Actively seek out your school's many resources. This will mean connecting with an academic advisor, signing up for a tutor if you need one, or getting involved with several on- or off-campus activities.

- Foster a valuable relationship with your instructors; ask for their assistance, feedback, and constructive criticism.
- Start a study group by looking for several classmates who are prepared, regularly attend classes, and take an active part in class discussions. Don't overlook a quiet student who may have true insight into the course; he or she can prove an asset. Approach those you've identified and suggest forming the group. If the answer is yes, decide on your group's mutual goals and the rules your group will follow.
- Coming to college can be a challenging and emotionally stressful experience; fortunately, your school offers counselors who can provide the understanding and skill to help you overcome your issues, so turning to one can be the right thing to do.

Getting Advice from Other Students

The Goal Setter: Liberal Arts Major at the Community College of Rhode Island

Having little idea what he wanted to do upon entering college, The Goal Setter elected to not declare a specific major; instead he chose general education courses to slowly get himself "into the student mindset." High school had been a struggle academically and personally, so a four-year school was not an immediate option. Previously, his only goal was to not leave school early, and now he realized he needed more structure. He connected with an advisor, and she suggested that he first take a self-assessment test and based on the results, come up with a set of both short-term and long-term goals. The advisor explained the value in doing such an exercise and cautioned that he not give up before achieving some or all of those goals. The Goal Setter heeded this advice, earned his associate's degree, and has since transferred to a four-year college, full of confidence that his next goal of a bachelor's diploma will be realized.

The Networker: Marketing Major at Bryant University, Rhode Island

Her high school counselor told The Networker that she was "not college material" and she retained that belief until her early thirties, when she decided that she had something to prove to the counselor *and to herself.* She employed interdependence, surrounding herself with students who practiced successful strategies and who regularly encouraged her. The result was a mostly successful first-semester experience. Following this positive outcome, she never looked back, except to wait for the day when she returned to her former high school to display her diploma to her former guidance counselor.

TIPS FOR CONFIDENCE BUILDING

Here are some time-tested strategies that will help you throughout your life. By following these steps, you will achieve *realistic and worthwhile* confidence:

- As often as possible, focus on your strong points rather than areas of weakness. In other words, be aware of what is good about you rather than what you are not proud of.
- Make a consistent effort to learn from your experiences — the good and bad (you will undoubtedly have many of both in your life).

- Find the courage to try something new and different, even when it appears too difficult or risky.

- When something bothers or disappoints you, take the time to examine your thoughts. Choose to react calmly and rationally rather than on impulse and your emotions.

- Expect that while some of what you achieve in life may be due to pure luck, a good deal more will likely be the result of your personal persistence and effort.

- Strive to be assertive. This means express how you feel, what you think, the beliefs you hold, and do so directly and sincerely. You have a right to say "no" to requests that are not genuine or reasonable.

- Continue to learn and vary your skills and talents long after you leave college. Embrace the idea that there is no end to learning throughout your life.

- Most important of all, believe in yourself. Identify what distinguishes you from everyone else and what you have to offer. Once you know these qualities, you will begin to cultivate them by applying them in everyday life.

Managing Your Time

You might be the kind of student who thinks it's normal to spend hours making flash-cards and outlining your notes in different colored ink. Or maybe you're an adrenaline junkie, accustomed to starting a twenty-page term paper the night before it's due.

The problem is both of these approaches carry certain inherent liabilities. Goof off and you'll probably bomb all your courses. Do nothing but cower in a library carrel for weeks on end and you'll wind up dull, pasty, and miserable. If you're like most of us, you'll learn more, get better grades, and have more fun in college if you operate somewhere in the middle.

By now, you've probably heard the Latin expression *carpe diem,* which translates to "seize the day" (as in, make time work for you). Mastering the art of time management is one key to your future success and happiness, but learning to actually make time work for you can be problematic. What can you do to take control of your own time? Read on to find out.

The Case for Time Management

Why bother? We know. Some students don't want to "waste" time on planning and managing their schedules. Instead, they prefer to go with the flow. Unfortunately, the demands of college (not to mention most careers) require serious, intentional strategies. Unless you can afford to hire a personal assistant, your previous slacker habits won't carry you through.

To psych yourself up, think of time management as part of your life skill set. If you're trying to remember all the things you need to get done, it's hard to focus on actually doing the work. Organizing your time well accomplishes three things: First, it optimizes your chances for good results, so you're not flying by the seat of your pants. Second, it enhances your life by saving you from stress and regret. And finally, it reflects what you value—it's all about doing your best.

Need more motivation? Remember that people who learn good time management techniques in college generally soar in their careers. Think about it: If you're more efficient at your job, you'll be able to accomplish more. That will give you a competitive advantage over your coworkers. Your bosses will learn to depend on you. They'll reward you with interesting projects, promotions, and educational and training opportunities. You'll feel empowered and will fill your workplace with positive vibes. You'll have time for a sizzling social life outside the office. Plus you'll make more money and need less Red Bull.

Taking Charge of Your Time

Freedom can be a dangerous thing. One of the biggest differences between high school and college is that you find yourself with far more independence—and greater responsibility—than you've ever known. If you are continuing your education after a break, you may also be contending with spouse/boss/child obligations, too. But it would be a gigantic mistake to assume that Oprah, rocket scientists, and other type-A folks have some kind of monopoly on organization and focus. You, the ordinary student, can also embrace your inner executive assistant—the one who keeps you on time, on task, and ready for a slice of the action. So how do you begin?

Setting Goals

Goals help you figure out where to devote the majority of your time. To achieve your goals, you need to do more than just think about them. You need to act! This requires setting some short-term and long-term goals. When determining your long-term goals, it is important to be honest and realistic with yourself. Goals should be challenging, but they should also be attainable. Be sure they align with your abilities, values, and interests. Do you want to go on to further schooling? Have you decided what career you want to pursue? Mulling over these questions can help you start thinking about where you want to be in the next 5 to 10 years. Dreaming up long-term goals can be exciting and fun; however, reaching your goals requires undertaking a number of steps in the short term.

Try to be very specific when determining your short-term goals. For example, if you're committed to becoming an expert in a certain field, you'll want to throw yourself into every class and internship that can help you on your way. A specific goal would be to review your school's course catalog, identify the courses you want to take, and determine when you must take them. An even more specific goal would be to research interesting internship opportunities in your field of study. The good news about goals is that each small step adds up.

Identify one long-term goal and identify three steps you can take to achieve your goal.

Long-Term Goal _____

Steps toward Your Goal

1. _____
2. _____
3. _____

Knowing Your Priorities

To achieve your goals, prioritize your life so that you're steadily working toward them.

- **Start out with a winner's mentality:** Make sure your studies take precedence. Having worked so hard to get to college, you cannot allow other activities to derail your schoolwork. Review your current commitments and prepare to sacrifice a few—for now. Whatever you do, talk to your family, your boss, and your friends about your college workload and goals so that everyone's on the same page. When you have a looming deadline, be firm. Emphasize that no amount of badgering will succeed in getting you to go to the James Bond theme party during finals week.

- **Next, start preparing for your future:** Visit your campus career center and schedule an assessment test to hone in on your talents and interests. Or, if you know what career you want to pursue, talk with a professional in that field, your guidance counselor, a professor, or an upper-class student in your chosen major to find out what steps you need to take to get the results you want, starting now. What skills and experiences should be on your résumé when you graduate that will make you stand out from the pack? Make a plan, prioritize your goals, and then make a time-management schedule.

- **Balance is key:** If you're realistic, planning for the future you want may demand big sacrifices. Be realistic about the present, too. Always include time in your schedule for people who are important to you and time on your own to recharge.

Embrace the 2-for-1 Rule. For every hour you spend in class at college, you should plan to study two hours more outside of class. That's the standard, so keep it in mind when you're planning your schedule. The bottom line is that you simply carry more responsibility for your education in college than you did in high school.

Own Your Class Schedule. Your schedule will impact almost every aspect of your college life. Before you register, think about how to make your schedule work for you.

> **TIP**
>
> **Share your Google or Outlook Calendar.** Keeping an electronic copy of your calendar allows you to share with others at a click of the button. Letting your family, friends, and employer know what is on your plate at any given moment can bridge any misunderstandings that may arise because of your school commitments and create a more supportive home and work environment.

- **Start with your biorhythms.** Do you study more effectively in the day or the evening or a combination of both? Ideally, you should devote your peak hours—when you're most alert and engaged—to schoolwork. Schedule other activities, like laundry, e-mail, exercise, and socializing, for times when it's harder to concentrate.

- **If you live on campus,** you might want to create a schedule that situates you near a dining hall at mealtimes or lets you spend breaks between classes at the library. Feel free to slot breaks for relaxation and catching up with friends. But beware the midday nap: You risk feeling lethargic afterward or even worse, oversleeping and missing the rest of your classes. If you attend a large college or university, be sure to allow adequate time to get from one class to another.

- **Try to alternate classes with free periods.** Also, seek out instructors who'll let you attend lectures at alternate times in case you're absent. If they offer flexibility with due dates for assignments, all the better.

- **If you're a commuter student or carry a heavy workload,** you might be tempted to schedule your classes in blocks without breaks. But before you do this, consider the following:
  - Falling behind in all your classes if you get sick
  - The fatigue factor
  - No last-minute study periods before tests
  - The possibility of having several exams on the same day

CONTROL FACTOR: KNOW WHAT YOU *CAN* AND *CAN'T* CONTROL

When it comes to planning your time between what you can and can't control, it helps to know the difference.

What You *Can* Control

- **Making good choices.** How often do you say, "I don't have time"? Probably a lot. But truth be told, you have a choice when it comes to most of the major commitments in your life. You also control many of the small decisions that keep you focused on your goals: when you wake up, how much sleep you get, what you eat, how much time you spend studying, and whether you get exercise. So be a woman or man with a plan. If you want something enough, you'll make time for it.

- **Doing your part to succeed.** Translation: Go to all your classes; arrive on time; buy all the required textbooks; keep track of your activities; complete every reading and writing assignment on time; take notes in class; and, whenever possible, participate and ask questions.

- **Managing your stress levels.** Organization is the key to tranquility and positive thinking. Manage your time well, and you won't be tormented with thoughts of all the things that need doing. Psychologists have found that free-floating anxiety can turn even your subconscious thoughts into a horror show. Want to avoid unnecessary stress? Plan ahead.

What You *Can't* Control

- **Knowing how much you'll need to study right off the bat.** Depending on the kind of high school you went to (and the types of courses you took there), or if it has been a while since you've had to study, you might be more or less prepared than your college classmates. If your studying or writing skills lag behind, expect to put in a little extra time until you're up to speed.

- **Running into scheduling conflicts.** If you find it hard to get the classes you need, you can seek help from a dean, an academic adviser, or someone in the college counseling center.

- **Needing a job to help pay your way.** Just follow the experts' rule of thumb: If you're taking a full courseload, do your best to avoid working more than fifteen hours a week. Any more than that and your academic work could suffer.

Four Time-Wasting Habits to Avoid

1. Procrastinating

Should you have to do assignments that seem incredibly long and boring? Shouldn't you be able to study with family members in the room, even if you can't get any work done with them around? Can't you occasionally blow off the outside reading? Yes, no, and no.

There are lots of reasons why we procrastinate. Maybe you're a perfectionist—in which case, avoiding a task might be easier than having to live up to your own very high expectations (or those of your parents or instructors). Maybe you object to the sheer dullness of an assignment, or you think you can learn the material just as well without doing the work. Maybe you even fear success and know just how to subvert it.

None of these qualify as valid reasons to put off your work. They're just lame excuses that will get you in trouble. Fortunately, doing tasks you don't like is excellent practice for real life.

Slacker alert: Procrastination is a slippery slope. Research shows that procrastinators are more likely to develop unhealthy habits like higher alcohol consumption, smoking, insomnia, poor diet, and lack of exercise. Make sure you get these tendencies under control early. Otherwise, you could feel overwhelmed in other aspects of your life, too.

Easy Tricks to Stop Procrastination

- **Break big jobs down into smaller chunks.** Spend only a few minutes planning your strategy and then act on it.

- **Reward yourself** for finishing the task, like watching your favorite YouTuber or playing a game with your kids or friends.

- **Find a quiet, comfortable place to work** that doesn't allow for distractions and interruptions. Don't listen to music, and turn off your phone. If you study in your room, shut the door.

- **Treat your study time like a serious commitment.** That means no phone calls, e-mail, text messages, or updates to your Facebook page. You can rejoin society later.

- **Consider the consequences if you don't get down to work.** You don't want to let bad habits derail your ability to achieve good results *and* have a life.

2. Overextending Yourself

Feeling overextended is a huge source of stress for college students. Why? Well, what constitutes a realistic workload varies significantly from one person to another. Being involved in campus life is fun and important; it's crucial not to let your academic work take a backseat.

- **Learn to say no—even if it means letting other people down.** Don't be tempted to compromise your priorities.

- **But don't give up all nonacademic pursuits.** On the contrary, students who work or participate in extracurricular activities often achieve higher grades than their less-active counterparts partly because of the important role that time management plays in their lives.

- **If you're truly overloaded with commitments and can't see a way out . . .** You may need to drop a course before the drop deadline. It may seem drastic, but a low grade on your permanent record is even worse. Become familiar with your school's add/drop policy to avoid penalties. If you receive financial aid, keep in mind that in most cases you must be registered for a minimum number of credit hours to be considered a full-time student and maintain your current level of aid. Be sure before you drop!

3. Losing Your Focus

Too many first-year college students lose sight of their goals. Translation: They spend their first term blowing off classes and assignments, then either get expelled, placed on probation, or have to spend years clawing their way back to a decent GPA. So plan your strategy and keep yourself motivated for the long haul.

4. Running Late

Punctuality is a virtue. Rolling in late to class or review sessions shows a lack of respect for both your instructors and your classmates. Arrive early and avoid using your phone in class, texting, doing homework for another class, falling asleep, talking, whispering, or leaving class to feed a parking meter. Part of managing your time is freeing yourself to focus on the present and on other people who inhabit the present with you. Note: Respecting others is a habit that can work wonders in your career and personal life.

TIP

Facebook Addict? Online tools like *StayFocused* allow you to block or limit your time on certain Web sites while you are studying so you can focus on the task at hand. Google "10 Online Tools for Better Attention & Focus" to find a program that works for you.

Two Indispensable Tools to Keep You on Track

Here's the deal. Once you enter college or the working world, you must immediately do the following: Write down everything you need to do; prioritize your tasks; and leave yourself constant reminders. The good news is that a little up-front planning will make your life infinitely easier and more relaxing. For one thing, you'll be less likely to screw up. On top of that, you'll free your brain from having to remember all the things you need to get done so you can focus on actually doing the work. Two key items will help you plan to succeed.

A Planner or Calendar

Find out if your college sells a special planner in the campus bookstore with important dates and deadlines already marked. Or, if you prefer to use an online calendar or the one that comes on your computer or smartphone, that's fine too. As you schedule your time, follow a few basic guidelines.

Pick a timeframe that works best for you. If you want a "big picture" sense of how your schedule plays out, try setting up a calendar for the whole term or for the month. For a more detailed breakdown of what you need to accomplish in the near future, a calendar for the week or even the day may be a better fit. Of course, there's no need to limit yourself—use more than one type of calendar if that works for you.

Enter all of your commitments. Once you've selected your preferred timeframe, it's time to record your commitments and other important deadlines. These might include your classes, assignment due dates, work hours, family commitments, and so on. Be specific. For instance, "Read Chapter 8 in history" is preferable to "Study history," which is better than simply "Study." To be even more specific, include meeting times and locations, social events, and study time for each class you're taking. Take advantage of your smartphone and set reminders and alarms to help keep you on top of all your activities and obligations.

Break large assignments like term papers into smaller bits, such as choosing a topic, doing research, creating an outline, learning necessary computer skills, writing a first draft, and so on. And give them deadlines. Estimate how much time each assignment will take you. Then get a jump on it. A good time manager often finishes projects before the actual due dates to allow for emergencies.

Watch out for your toughest weeks during the term. If you find that paper deadlines and test dates fall during the same week or even the same day, you can alleviate some of the stress by finding time to finish some assignments early to free up study and writing time. If there's a major conflict, talk it over with your professor and find a way to work around it. Professors will be more likely to help you if you come to them plenty of time in advance.

Update your planner/calendar regularly. Enter all due dates as soon as you know them. Be obsessive about this.

Check your planner/calendar every day (at the same time of day if that helps you remember). You'll want to review the current week and the next week, too.

When in doubt, turn to a type-A classmate for advice. A hyper-organized friend can be your biggest ally when it comes to making a game plan.

A To-Do List

The easiest way to remember all the things you need to do is to jot them down in a running to-do list—updating as needed. You can do this on paper or use an online calendar or smartphone to record the day's obligations. Techies love the GTD® ("Getting Things Done"®) system for taking control of tasks and commitments. Google it to learn how it works.

1. **Prioritize.** Rank items on your list in order of importance. Alternately, circle or highlight urgent tasks. Exclamation points and stars—it's all good.

2. **Every time you complete a task, cross it off the list.** (This can be extremely satisfying.)

3. **Move undone items to the top of your next list.** (Less satisfying, but smart and efficient.)

4. **Start a new to-do list every day or once a week.** It shouldn't be just about academics. Slot in errands you need to run, appointments, e-mail messages you need to send, and anything else you need to do that day or week.

Advice from Other Students

Martha Flot, Education Major in Florida

"I learned a long time ago that if I don't start my work early, it's not going to happen. I always open my books right after the kids are off to school, and begin with the easiest assignments. I feel really productive and get into the swing of things before tackling the harder stuff. It's kind of like the warm-up before practice."

- **Digitally bolster your memory.** "I keep everything in my smartphone calendar—for me, that's the best way to stay organized. I set reminders for all of my study groups and upcoming assignments. If it's a big exam, I'll set the reminder a week in advance to give myself plenty of time to prepare."

- **Exercise.** "I always try to exercise before I sit down for an exam or a long study session, too. Studies show that exercise boosts your blood circulation, so you can think better and feel more awake. For me, it makes a huge difference."

- **Beware of over-committing.** "I used to be a huge people pleaser. Trying to please everyone and juggling my role as a mother, wife, and student, I learned fast that I couldn't do that and still get all my work done. Once I started prioritizing, my friends and family have been responsive and supportive. It helps having a husband who manages his time well; you grow and learn from it."

EASY WAYS TO MAXIMIZE YOUR TIME

- **Carry work with you.** If you have a lull between classes, use it to review material from the previous class and prepare for the next one. Take advantage of waiting time (on the bus or between appointments) to study. You'll be more likely to remember what you've learned in class if you review or copy your notes as soon as you reasonably can.

- **Discipline yourself with routines.** You might want to get up early to prepare, or set fixed study hours after dinner or on weekend afternoons.

- **Don't multitask.** Even though you might be quite good at it, or think you are, the reality is—and research shows—that you'll be able to do your most effective studying and retain the most information if you concentrate on one task at a time.

- **Study with friends.** You can help each other grasp tricky concepts and memorize important facts and dates.

- **Be flexible.** Disruptions to your plans don't come with ample warning time. Build extra time into your schedule so that unanticipated interruptions don't prevent you from meeting your goals.

John Dietz, Architecture Major in Florida

"My first two years of college forced me to be a morning person. But as an upperclass-man, I have the freedom to pick classes that start in the afternoon, so I've reverted to being nocturnal: I usually study or work in my design studio until 2 or 3 a.m."

- **Go digital.** "I take my computer to all my classes, so I keep a detailed calendar there. My work schedule changes frequently, so I always type that in along with all my assignments."

- **Beware of perfectionism.** "As an architect, you could spend your whole life designing something. Often I really have to tell myself to stop and go on to the next thing."

- **Find a part-time job that offers flexible hours and lets you study.** "I work at the gym on campus, where each shift is just three hours long. They only hire students, so they're very accommodating if I need to change my schedule. Plus, mostly I get to sit at the check-in desk and review my notes."

Carolina Buckler, Business and Political Science Major in Indiana

"Having a double major means a heavier workload, but it's doable in my subjects. My roommate — who's studying engineering and puts in a lot more hours than I do — couldn't have handled a heavier workload because of his major."

- **Start things sooner rather than later.** "That especially helps with group projects because it's hard to find time in everyone's schedule to get together. If you meet early, you can divide up the work."

- **Make sure your employer knows your academic commitments.** "I work twelve to fifteen hours a week as a teacher's assistant in the political science department. The professors will automatically understand if I need to take a study day. Around finals, they give everyone a week off."

- **Socialize at mealtimes.** "My friends and I meet for dinner at 5 p.m. It sounds ridiculously early, but I've found that it makes me less likely to waste time: Instead of trying to start something for an hour or so before dinner, I get back around 6:30 and jump right into homework."

3

Writing Ethically and Responsibly

Thanks to technology, it's easier than ever for students to cheat — so cheaters are sprouting like mushrooms. Thanks to technology, it's also much easier for colleges to catch cheaters. And administrators are cracking down on cheating by making the penalties increasingly harsh.

To complicate matters, there are plenty of students who cheat *without even knowing that they're cheating.* Of course, in a perfect world, they'd get lighter sentences than the people who cheated intentionally. But colleges aren't perfect worlds. They're wonderful institutions of learning that don't like to be taken advantage of.

So let's clear a few things up.

Defining "Cheating"

Cheating comes down to two things: Faking your own work, and helping other students fake theirs.

Some of the Most Obvious Forms of Cheating

- Buying an essay from someone else
- Texting answers during an exam
- Sharing the details of a test with students who haven't taken it yet
- Copying someone else's homework
- Peeking at someone else's test paper
- Letting other people cheat off you
- Stealing a test
- Writing answers to the test in crazy small letters on your gum wrappers or on the inside of your bottled water label. (Note: Professors are onto these tricks.)
- Plagiarizing: The most common (but equally problematic) form of cheating

The trouble with plagiarism is that a lot of students don't completely understand what it is. Plagiarism is a fancy word that, according to the *Oxford English Dictionary,* means "taking someone else's work or ideas and passing them off as one's own." Fun fact: The word *plagiarism* comes from the Latin word for *kidnapping*. Get the picture?

It's hard to believe that anybody *really* thinks it's OK to cut and paste whole sentences from the Internet into their essays. But given that some people don't think twice about downloading copyrighted music tracks and videos, maybe the concept of "borrowing" isn't as clear as it used to be. What's your stance? Have you ever lifted passages off a Web site, maybe even changing a couple of words to make it sound more like you? Are you inclined to believe that once something is on the Web, it's public domain? If so, please know it's NOT so. The fact remains that copying or paraphrasing anything off the Internet, or from any another source, and using it without citing the source is cheating.

Beware: Plagiarizing with intent is one thing. But many college students who plagiarize by accident — they copy quotations into their notes but forget to add quotation marks and later can't tell what's their own writing and what they borrowed from a source — are also convicted of plagiarism simply because they forget to indicate which parts of an essay are their own and which parts belong to another author. We repeat: Colleges are on a crusade to thwart cheating. If your high school was lax about footnotes or paraphrasing, you need to figure out the rules fast.

The Cheating Problem

In a recent survey of 36,000 high school students by the Josephson Institute of Ethics, 60 percent admitted to cheating on a test during the previous year. Thirty-five percent had cheated on multiple tests. A third of them had committed plagiarism, cutting and pasting from the Internet. What's worse, according to recent studies by Donald L. McCabe at Rutgers University, the number of students who think that copying material from the Web is "serious cheating" has plummeted to only 29 percent.

Cheating typically begins during junior high, which is—no surprise—around the same time that grade pressure and academic workloads ramp up. In college, the pressure to get good grades becomes even more intense. Maybe you're trying to get into a competitive graduate program, win a scholarship, or land a high-paying job. Maybe you're involved in a zillion clubs, sports, or volunteer activities. Maybe you have a job and/or kids. Maybe you're taking metaphysics. Whatever it is, you could start to feel overextended. And from there, you might start to justify cheating in your mind. Big mistake.

Why You Shouldn't Cheat

Because it's wrong. Because it's lazy and contemptible. Because getting caught could set off a firestorm and totally screw up your future. Because cheating is bad for your self-image and can trigger severe guilt and anxiety.

Because attending college is ultimately about learning new things, challenging yourself, and building your integrity. If you try to scam your way through, you've defeated the whole point of this exercise.

And here's the real drag: Cheating has a nasty way of seeping into other parts of your life, like your career, your finances, and your personal relationships, where it can cause long-term damage. Once you've cheated on a few tests, it might not seem like a big leap for you to start padding your résumé or fudging your taxes.

Why It's Easy to Get Caught

College professors have more time and leeway to investigate their suspicions and better resources to back them up. Programs like Turnitin.com let instructors scan essays and crosscheck them against books, newspapers, journals, and student papers, as well as against material that's publicly accessible on the Web. Even a tiny, nine-word snippet could give you away.

How *Not* to Cheat: Ten Essential Tips

1. **Avoid friends who pressure you to bend the rules.** Writing a paper is really hard. Doing advanced math and science homework is really hard. Studying for exams is lonely, boring, and *really* hard. But trying to beat the system doesn't pay. Remind yourself of the consequences of cheating. Explain to your friends that you are on a valiant quest for honest effort. Make them watch a lot of movies about Abraham Lincoln. As a last resort, find new friends.

2. **Join a study group.** If you're struggling to get through a daunting course, get together with other students to compare notes and help each other grasp tricky concepts. A study group gives you a support system and a more positive belief in yourself. It teaches you persistence and discipline because the group structure involves meeting promptly at set times for reviews. A study group can also make

THE PENALTIES FOR CHEATING

Cheating is a much bigger deal in college than it was in high school. Remember, you're not a minor anymore. Once you're over 18 and are caught cheating, you'll be reprimanded as an adult.

- "At minimum, you're looking at an F for the entire course and very likely academic probation or even dismissal," says Dr. Thomas Skouras, a professor at the Community College of Rhode Island. "In most cases now, instructors have to adhere to the school's policy on cheating, so they can't bend the rules even if they want to."

- And it gets scarier than that: If caught cheating, you could end up with a Conviction of Plagiarism on your college transcript. That's the same transcript you'll need to use for graduate school and job applications.

- Plagiarism is different from other student offenses in that it isn't protected under federal confidentiality laws. Think about it: "A student who has stalked someone on campus and has a history of psychiatric illness might not have that information on his transcript," Prof. Skouras adds. "A conviction of cheating is much harder to suppress."

Note: How often are convictions of plagiarism overturned? Almost never. Most instructors won't go forward with the charges unless they have substantial evidence to back them up.

learning easier and more fun. Other members of the group may have noticed important points from class that you didn't catch. Plus, once you understand the material well, any impulse to cheat will cease to be an issue.

3. **Don't procrastinate.** Here's the deal: If you want to write a thorough and honest essay, you need to start early. College papers aren't like movie reviews. You're required to do lots of outside research. Then you have to weed through it all to figure out what's valuable. Next, you have to incorporate the highlights into an outline, a first draft, and ultimately, an original, dazzlingly brilliant work that's all your own. All of that takes time. If you leave things too late, you'll be more tempted to cheat.

> **TIP**
>
> **Make a pledge to successfully pass the course as a team — the honest way.** "I chose to form a group more than a decade ago with three other doctoral candidates and we followed through on our promise to graduate together," says Prof. Skouras. "It really mattered that we were each rooting for the others to succeed."

4. **Don't muddle your notes.** It's vital that you keep your own writing separate from the material you've gathered from other sources. Why? Because it's surprisingly easy to mistake someone else's words for your own, especially after you get two hours into writing and your brain turns numb. So document everything. Be obsessive about this.

5. **Be a stickler for in-text citations.** It happens all the time: At the end of an essay, a student provides a full listing of all the works he or she has cited. But in the paper itself, there are no references to be found. "In this case, you're looking at a low C at best," says Prof. Skouras. "Your instructor has no choice but to take off major points since it's impossible to tell the difference between your writing and your references."

6. **Familiarize yourself with the proper formatting for a research paper.** The MLA style is pretty much standard. If your instructors require a different style, they will let you know. If you need to learn the basic guidelines and rules for citations, The Owl at Purdue University is a great source — well written and user-friendly (**http://owl.english.purdue.edu**). You might also want to speak to a reference librarian. A reference librarian has a graduate degree in gathering research and can be one of your biggest allies in college. Alternately, pay a visit to the writing center on campus or talk to your instructor for advice. Many college libraries offer tutorials in MLA formatting. Getting one early in the semester can give you a big leg up.

> **TIP**
>
> **Respect deadlines.** When you were in high school, your teachers might have negotiated due dates. In college, it's almost impossible to get an extension on an assignment. Your old stalling tactics ("My printer broke/I have the flu/I've been working with NASA on a nuclear laser shield — so can I get that essay to you on Monday?") won't fly.

> **TIP**
>
> **Flaunt your knowledge.** You must not only list the references you've used to research your topic, but you must also demonstrate that you know where they belong in your narrative.

7. **Be sure to list all of your research sources.** If you're not sure how to list a citation or if you're not sure that your source is valid, don't just put it down and keep your fingers crossed. Talk to your instructor, or ask a reference librarian for help.

8. **Master the art of paraphrasing.** Paraphrasing means restating someone else's ideas or observations in your own words and sentences. You don't have to put the text in quotation marks, but a citation acknowledging the original source is still needed. (See *The Rules of Paraphrasing* below for examples.)

9. **If you need help, seek it early.** This sounds painfully obvious, but it's important to go to the writing center or the librarian *well before your paper is actually due.* Revision takes time—and chances are, your paper will need more than a few tweaks.

10. **If you hand something in and then realize that you used material without giving credit to the source, alert your instructor immediately.** Don't just hope it will slip through. Better to risk half a grade on one essay than your whole college career, right?

> **TIP**
>
> **When copying research material into your notes, write the name of its source and page number directly after it.** Likewise, when you copy something from the Internet, add a URL in brackets at the end. Use quotation marks around all cited materials. You might also try highlighting your research in a bright color to set it apart from your notes. All of this will make things easier when it's time to make your footnotes.

The Rules of Paraphrasing

Paraphrasing doesn't mean copying a quote and swapping out a few words. It doesn't mean changing two or three words in a sequence, either. It means rephrasing someone else's quote altogether while retaining its essential meaning. Consider these examples:

- If the quote is "The likelihood of an increase in the growth rate appears dim," you might change it to "The economy improving in the near future is improbable, according to Dr. X, an economist at the University of Y."

- Likewise, "Google has been working to build cars that can drive themselves," could be rewritten as "One of Google's latest projects: a robotic car that takes humans out of the driver's seat."

If you're having trouble paraphrasing something, try this trick: Put away your source material, call up a friend or your mom, and explain the point you're trying to summarize. Chances are you'll come away with something that's clear, concise, and in your own words.

A word of warning: When you paraphrase someone else's opinions or insights, you still have to document the source. The upside? You don't have to frame the passage in quotation marks.

Writing Activities

Writing Activities

Patterns of Development*

Prewriting Activities

Trying out patterns of development as single paragraphs or extended multi-paragraph examples is a good way to find a pattern that works well, given your topic, audience, and purpose.

Narration: Paragraphs or Essays

Narration tells a story about an event or a sequence of events in order to explain something. Try completing the following prompts to get ideas for a narrative paragraph or essay.

➤ I would never have been able to do _____ if it weren't for the time when _____.

➤ At the time, I had no idea how the events of the day when _____
_____ [something happened] _____
would affect me.

➤ The most exciting experience of my life was _____
_____
because _____.

Now write a sentence of your own that could jump-start a narrative:

_____
_____
_____

* Activities for the Guided Writing Assignment in Chapter 10, *Successful College Writing*, Seventh Edition

Description: Paragraphs or Essays

Descriptive writing uses sensory details to contribute to a dominant impression. Try completing the following prompts to get ideas for a descriptive paragraph or essay.

➤ The taste of _____ always
reminds me of _____.

➤ _____ never smells
better than it does when _____.

➤ _____'s voice makes
me feel _____.

Now write a sentence of your own that could jump-start a description:

_____

_____

_____

Illustration: Paragraphs or Essays

Illustration uses examples to explain unfamiliar concepts. Try completing the following prompts to get ideas for an illustration paragraph or essay.

➤ All of my favorite _____ have one trait
in common: _____.

➤ I often have to explain _____,
and the examples I use are _____

_____.

➤ _____, _____,
and _____ are all good examples of _____

_____.

Now write a sentence of your own that could jump-start an illustration:

_____

_____

_____

Process Analysis: Paragraphs or Essays

Process analysis explains, step by step, how something works or how to do something. Try completing the following prompts to get ideas for a process analysis paragraph or essay.

➤ I have insider knowledge of the way _____

works, and it's not what most people think.

➤ You might be surprised at how easy it is to _____

_____.

➤ When I _____, I _____

_____ first, then _____, and finally

_____.

Now write a sentence of your own that could jump-start a process analysis:

_____

_____

_____

Comparison and Contrast: Paragraphs or Essays

Comparison and contrast analyzes the similarities and differences between two people, places, policies, activities, ideas, or other things. Try completing the following prompts to get ideas for a comparison and contrast paragraph or essay.

➤ _____ and _____

may seem very different, but they have more in common than you might think.

➤ I thought I would like _____ more than

_____, but it turned out otherwise.

➤ The toughest decision I ever had to make involved choosing between _____

_____ and _____,

both of which were _____.

Now write a sentence of your own that could jump-start a comparison and contrast analysis:

_____

_____

_____

Classification and Division: Paragraphs or Essays

Classification and division writing looks closely at the parts that make up a whole or different categories or types of something. Try completing the following prompts to get ideas for a classification and division paragraph or essay.

➤ Based on my experience as a(n) _____,
_____ can be divided into the following types: _____
_____.

➤ All of the _____ I've ever seen can be
categorized as _____, _____,
_____, or _____.

➤ On this campus, the food options can be classified as follows: _____
_____
_____.

Now write a sentence of your own that could jump-start a classification and division paragraph or essay:

_____

_____

_____

Definition: Paragraphs or Essays

A definition or extended definition conducts a close analysis of a complicated idea or word. Try completing the following prompts to get ideas for a definition paragraph or an extended definition essay.

➤ Many people are not aware that _____
means _____
and not _____.

➤ When I first heard of _____,
I thought it meant _____.

Now write a sentence of your own that could jump-start a definition paragraph or essay:

_____

_____

_____

Cause and Effect: Paragraphs or Essays

Cause and effect paragraphs and essays show how one or more causes lead to or influence something else. Try completing the following prompts to get ideas for a cause and effect paragraph or essay.

➤ I'm glad that _____ happened; because of
   it, _____.

➤ The unexpected consequences of _____
   included _____ and _____.

➤ When _____ happened, we had to know why.
   After a long search, we learned _____.

Now write a sentence of your own that could jump-start a cause and effect paragraph
or essay:

_____

_____

_____

Argument: Paragraphs or Essays

An argument aims to convince or persuade readers to believe something or take some
action. Try completing the following prompts to get ideas for an argument paragraph
or essay.

➤ Because _____ causes problems such
   as _____ and _____, we
   should take action to _____.

➤ Every _____ should have the
   opportunity to _____, and that dream can come
   true if _____.

➤ Even more than _____, children need
   _____, and _____
   can help.

Now write a sentence of your own that could jump-start an argument paragraph or
essay:

_____

_____

_____

Essay Development Activities

Identifying Possible Topics for an Essay That Combines Patterns of Development

Reread the ideas you've generated above and choose one or more that contain an idea you might want to use in an essay that combines patterns of development. Look particularly closely at any ideas you find yourself addressing more than once in the prompts you have completed.

➤ A possible preliminary topic is _____
_____
_____.

➤ Another possible preliminary topic is _____
_____
_____.

➤ A third possible preliminary topic is _____
_____
_____.

Identifying the Readers I Want to Reach in an Essay That Combines Patterns of Development

Figuring out what your audience already knows and does not know about the topic you choose will be extremely important. If you consider what they already believe or know, you will be able to identify patterns that will work more effectively to reach them. Complete the following prompts to analyze the audience you expect to reach:

➤ My audience includes _____.

➤ They may already know _____
about this topic, but they may not know _____
_____.

➤ I need to tell this audience about _____
_____ so they
will understand my perspective on the topic.

➤ When they read my essay, I want them to feel _____
_____.

➤ My purpose for writing is to _____.

Brainstorming Ideas for an Essay That Combines Patterns of Development

Which of the patterns will be most useful to you in drafting an essay on one of your preliminary topics? Choose at least two or three patterns and spend five minutes brainstorming all the ideas you can think of for a paragraph or section using that pattern.

Pattern

_____

Ideas for use

_____

_____

_____

_____

_____

_____

_____

Pattern

_____

Ideas for use

_____

_____

_____

_____

_____

_____

_____

Pattern

_____

Ideas for use

_____

_____

_____

_____

_____

_____

_____

Moving from Topic to Preliminary Thesis for an Essay That Combines Patterns of Development

Fill in the blanks to start thinking about the point you want to make in your essay.

➤ Many people will be surprised to find out that _____.

➤ I used to believe _____, but now I think _____.

➤ This may sound strange, but [the topic] makes me think about _____ because _____.

➤ At first I did not understand [the topic], but now I think of it as _____.

➤ A new insight my readers should have about [the topic] is _____.

Now, write your own generalization that can serve as a preliminary thesis:

_____

_____

_____

Creating a Graphic Organizer or Outline to Plan Your Essay Combining Patterns of Development

You may use whatever organizational method makes sense for the patterns you choose and the topic and audience you aim to reach. An effective way to begin is to create a graphic organizer or outline that notes which pattern you will use to make a given point.

Drafting, Reviewing, Revising, and Editing Your Essay Combining Patterns of Development

Pay attention to the pattern that seems to govern your overall essay. When you are sure which main pattern you want to use, go to the chapter in this workbook detailing that pattern and complete the activities there for drafting, getting feedback, revising, and editing your work.

5

Narration*

Prewriting Activities

Finding Ideas for a Narrative Essay Topic

What story can you include in your narrative? Try these prompts while you're starting to think about a topic:

➤ The _____ [superlative adjective — funniest/scariest] _____ thing that I ever experienced happened when _____ [person] _____ did
_____ [action] _____ because _____ [reason] _____.

➤ When my _____ [relation to me — mother/granddad/pet snake] _____ did
_____ [action] _____, I realized _____ [surprising thing] _____
_____.

➤ _____ [experience] _____ was almost a[n] _____ [really good or bad thing] _____.

➤ _____ [person] _____ didn't want to do _____ [action] _____ but did it anyway because _____ [reason] _____.

➤ _____ [person] _____ discovered that she/he was [different from/not different from] others in the _____ [place or community] _____ when _____ [event] _____ happened.

Help a classmate! Write a "mad lib" with blanks and ask others to complete it:
_____
_____
_____

* Activities for the Guided Writing Assignment in Chapter 11, *Successful College Writing*, Seventh Edition

Collaborating to Brainstorm Ideas for a Narrative Essay Topic

If you're having trouble thinking of ideas, try brainstorming with a group of class-mates. Spend five minutes writing as many sentences as you can in response to one or more of the following prompts:

➤ The moment when everything changed for me was _____
_____.

➤ The moment when everything changed for my family was _____
_____.

➤ The moment when everything changed for _____
was _____.

After five minutes, each member of the group should choose one or two of the sen-tences and briefly share the narrative(s). As each person tells a story, the other group members should ask questions, and the storyteller can make notes about details, sequence of events, and other important ideas that the story needs to include. Deter-mine which of the narrative options that each person presents would make the most compelling essay.

Identifying a Conflict in Your Narrative

What conflict or important choice faced you (or the person your narrative is about)? Try responding to any of these prompts that are relevant, or create a statement of your own that identifies the conflict in your story.

➤ [I/The person I'm writing about] would never have _____
if [I/the person] hadn't been afraid of _____
_____.

➤ When [I/the person I'm writing about] heard _____,
_____ [I/the person]
knew that it was important to _____.

➤ [I/The person who is featured in the narrative] had to choose between _____
_____, which mattered because
_____, and
_____, which mattered because
_____.

Exploring Topic Ideas for a Narrative Essay

What details should you include in your narrative? Choose the prompt above that has produced the story you most want to tell, and try at least two of the following ideas to start collecting details for use in your narrative essay.

➤ Look at photos or videos that relate in some way to the event you will narrate. What do you see? Who is in the photos and videos? Where were the images taken? What else about your narrative do they remind you of?

➤ Take five minutes and make a list of all the words and phrases that come to mind when you think about the experience you will narrate. Circle the ones that seem most important. How can you use them as you tell the story?

➤ Talk to people who remember the experience you want to narrate. What do they recall about it? How are their memories like and unlike yours?

➤ Take a photo of an object, person, or place related to your experience. Print the image in the middle of a blank piece of paper. Use the space around the image to describe its significance in your narrative and to make notes about how to include the photo in your essay.

➤ Write down dialogue from an incident you will include in your narrative essay, or recreate the dialogue in a recording. Who said the words and why? What was the mood and tone of the dialogue?

Identifying a Preliminary Topic for a Narrative Essay

What will your narrative be about? The topic can be one that you started with on p. 35, or it can be an idea that came to you while you were exploring something else in one of the activities above.

➤ My preliminary topic is _____
_____
_____.

Identifying Sensory Details for a Narrative Essay

How can you make your story immediate and interesting for readers? Details make a narrative come alive. Brainstorm as many of the following prompts as possible, identifying sensory details that reinforce your point of view on the topic and the setting you will describe.

➤ something seen, observed, watched that is important to the story

EXAMPLES: the mirage that appeared to be a pool of water on the steaming blacktop, the uneven layers of the collapsing wedding cake

_____

_____

_____

➤ dialogue or other sound heard or overheard that contributes to the story

EXAMPLES: "Why can't I come in?" my little brother whined; the whistle of a freight train in the middle of the night as it passed behind our house going far away

_____

_____

_____

➤ an aroma, smell, or stench that figures importantly in the story

EXAMPLES: the scent of lilacs reminding me of final exam time, the rotting vegetable smell from the bottom of the garbage bag as we rummaged for our lost lottery ticket

_____

_____

_____

➤ something tangible or textured that contributes to the story

EXAMPLES: the sharp blade that I wasn't supposed to touch, the grimy fur of the stray kitten

_____

_____

_____

➤ a flavor or taste that matters to the story

EXAMPLES: the deliciously charred taste of the marshmallows that had fallen into the campfire, sweet and juicy little tomatoes from my uncle's backyard

_____

_____

_____

Thinking about the Setting for a Narration

A narrative essay should set a scene.

➤ The story I am telling happened when [I/the person I am writing about] was
_____ years old, in _____
[year or era].

➤ The story is most strongly tied to _____ [place].

➤ Whenever I think of [this story], I remember being _____
_____ and
doing _____.

➤ When I remember this time and place, I always think of _____
_____, _____,
and _____.

Thinking about Action for a Narration

A good narrative includes some kind of action. Try at least one of the following activities to enliven the action in your narrative.

➤ Draw a picture of the action in your narrative. Who is in the picture? What is happening?

➤ Identify a verb to describe every action in your story. Then try finding at least three more precise synonyms for each verb, using a dictionary if necessary. Which verbs are liveliest?

➤ Record yourself three separate times telling the active event of your narrative. Play your narratives back for a friend. Which version is best? Why?

Finding a Perspective on the Preliminary Topic for Your Narrative Essay

➤ Thinking about this topic makes me feel _____
_____.

➤ Others involved in the event I will narrate felt _____
_____.

➤ I want anyone who reads my narrative essay to know that _____
_____.

➤ The best way to show my point of view is to include _____
_____, and _____.

Identifying the Readers I Want to Reach in My Narrative Essay

➤ My audience includes _____.

➤ Their experiences have probably been [similar to/ different from] the one I am describing.

➤ I need to tell this audience about _____ _____ so they will understand my perspective on the topic.

➤ When they read my essay, I want them to feel _____ _____.

➤ My purpose for writing is to _____.

Thesis Activities

➤ My preliminary topic (p. 37) is _____.

Narrowing and Focusing a Topic for a Narrative Essay

Can you tell the story in your narrative briefly, and will it support some kind of point you're making? Will you be able to tell the story and make the point in an essay of the assigned length? Sometimes a narrower topic allows you to create a better narrative essay.

➤ If I had five minutes to explain why this story is important, I would start with

_____

_____.

Identifying a Point for Your Narrative Essay

To me, the single most important thing about this narrative is (pick one and complete the sentence)

- that it made me realize _____.

- that it made someone else realize _____.

- that it started _____.

- that it ended _____.

- that it changed _____.

- that _____

_____.

Moving from Topic to Preliminary Thesis for a Narrative Essay

Fill in the blanks to start thinking about the point you want to make about your narrative.

1. Many people will be surprised to find out that _____
   _____.

2. I used to believe _____, but now I
   think _____.

3. This may sound strange, but [the story] makes me think about _____
   _____ because _____.

4. I did not expect what happened to make much of an impression on me, but
   _____.

5. The reason my readers should care about [the story] is _____
   _____.

Now, invent your own assertion about your topic that can serve as a preliminary thesis.

_____

_____

_____

Testing Your Thesis

Tell the story you will include in your narrative essay to a classmate, friend, or peer group. Ask this person to respond to these questions.

➤ What is the takeaway from this narrative? _____

_____

➤ The point of the story is to _____

_____

Do their responses match the point you were trying to make? If not, consider whether you should change the narrative or reconsider the point the story is making.

Drafting Activities

Planning the Placement of Your Thesis

In a narrative essay, a thesis stating the point of your narrative will usually appear at the beginning of the story or at its end, or it can be unstated, just implied.

➤ Do readers need to hear the story before the thesis will make sense? If so, stating the thesis in your introduction does not make sense.

➤ Should I state the thesis directly, or should it be implied? Even if you decide not to state it directly, be sure that the thesis is clear to readers.

Deciding Where to Begin

For many people, the best way to begin a narrative essay is to tell the story first, since the story is probably the part of the essay you can draft most easily. However, if you have an idea for a solid jumping-off place that will help you write coherent body paragraphs, you can begin with an introduction. (You can even begin by writing the conclusion first if you feel that it will be the easiest place to get started.)

Brainstorming Ways to Get Readers' Attention

Keeping your narrative and your preliminary thesis in mind, try your hand at these effective ways to start an introduction:

➤ a quotation (something you said, something someone said to you, a relevant snippet of dialogue from the narrative)

_____

_____

➤ an anecdote or story (something that sheds light on the subject you're describing or explains how you came to realize the importance of your topic)

_____

_____

➤ a provocative statement (a surprising or shocking comparison or an unexpected revelation)

_____

_____

➤ a question that prompts readers to think about how they will answer it

_____

_____

➤ a hypothetical situation ("Have you ever tried to . . . .?") that invites others to imagine being in someone else's place

_____

_____

➤ a comparison of the topic with something more familiar to your readers

_____

_____

Drafting an Introduction

Choose the opening you like most from the examples you've created, and start a new draft that begins with that opening. How easily can you move from this catchy opening to your narrative? Try one of the following activities if you are having trouble creating an introduction.

1. Write your opening sentence at the top of a page and label it "A." Then write the main point of your narrative at the bottom of the page and label it "B." Ask a classmate or friend to write three to five words or phrases that can get you from A to B.

2. Using any of the words or phrases that seem useful, write three sentences to connect your opening to the beginning of your narrative. The final sentence should wrap up the introductory paragraph and also set up the first sentence of the narrative that will follow. If you have decided to include an explicit thesis statement in your introduction, the final sentence will probably be your thesis.

Trying Options for Organizing Body Paragraphs

A narrative is usually organized by sequencing events in a clear order, and details should build tension to the climactic moment of the essay. If you aren't certain what organization makes sense for your narrative essay, try completing any option that seems viable. Use the option you choose as the basis for an outline or graphic organizer that you can follow as you draft your narrative.

By Time
Chronological order (starting at the beginning and moving forward)

➤ First, _____ .

➤ Then, _____ .

➤ Finally, _____ .

Out of order (flashback or arrangement by association)

➤ A little while ago, _____ .

➤ Before that, _____ .

➤ Now, _____ .

In Order of Importance, Familiarity, or Interest
Least to most important, familiar, or interesting (saving the best for last)

➤ Least _____ .

➤ More _____ .

➤ Most _____ .

Most to least important, familiar, or interesting (starting strong)

➤ Most _____.

➤ Less _____.

➤ Least _____.

Try it yourself!

Topic of first body paragraph: _____

    Details to include in the paragraph:

    • _____

    • _____

    • _____

Topic of second body paragraph: _____

    Details to include in the paragraph:

    • _____

    • _____

    • _____

Topic of third body paragraph: _____

    Details to include in the paragraph:

    • _____

    • _____

    • _____

(Continue until you have outlined or sketched a plan for all your body paragraphs.)

Drafting a Conclusion

Your conclusion should reinforce the point of your narrative without being repetitive or boring. If you have not stated the thesis explicitly in the introduction or body of your narrative essay, you should either state it explicitly or imply it in your conclusion.

➤ The point of this narrative is _____

_____.

➤ Readers should know that I feel _____

_____.

➤ Readers should feel _____

_____.

➤ A detail that suggests my thesis is _____

_____ .

➤ A reason that I chose to tell the story here and now is that _____

_____ .

Try it yourself!

Draft a conclusion that reminds readers — or explicitly tells them for the first time — what the point of your story is:

_____

_____ .

Creating an Intriguing Title

Your title should indicate your topic and say something about it that will interest readers. Try the following ideas to create an intriguing title that your audience will want to read:

➤ Alliteration: My story is about _____

and some words that begin with the same sound and relate to my point are

_____ .

➤ Groups of three: Three things that are important to the narrative are _____

_____ , _____

_____ , and _____ .

➤ Question: People ask _____

_____ about my story.

➤ Quotation: Someone said " _____

_____ " about my narrative.

➤ Try out a title of your own: _____

Feedback Activities

Getting Your Questions Answered by Peer Reviewers

You'll get better feedback from peer reviewers if you ask for specific help with comments and questions like these:

➤ I'm not sure whether or not _____ is working.

➤ Does the story about _____ make sense?

➤ My biggest concern is _____ .

Now write the question with which you *most* want your peer reviewers' help:

_____

_____

Asking Reviewers for Feedback about a Narrative Essay

To find out if reviewers are getting the impressions you want to give in your narrative essay, have them answer the following questions.

➤   What is the thesis? Does it need to be clearer? Should it be implied rather than stated directly (or vice versa)?

➤   How clearly is the narrative told? How clear is the point of the story?

➤   What questions are not answered that should be answered?

➤   Is the point of the narrative clear?

➤   What details work well for the narrative? What do you like about them?

➤   Which details are weakest? Which ideas need further development?

➤   Does the essay's organization make sense?

➤   How well does the essay hang together? How effective are the transitions between paragraphs?

➤   How enticing is the introduction? Which parts make you want to keep reading? What is less interesting?

➤   How well does the conclusion end the essay? What works best to bring the essay to an end? What should change?

➤   How effective is the title? Why?

➤   My favorite part of this essay is _____

_____

because _____ .

➤   The part that I think needs the most improvement is _____

_____

because _____ .

Conducting a Self-Review

Put your draft aside for at least one day. Then, read it again, doing your best to pretend that you have never seen it before. Use the Rubric for Assessing Narration Essays, and rate the draft yourself. (Your instructor may use other criteria for assessing student writing, so be sure to check with him or her about expectations.)

Rubric for Assessing Narration Essays

	Exceeds expectations	Meets expectations	Needs improvement	Does not meet expectations
Focus, purpose, and audience	The narrative focuses on a specific incident from the writer's experience for the purpose of expressing a view or feeling for, informing, or persuading the target audience. The introduction briefly establishes the setting and purpose, sets the tone, and gives the audience a reason to read. A clear thesis gives purpose to the narrative and controls all development.	The thesis addresses an appropriately limited incident that is meaningful to the audience and that meets the assignment. The introduction indicates the writer's purpose — to tell a story in order to make a point or share an insight or life lesson — but the point may be too obvious or too personally confessional for an academic audience. The thesis focuses all or most of the development.	A thesis is apparent but the paper addresses a topic too broad to be described as an incident (such as the senior year in high school) or that fails in some other way to satisfy the assignment's requirements or appeal to the target audience. Body paragraphs may be analytical rather than narrative (for example, "I learned three things about myself in my senior year"). Some irrelevant content may be included.	No clear thesis or narrative point is evident, or the paper does not have a clear purpose or engage the reader's favorable attention. Impressions and vague abstract statements may generally relate to an identified topic but do not form a narrative sequence. Irrelevant material may intrude or contradictory material may confuse the reader about the paper's focus or purpose.
Development	The paper offers well-chosen, concrete details and images along with natural dialogue to vividly recreate the incident being narrated. Unobtrusive, insightful commentary or explanation supports the thesis and engages the audience's favorable attention. Exposition and forecasting statements offer helpful context. Characters seem real.	Details and dialogue serve to engage the audience and accomplish the narrative purpose, and are sufficient to adequately support the thesis, but may not be fully integrated, leaving the reader to wonder at their significance. Content is relevant, with no disruption of essay or paragraph unity and no distortion or visible bias. Characters are appropriately developed.	Details and dialogue are sparse, overbalanced by statements that tell about the incident rather than relating or narrating it directly. Analytical or explanatory observations may inappropriately constitute the bulk of the essay's development. Irrelevant observations or opinions may intrude and distract the reader or obscure the point. Characters are developed but may be depicted unrealistically.	Few or no details or dialogue is included. General statements are vague or they distort or confuse the thesis rather than serving to validate or clarify it. No effort to recreate a scene or narrate an incident is apparent. No exposition is offered, or it is not clearly related to the incident. Characters are flat and undeveloped, so they are unengaging.

	Exceeds expectations	Meets expectations	Needs improvement	Does not meet expectations
Organization and coherence	A clear chronological sequence governs development at both essay and paragraph levels. Flashbacks and forecasting statements are used effectively throughout and are marked clearly with well-chosen transitional devices. Dialogue proceeds naturally and changes in speaker are clearly marked. Explanatory discourse is woven through the narrative and relates consistently to linking elements in the introduction and conclusion, framing the incident and reinforcing the thesis.	Development is reasonably organized throughout, arranged to show the chronological sequencing of sentences narrating the incident, but may be perfunctory. Exposition and forecasting statements are signaled with adequate transition. Indirect quotation may replace dialogue. Transitions are adequate but may be used repetitively. Focusing statements in the introduction and conclusion help provide context. The narrative purpose is achieved.	Chronological organization is attempted but inconsistent, so coherence is weak. The reader can discern a sequence of events but can only follow it with difficulty, as exposition and explanation are inserted with little transition. Conversations are not represented as dialogue. Transitions are used improperly, randomly, or repetitively. The introduction and conclusion fail to clarify the narrative purpose or create a context.	The essay has no discernible organization at essay or paragraph level. Unconnected impressions fail to provide a cohesive narrative structure. No expository or explanatory content is introduced, and the essay employs inadequate or misleading transitional devices or organizational cues. No contextualizing statements are included in either introduction or conclusion; the narrative purpose is obscure.
Style and structure	Design of introductory and body elements engage the audience's favorable attention and guide it through the essay's content, arranged in coherent body and dialogue paragraphs. A conclusion prompts rethinking of the topic or promotes new insight. The paper achieves variety in sentence pattern and type. Tone is skillfully controlled and avoids being too stiff, informal, or familiar; word choice is apt and artful.	The introduction addresses the topic, sets the tone, and guides the reader into the body of the paper, which is developed in multiple separate paragraphs and dialogue. A functional conclusion is present. The writing employs little variety, but sentence construction is competent. Tone and diction are generally appropriate to audience or purpose, but may be self-conscious, colloquial, repetitive, or imprecise.	The essay uses spacing or indention, but paragraphing is weak. Introductory and concluding elements may not be present to frame the narrative. In dialogue, changes in speaker are not properly signaled by the beginning of a new paragraph. Sentences employ faulty or mixed constructions, with little or no variety in pattern or type. Tone and diction are inappropriately stiff or informal for the purpose and audience.	Paragraphing is absent or insufficient to meet the demands of the writing situation, with no distinct introductory or concluding elements included. Dialogue is not represented or the speaker of a given passage cannot be definitively identified. Sentences are difficult to interpret; the writer does not demonstrate control of grammar or paragraph structure. Tone and diction are contradictory or inappropriate.

	Exceeds expectations	Meets expectations	Needs improvement	Does not meet expectations
Precision and editing	The writer reveals mastery of all elements of grammar, usage, and mechanical conventions. Verb tenses are consistent, with appropriate shifts in passages of exposition and forecasting. Uses of second person perspective and passive voice are absent. Dialogue is punctuated properly and is interspersed with exposition and explanation to provide variety to the eye when perusing the page. The writer executes the assignment memorably with no careless errors.	The essay is largely free of error in grammar, punctuation, and use of mechanical conventions, though occasional lapses occur. Verb tenses may shift, and inappropriate shifts in person may occasionally be included, but do not create confusion. Dialogue is punctuated well, with only minor and infrequent error. The paper is neat, legible, and clear, with formatting of manuscript conventions applied consistently. The paper satisfies the assignment with only scattered editing errors.	The essay is weakened with frequent errors in grammar, punctuation, and the use of mechanical conventions. Punctuation of dialogue includes frequent errors; shifts in verb tense and perspective are pervasive and distracting. The submission may be crumpled, stained, or torn. Errors in manuscript formatting conventions draw unfavorable attention. Numerous editing errors distract the reader, though perhaps cause little or no confusion.	Verb and pronoun usage, sentence constructions, and diction are consistently faulty. Sentence structure is dysfunctional. Punctuation is unconventional. The reader is unable to follow attempts at dialogue. Careless or illegible writing is confusing. Stains, rips, blots, or printing errors distract the reader and may make parts of the paper unreadable. The writer fails to observe manuscript conventions or to satisfy other demands of the assignment. Errors throughout are serious enough to cause confusion and misunderstanding of meaning.

Gathering Responses and Collecting Your Thoughts

Gather all the reviewer responses. Make notes about what you and your reviewers agree and disagree on, moving from most important issues, such as the interest of the narrative, the effectiveness of the story's point, the organization, and the support for ideas, to least important, such as spelling and comma placement. List areas where you agree that improvement is needed, and make a plan about what you need to revise. Think about areas of disagreement, too. You make the final decisions about what changes to make, so determine which comments you need to respond to and which you can ignore.

Revision and Editing Activities

Identifying Options for Revision Planning

After you have gathered revision comments on your early draft from peer reviewers and your instructor (pp. 45–46), choose one of the following strategies to begin making your revision plan.

➤ Create a storyboard. On a sticky note or note card, write the main point of your narrative, and put it at the top of your work area. Using separate sticky notes or note cards for each paragraph or example, write down important features such as topic sentences and supporting details. Does your organization make sense? Do the parts work together? Does every paragraph help to advance the story and clarify the point it makes? Using sticky notes or note cards of a different color, add notes to each paragraph about how you will strengthen, change, or delete content based on your reviewers' comments and your own. Take photos of the parts of the storyboard so you'll have a record of what you decide, even if you lose your notes.

➤ Create a graphic organizer. Using either paper and pencil or a digital document, create text boxes representing each introductory paragraph, body paragraph, and conclusion paragraph, and write the main idea of each paragraph in the box. Below it, leave room to revise the main idea. To the right of each main idea box, draw additional boxes for changes, additions, and deletions you have decided to make to supporting details, transitions, and other material in that paragraph.

➤ Make an annotated outline. Using formal complete sentences or informal phrases, make an outline that shows the current main ideas, supporting details, and organization of your draft. Using highlighters, colored pens, different colors of type, or some other method that will make your changes clearly visible, annotate your outline to show the changes you plan to make to your thesis, dominant impression, organization, supporting ideas, introduction, conclusion, and so on.

➤ Make a plan of your own: _____
_____
_____
_____

Revising a Narrative Essay

Following the plan you've created, write a complete revised draft. Repeat as needed until you feel that you have a solid draft that is nearly final.

Using Your Common Issues to Focus Editing of Your Narrative Essay

Edit for grammar, punctuation, and other common problems you have.

➤ The two kinds of problems that teachers or peer reviewers point out most often in my writing are _____ and
_____.

➤   I know I sometimes struggle with _____.

Review the information in Part 3 (pp. 190–247) about the errors you have identified above. Then reread your draft again, correcting any such errors (and any other issues) that you find.

Proofreading

➤   Run the spell checker and carefully consider every suggestion. Do not automatically accept the suggestions! Remember that spell checkers cannot identify problems with certain kinds of words, such as homonyms and proper nouns (names), so check the spelling of such words yourself. Write the words you have misspelled on a spelling checklist you can use to identify and avoid words that give you trouble.

➤   Read your essay aloud slowly, noting and correcting any issues that you find.

➤   Read your essay aloud backwards, word by word, looking for repeated words and similar mistakes that are easy to miss in work that is very familiar. Correct any problems you see.

When your work is as error-free and professional as you can make it, submit your essay.

6

Description*

Prewriting Activities

Brainstorming Memories to Find a Good Descriptive Topic

Prod your memory with questions about sensory details.

➤ The most delicious thing I have ever eaten is _____.

➤ A sound that always makes me happy is _____.

➤ The ugliest place I have ever seen was _____.

➤ I experienced the worst pain of my life when _____.

➤ For me, the smell of _____ is always associated
  with _____.

➤ The object I cherish most is _____
  because _____.

➤ The person who makes me feel most _____ is
  _____
  because _____.

Try one of your own.

_____

_____

_____

_____

* Activities for the Guided Writing Assignment in Chapter 12, *Successful College Writing*, Seventh Edition

Freewriting to Expand Ideas for a Descriptive Essay

Choose the prompt above that creates the *most vivid* ideas in your mind and spend five minutes freewriting (or record yourself speaking) without stopping, giving every detail you can think of about the sense, thing, place, person, or feeling you've identified. You can use words, phrases, or complete sentences; you can jump from one idea to another if a new thought comes to mind. Time yourself, and don't stop writing or speaking until the time is up.

Identifying a Useful Preliminary Topic for a Descriptive Essay

What person, place, animal, plant, thing, or idea seems like a good preliminary topic for a descriptive essay? The topic can be one that you started with on p. 52, or it can be an idea that came to you while you were freewriting about something else.

➤ My preliminary topic is _____
_____
_____.

Finding a Perspective on the Preliminary Topic

➤ Thinking about this topic makes me feel _____
_____.

➤ I want anyone who reads my essay to know that _____
_____.

➤ The best way to show my point of view is to include _____,
_____, and _____.

Identifying the Readers You Want to Reach

➤ My audience includes _____.

➤ They might be interested in this topic because _____
_____
_____.

➤ I need to tell this audience about _____
_____

so they will understand how I feel about the topic.

➤ When they read my essay, I want them to feel _____

_____.

➤ My purpose for writing is to _____.

Finding Sensory Details to Support the Impression of a Descriptive Essay

Brainstorm as many of the following prompts as possible, identifying sensory details that reinforce your point of view on the topic and the setting you will describe.

➤ something seen, observed, or watched that connects to the setting and contributes to the dominant impression

EXAMPLES: bright dots on a Twister mat, a sunset turning the ocean pink

_____

_____

_____

➤ something heard or overheard that connects to the setting and contributes to the dominant impression

EXAMPLES: the faraway-motorcycle sound of a hummingbird, impatient honking behind me as my car wheezed and died

_____

_____

_____

➤ an aroma, smell, or stench that connects to the setting and contributes to the dominant impression

EXAMPLES: the cloyingly sweet smell of baby powder lingering in a room she had left, the scent of cut grass perfuming a summer night

_____

_____

_____

➤ something tangible or textured that connects to the setting and contributes to the dominant impression

EXAMPLES: sharp gravel pinching my bare feet, the mule's flannel-soft ears

_____

_____

_____

➤ a flavor or taste that connects to the setting and contributes to the dominant impression

> EXAMPLES: my grandfather sprinkling salt on a juicy slice of watermelon, the herbal sore-throat remedy that tasted like the sole of a muddy army boot

_____

_____

_____

Using Specific Words to Emphasize the Feeling Readers Should Take Away from a Descriptive Essay

Reread your supporting details and cross out any that are irrelevant or that give a different impression than the one you want readers to get. You may want to ask a classmate or peer group if the details you plan to keep are effective.

Finding Figures of Speech to Enliven a Description

Practice making comparisons to bring your topic to life.

➤ If this topic were a person, it would be _____
because _____.

➤ _____ reminds me
of _____ because
_____.

➤ People say that _____ is
like _____, but I don't
think that is true because _____
_____.

Now try writing your own comparison.

_____

_____

_____

Thesis Activities

➤ My preliminary topic (from p. 53) is _____
_____.

Narrowing and Focusing a Topic for a Descriptive Essay

Is your preliminary topic something that you can describe in an essay of the assigned length? Sometimes a narrower topic allows you to create a better description.

➤ To me, the single most important thing about this topic is (pick one and complete the sentence)

- that it made me realize _____.
- that it is unique because _____.
- that it reminds me of _____.
- that the person's character is _____.
- that _____
  _____.

➤ If I had five minutes to explain why I have strong feelings about this topic, I would start with _____
_____.

Moving from Topic to Thesis for a Descriptive Essay

Fill in the blanks to start thinking about making some kind of assertion (that is, expressing an opinion or taking a stand) about your topic.

1. Many people are surprised to find out that (my topic) is _____
   _____.

2. I used to believe _____ about (my topic), but now I think _____
   _____.

3. This may sound strange, but (my topic) reminds me of _____
   because _____.

4. I did not expect (my topic) to make much of an impression on me, but _____
   _____.

5. The reason audiences should care about (my topic) is _____
   _____.

6. An ordinary _____ is like _____,
   but (my topic) is different because _____
   _____.

7. Invent your own assertion about your topic.
   _____
   _____
   _____

Creating a Preliminary Thesis Statement for a Descriptive Essay

Remember that a thesis statement needs a topic—but it also needs to make some kind of assertion about the topic. In a descriptive essay, the thesis should emphasize the dominant impression you want your writing to make on readers.

➤ _____ has brightened my life since the day _____.

➤ I changed my mind about _____

   after experiencing _____.

Reread the ideas you've come up with about your topic on pp. 52–55, and try writing a thesis statement of your own.

_____

_____

_____

_____

Developing a Dominant Impression for a Descriptive Essay

The main idea in a descriptive essay is a dominant impression—an overall attitude, mood, or feeling that readers are left with.

➤ What dominant impression should your thesis evoke? Write a few words that evoke the same impression in you, and refer to them frequently as you write.

Thinking about the Setting for a Description

A descriptive essay evokes a very particular setting.

➤ The memory I am writing about happened when I was _____ years old, in _____ (year or era).

➤ The memory is most strongly tied to _____ (place).

➤ Whenever I think of (my topic), I remember being _____

   _____

   and doing _____.

➤ When I remember this time and place, I always think of _____,

   _____, and _____.

Drafting Activities

Deciding Where to Begin Your Draft

What part of the draft are you most excited about writing or do you feel best prepared to begin? Start with that part. If you know how you want to tell your story but not how you want to introduce or conclude, begin with body paragraphs. If you have an idea for a solid jumping-off place that will help you write coherent body paragraphs, begin with an introduction. You don't need to write the draft in what will be its final order; just get started.

Brainstorming Ways to Get Readers' Attention

Keeping your thesis, setting, and dominant impression in mind, try your hand at these effective ways to start an introduction.

➤ a quotation (something you said, something someone said to you, a quotation from a book or film, etc.)

_____

➤ an anecdote or story (something that sheds light on the subject you're describing or explains how you came to realize the importance of your topic)

_____

➤ a provocative statement (a surprising or shocking comparison or an unexpected revelation)

_____

➤ a question that prompts readers to think about how they will answer it

_____

➤ a hypothetical situation that invites others to imagine being in someone else's place

_____

➤ a comparison of the topic with something more familiar to readers

_____

Drafting an Introduction

Choose the opening you like most from the examples you've created, and start a new draft that begins with that opening. Then write the preliminary thesis that you created on p. 57. How easily can you move from a catchy opening sentence to your preliminary thesis?

1. Write no more than three sentences to connect your opening and your thesis.

2. Copy and paste your opening statement, connecting sentences, and preliminary thesis into a new document. Revising any of the sentences as needed, write a complete introductory paragraph.

Trying Options for Organizing Body Paragraphs

If you aren't certain what organization makes sense for your descriptive essay, try completing as many of the following options as you can. Which one best reinforces the dominant impression you want your essay to give? Use the option you choose as the basis for an outline or graphic organizer that you can follow as you draft.

By Time

Chronological order (starting at the beginning and moving forward)

➤ First, _____.

➤ Then, _____.

➤ Finally, _____.

Reverse chronological order (starting at the end and moving backward)

➤ Now, _____.

➤ Earlier, _____.

Out of order (flashback or arrangement by association)

➤ A little while ago, _____.

➤ Before that, _____.

➤ Now, _____.

By Place

➤ If I moved around my topic while describing it, I would begin with _____

_____

and end with _____.

In Order of Importance, Familiarity, or Interest

Least to most important, familiar, or interesting (saving the best for last)

➤ Least _____.

➤ More _____.

➤ Most _____.

Most to least important, familiar, or interesting (starting strong)

➤ Most _____.

➤ Less _____.

➤ Least _____.

Try it yourself!

Topic of first body paragraph: _____

Details to include in the paragraph:

• _____

• _____

• _____

Topic of second body paragraph: _____

Details to include in the paragraph:

• _____

• _____

• _____

Topic of third body paragraph: _____

Details to include in the paragraph:

• _____

• _____

• _____

(Continue until you have outlined or sketched a plan for all your body paragraphs.)

Drafting a Conclusion

Your conclusion should reinforce the dominant impression you are giving in your essay without being repetitive or boring.

➤ The dominant impression I want this description to give is _____

_____.

➤   Readers should know that I feel _____

_____ .

➤   Readers should feel _____ .

➤   A fact, story, or detail that reminds readers of my thesis is _____

_____ .

➤   A reason that I chose to describe this topic and this setting here and now is that

_____ .

Try it yourself!

Draft a conclusion that reminds readers of your dominant impression without repeating your thesis exactly as you've stated it in the introduction:

_____

_____

_____

_____

Creating an Intriguing Title

Your title should indicate your topic and say something about it that will interest readers. Try the following ideas to create an intriguing title that your audience will want to read.

➤   Alliteration: My topic is _____

and some words that begin with the same sound and relate to my topic are

_____ .

➤   Groups of three: Three things I talk about in the essay are _____

_____ , _____

_____ , and _____ .

➤   Question: People ask _____

_____ about my topic.

➤   Quotation: Someone said "_____

_____ " about my topic.

➤   Try out a title of your own: _____

Feedback Activities

Getting Your Questions Answered by Peer Reviewers

You'll get better feedback from peer reviewers if you ask for specific help with comments and questions like these.

➤ I'm not sure whether or not _____ is working.

➤ Does the story about _____ make sense?

➤ My biggest concern is _____.

Now write the question with which you *most* want your peer reviewers' help.

_____

_____

_____

_____

Asking Reviewers for Feedback about a Descriptive Essay

To find out if reviewers are getting the impressions you want to give in your descriptive essay, have them answer the following questions.

➤ What is the thesis? What is your dominant impression?

➤ How well do the topic sentences of the body paragraphs support the dominant impression?

➤ What important questions do you have that are not answered by the essay?

➤ What details work best for this essay? What do you like about them?

➤ Which details are weakest? Which ideas need further development?

➤ Does the essay organization make sense?

➤ How well does the essay hang together? How effective are the transitions between paragraphs?

➤ How enticing is the introduction? Which parts make you want to keep reading? What is less interesting?

➤ How well does the conclusion end the essay? What works best to bring the essay to an end? What should change?

➤ How effective is the title? Why?

➤ My favorite part of this essay is _____

_____

because _____.

➤ The part that I think needs the most improvement is _____

_____

because _____.

Conducting a Self-Review

Put your draft aside for at least one day. Then, read it again, doing your best to pretend that you have never seen it before. Use the Rubric for Assessing Description Essays, and rate your draft yourself. (Your instructor may use other criteria for assessing student writing, so be sure to check with him or her about expectations.)

Rubric for Assessing Description Essays

	Exceeds expectations	Meets expectations	Needs improvement	Does not meet expectations
Focus, purpose, and audience	The description focuses on a specific person, place, or thing from the writer's experience in order to express a view or feeling, inform, or persuade the target audience. The introduction briefly establishes the focus of attention, sets an engaging tone, and gives the audience a reason to read. A clear thesis gives the essay a meaningful purpose and controls all development.	The thesis addresses an appropriately limited, specific subject of description that engages the audience and meets the assignment. The introduction indicates the writer's purpose—describing in order to share, teach, or convince—but the subject may be overly personal for an academic writing situation. The thesis statement and topic sentences effectively focus content at the essay and body levels.	A focus of description is apparent, but the thesis fails to clarify the purpose for the writing, satisfy the assignment's requirements, or appeal to the target audience. The introduction is sparse or vague. Body paragraphs may follow an analytical, explanatory, or narrative pattern of development rather than using description. Some irrelevant content may be included.	No clear thesis or focal point for description is evident, or the paper does not have a clear purpose or engage the reader's favorable attention. Impressions and generalizations may refer to an identified topic but do not develop or recreate a specific image, impression, moment, or place. Irrelevant material may intrude or contradictory material may confuse the reader about the paper's focus or purpose.

	Exceeds expectations	Meets expectations	Needs improvement	Does not meet expectations
Development	The paper offers specific, clear details and images evoking multiple sensory responses to depict the subject of description. Natural, insightful commentary or explanation clarifies the purpose for which the imagery is offered and engages the audience's favorable attention. Imagery is constructed of strong, concrete nouns and avoids using too many intensifiers or modifiers.	Details serve to engage the audience and accomplish the description's purpose. Imagery may be primarily visual or focus on only one of the senses. Details adequately support the thesis, but may be more ornamental than functional. Content is relevant, with no disruption of essay or paragraph unity and no distortion or visible bias. Imagery evokes feeling or understanding but avoids sentimentality or overreliance on modifiers.	Details and specifics are sparse, and development is comprised of general observations rather than concrete imagery relating directly to the subject of description. Most imagery is included for the sake of ornament. Personal observations or opinions may be less helpful or meaningful than merely distracting. Imagery is trite and figures of speech predominate rather than original imagery, making the essay either dry or overly sentimental.	Few or no details or concrete, specific images are included. General statements are vague or they obscure the thesis rather than serving to validate or clarify it. No recreation or depiction of a scene or other subject of description is discernible. If imagery is present, its purpose is not clearly related to the support of a thesis or the achievement of a purpose. Very little sensory stimulation occurs, as imagery is undeveloped, relying heavily on repetitive intensifiers and modifiers.
Organization and coherence	A clear organizing principle (spatial, emphatic, or other) governs the arrangement of content at both essay and paragraph levels. Organizing cues are used effectively. Each body paragraph has its own internal organization which relates to linking elements in the introduction, other body paragraphs, and conclusion. The reader understands at every point what is being described, why it is being described, and how the description relates to the essay's purpose.	Development is reasonably organized throughout, arranged according to some logical principle, but may be predictable or mechanical. Shifts in the reader's field of vision are signaled with adequate transition. Body paragraphs follow the sequence mapped in the introduction and summarized in the conclusion, but the rationale behind the sequencing itself may be unclear. Transitions are adequate but may be used repetitively. The essay's descriptive purpose is adequately achieved.	A strategy is attempted for sequencing material but is not implemented consistently, so arrangement of content seems uncontrolled. The reader can follow a sequence of impressions but only with difficulty, as exposition and explanation are inserted with little transition. Organizing cues are used improperly, randomly, or repetitively. The introduction and conclusion fail to clarify the thesis, and the body paragraphs lack coherence, so the essay's descriptive purpose is not achieved.	The essay has no discernible organization at essay or paragraph level. Random impressions fail to provide a cohesive structure at either the essay or the paragraph level. No explanatory content is introduced, and the essay employs inadequate or misleading transitional devices or organizational cues. No contextualizing statements are included in either introduction or conclusion; the paper seems comprised of general impressions largely unconnected to a descriptive purpose.

	Exceeds expectations	Meets expectations	Needs improvement	Does not meet expectations
Style and structure	Design of introductory and body elements engages the audience's favorable attention and guides it through the essay's content, arranged in coherent body and dialogue paragraphs. A conclusion prompts rethinking of the topic or promotes new insight. The paper achieves variety in sentence pattern and type. Tone is skillfully controlled and avoids being too stiff, informal, or familiar; word choice is apt and artful.	The introduction addresses the topic, sets the tone, and guides the reader into the body of the paper, which is developed in multiple separate paragraphs. A functional conclusion is present. The writing employs some variety of pattern or type, and sentence construction is competent. Tone and diction are generally appropriate to audience or purpose, but may be too formal or informal for the rhetorical situation.	The essay uses spacing or indention, but paragraphing is weak. Introductory and concluding elements may not be present to frame the purpose for which the subject is being described. Changes in subtopics are not properly signaled by the beginning of a new paragraph. Sentences employ faulty or mixed constructions, with little or no variety in pattern or type. Tone and diction are inappropriately stiff or informal for the purpose and audience.	Paragraphing is absent or insufficient to meet the demands of the writing situation, with no distinct introductory or concluding elements included. Shifts in person or verb tense are frequent and random. Sentences are difficult to interpret; the writer does not demonstrate control of grammar or paragraph structure. Tone and diction are contradictory or inappropriate.
Precision and editing	The writer reveals mastery of all elements of grammar, usage, and mechanical conventions. Verb tenses are consistent, with appropriate shifts in passages of exposition and forecasting. Uses of second person perspective and passive voice are absent or appropriate if included. Sequential modifiers are punctuated properly and are interspersed with exposition and explanation to provide variety. The writer executes the assignment memorably with no careless errors.	The essay is largely free of errors in grammar, punctuation and use of mechanical conventions, though occasional lapses occur. Inappropriate shifts in verb tense and person may occasionally be included, but do not create confusion. Sequential modifiers are punctuated correctly, with only minor and infrequent error. The paper is neat, legible, and clear, with formatting of manuscript conventions applied consistently. The paper satisfies the assignment with only scattered careless errors.	The essay is weakened by frequent errors in grammar, punctuation, and the use of mechanical conventions. Punctuation of sequential modifiers includes frequent errors; shifts in verb tense and perspective are pervasive and distracting. The submission may be crumpled, stained, or torn. Errors in manuscript formatting conventions draw unfavorable attention. Numerous careless errors distract the reader, though perhaps cause little or no confusion.	Verb and pronoun usage, sentence constructions, and diction are consistently faulty. Sentence structure is dysfunctional. Punctuation is unconventional. Careless or illegible writing is confusing. Stains, rips, or printing errors distract the reader and may make parts of the paper unreadable. The writer fails to observe manuscript conventions or to satisfy other demands of the assignment. Errors throughout are serious enough to cause confusion and misunderstanding of meaning.

Gathering Responses and Collecting Your Thoughts

Gather all the reviewer responses. Make notes about what your reviewers agree and disagree on, moving from most important issues, such as thesis, dominant impression, organization, interest, and support for ideas, to least important, such as spelling and comma placement. List areas where you agree that improvement is needed, and make a plan about what you need to revise. Think about areas of disagreement, too. You make the final decisions about what changes to make, so determine which comments you need to respond to and which you can ignore.

Revision and Editing Activities

Identifying Options for Revision Planning

After you have gathered revision comments on your early draft from peer reviewers and your instructor (pp. 62–63), choose one of the following strategies to begin making your revision plan.

➤ Create a storyboard. On a sticky note or note card, write your thesis statement or dominant impression, and put it at the top of your work area. Using separate sticky notes or note cards for each paragraph or example, write down important features such as topic sentences and supporting details. Does your organization make sense? Do the parts work together? Does every paragraph help to support the dominant impression? Using sticky notes or note cards of a different color, add notes to each paragraph about how you will strengthen, change, or delete content based on your reviewers' comments and your own. Take photos of the parts of the storyboard so you'll have a record of what you decide, even if you lose your notes.

➤ Create a graphic organizer. Using either paper and pencil or a digital document, create text boxes representing each introductory paragraph, body paragraph, and conclusion paragraph, and write the main idea of each paragraph in the box. Below it, leave room to revise the main idea. To the right of each main idea box, draw additional boxes for changes, additions, and deletions you have decided to make to supporting details, transitions, and other material in that paragraph.

➤ Make an annotated outline. Using formal complete sentences or informal phrases, make an outline that shows the current main ideas, supporting details, and organization of your draft. Using highlighters, colored pens, different colors of type, or some other method to make your changes clearly visible, annotate your outline to show the changes you plan to make to your thesis, dominant impression, organization, supporting ideas, introduction, conclusion, and so on.

➤ Make a plan of your own. _____

_____

_____

Revising a Descriptive Essay

Following the plan you've created, write a complete revised draft. Repeat as needed until you feel that you have a solid draft that is nearly final.

Using Your Common Issues to Focus Editing of Your Descriptive Essay

Edit for grammar, punctuation, and other common problems you have.

➤ The two kinds of problems that teachers or peer reviewers point out most often in my writing are _____ and

_____.

➤ I know I sometimes struggle with _____.

Review the information in Part 3 (pp. 190–247) about the errors you have identified above. Then reread your draft again, correcting any such errors (and any other issues) that you find.

Proofreading

➤ Run the spell checker and carefully consider every suggestion. Do not automatically accept the suggestions! Remember that spell checkers cannot identify problems with certain kinds of words, such as homonyms and proper nouns (names), so check the spelling of such words yourself. If you keep track of the words you commonly misspell, you can improve your spelling, so consider a spelling-mistake list based on what you find.

➤ Read your essay aloud slowly, noting and correcting any issues that you find.

➤ Read your essay aloud backwards, word by word, looking for repeated words and similar mistakes that are easy to miss in work that is very familiar. Correct any problems you see.

When your work is as error-free and professional as you can make it, submit your essay.

7

Illustration*

Prewriting Activities

Finding Ideas for an Illustration Essay Topic

An illustration essay uses multiple examples to support a generalization or clarify an unfamiliar concept. To identify a generalization or concept that can serve as the topic for your illustration essay, try the following prompts.

➤ Most people don't understand _____, but I do.

➤ A big problem that many people aren't aware of is _____

_____.

➤ The common thread that connects all my favorite films is _____

_____.

➤ The biggest problems facing my community have _____

_____ in common.

Try it yourself!

Identify a general truth or a concept that you can illustrate with examples.

_____

_____

_____

*Activities for the Guided Writing Assignment in Chapter 13, *Successful College Writing*, Seventh Edition

Clustering to Brainstorm Ideas for an Illustration Essay Topic

To generate ideas for the topic of an illustration essay, try clustering. Write an idea, either for an example or for a concept you will illustrate with examples, in the middle of a sheet of paper and circle it. Then, write more words and phrases that relate to the central word, circling each and joining them to the central circle. Keep going, generating ideas related to circled concepts as you think of them, until the paper is filled. (You can also use software for digital clustering diagrams if you prefer.)

➤ What ideas were most productive for you, prompting the largest clusters of circled words and phrases?

➤ Are any ideas unexpectedly unproductive, going nowhere on your diagram? Pay attention to what doesn't work as well as to what does.

Identifying a Preliminary Topic for an Illustration Essay

What general statement or concept will you illustrate in your essay? The topic can be one that you started with on p. 68, or it can be an idea that came to you while you were exploring something else in one of the activities above.

➤ My preliminary topic is _____
_____
_____ .

Finding a Perspective on the Preliminary Topic for Your Illustration Essay

In order to find examples that will work well for your illustration, you should consider your point of view of the topic.

➤ This topic makes me feel _____
_____ .

➤ I want anyone who reads my illustration essay to know that _____
_____ .

➤ The best way to show my point of view is to include _____ ,
_____ , and _____ .

Identifying the Readers I Want to Reach in My Illustration Essay

Figuring out what your audience already knows and does not know about the topic will be extremely important. If you consider what they already believe or know, you will be able to identify examples that can more effectively illustrate the concept you are explaining. Complete the following prompts to analyze the audience you expect to reach.

➤ My audience includes _____.

➤ They may already know _____
about this topic, but they may not know _____
_____.

➤ I need to tell this audience about _____
_____ so they
will understand my perspective on the topic.

➤ When they read my essay, I want them to feel _____
_____.

➤ My purpose for writing is to _____.

➤ To succeed in this purpose, I will probably need to use _____ (one
or two/ three or four/five or more) _____ examples.

Exploring Example Ideas for an Illustration Essay

What examples should you use to illustrate the generalization or concept of your topic? Respond to any of the following prompts that are appropriate for your illustration essay.

➤ The field or discipline that will provide the most compelling examples for my
audience is _____
because _____.

➤ An example that everyone associates with this topic is _____
_____.

It is (useful/not useful) for my illustration essay because _____
_____.

➤ A visual that would clarify the topic is _____.

➤ My own experience with _____
could be used as an example because _____
_____.

➤ Other examples might include _____,
_____,
and _____.

➤   I (need/do not need) to use sources from research.

➤   Additional sources I could use include _____
_____, and
I can find them _____.

Identifying Strong, Vivid Examples for an Illustration Essay

Detailed examples make an illustration come alive. Brainstorm as many of the following prompts as possible to try out different patterns of development for the examples you will include, and be sure to include vivid details to interest readers.

➤   narrative examples

   EXAMPLE: a personal anecdote to illustrate the concept of de-cluttering

   _____

   _____

   _____

➤   descriptive examples

   EXAMPLE: a detailed description of a local grocery store's cereal aisle to illustrate the concept of choice overload

   _____

   _____

   _____

➤   process analysis examples

   EXAMPLES: a description of the process of writing an essay to illustrate the idea of multitasking

   _____

   _____

   _____

➤   causal analysis examples

   EXAMPLES: a discussion of the effect of a neighborhood cleanup to illustrate the "broken windows" theory

   _____

   _____

   _____

➤ Try creating an example from any pattern of development that seems useful.

_____

_____

_____

Choosing Visuals or Other Media to Enliven an Illustration Essay

If you have access to photos or other media that will help create a vivid impression of the generalization you are illustrating, consider including one or more of them in your essay. Video and audio files can be used in an essay that you will post online.

Thesis Activities

➤ My preliminary topic (p. 69) is _____.

Narrowing and Focusing a Topic for an Illustration Essay

Will you be able to clarify the concept or support the generalization in an essay of the assigned length? Sometimes a narrower topic may allow you to create a better illustration essay.

➤ If I had five minutes to explain the concept or generalization to people who are

not familiar with it, I would start with _____

_____.

Identifying a Point for Your Illustration Essay

To me, the single most important thing about the topic I am trying to illustrate is (pick one and complete the sentence)

- that it clarifies _____.
- that it helps people understand _____.
- that it proves _____.
- that it is exciting because _____.
- that it is important because _____.
- that _____

_____.

Moving from Topic to Preliminary Thesis for an Illustration Essay

Fill in the blanks to start thinking about the point you want to make in your illustration essay.

1. Many people will be surprised to find out that _____

_____.

2. I used to believe _____, but now
   I think _____.

3. This may sound strange, but (the topic) makes me think about _____
   _____ because _____.

4. At first I did not understand (the topic), but now I think of it as _____
   _____.

5. A new insight my readers should have about (the topic) is _____
   _____.

Now, write your own generalization that can serve as a preliminary thesis.

_____

_____

_____

Testing Your Thesis

In a sentence or two, explain your proposed thesis for your illustration essay to a classmate or friend who is part of your audience, and briefly tell him or her about the example or examples you will use to support the thesis. Ask for responses to these questions.

➤ How much do you understand about the generalization being illustrated?

_____

_____

➤ How does the plan for this illustration essay seem likely to expand your under-standing of generalization, idea, or concept?

_____

➤ What interests you most about this topic? Why? _____

_____

Do the reviewer's responses suggest that you are on the right track? If not, consider whether you should rethink your topic, review your assumptions about what your audience knows and cares about, or reconsider the examples you will use.

Drafting Activities

Deciding Where to Begin

Begin at the easiest point for you to get started. If starting with the example that is most personal or most familiar will help you get your draft underway, begin there. If you know you want to include an image or video clip as an example, begin with that. You can start with the introduction, of course, but you do not have to begin at the beginning; you can draft the introduction and conclusion after completing the body of your essay if you like.

Brainstorming Ways to Get Readers' Attention

Keeping your preliminary thesis in mind, try your hand at these effective ways to start an introduction.

➤ a quotation (something you said, something someone said to you, a relevant snippet of dialogue that will be part of one of your examples)

_____

_____

➤ an anecdote or story (something that sheds light on the subject you are describing or explains how you came to realize the importance of your topic)

_____

_____

➤ a provocative statement (a surprising or shocking announcement or an unexpected revelation)

_____

_____

➤ a question that prompts readers to think about how they will answer it

_____

_____

➤ a hypothetical situation that invites others to imagine being in someone else's place

_____

_____

➤ a comparison that shows how your unfamiliar concept is like something more familiar to your readers

_____

_____

Drafting an Introduction

Choose the opening you like most from the examples you've created, and start a new draft that begins with that opening. How can you move from this catchy opening to your first example?

➤ Where will you state your thesis—right after the opening, at the end of the introduction, or somewhere else?

➤ What background information will readers need right up front to make sense of your examples? How can you incorporate it smoothly?

➤ How will you help readers get a sense of the scope of the examples you will use to illustrate your thesis?

Trying Options for Organizing Body Paragraphs

If you aren't certain what organization makes sense for the examples that will support your thesis, try completing the most viable option listed below. Use the option you choose as the basis for an outline or graphic organizer that you can follow as you draft.

By Time

➤ Chronological order: start at the beginning and move forward in time

➤ Reverse chronological order: move from most recent time to earliest

In Order of Importance, Familiarity, or Interest

➤ Least to most important, familiar, or interesting: save the best for last

➤ Most to least important, familiar, or interesting: start strong

Try it yourself!

➤ Organization plan for examples: _____

Topic of first body paragraph: _____

➤ I will develop the example(s) using the _____ pattern.
Details to include in the paragraph:

  • _____

  • _____

  • _____

Topic of second body paragraph: _____

➤ I will develop the example(s) using the _____ pattern.
Details to include in the paragraph:

  • _____

  • _____

  • _____

Topic of third body paragraph: _____

➤ I will develop the example(s) using the _____ pattern.

Details to include in the paragraph:

- _____

- _____

- _____

(Continue until you have outlined or sketched a plan for all your body paragraphs.)

Drafting a Conclusion

Your conclusion should reinforce the way your examples have illustrated your generalization and make a final statement.

➤ These examples illustrate _____

_____.

➤ This illustration is important because _____.

➤ Readers should feel _____.

Try it yourself!

Draft a conclusion that reinforces your thesis and ties the whole essay together.

_____

_____

_____

Creating an Intriguing Title

Your title should indicate the topic of your illustration essay and say something about it that will interest readers. Try the following ideas to create an intriguing title that your audience will want to read:

➤ Alliteration: My generalization relates to _____

and some words that begin with the same sound and relate to my examples are

_____.

➤ Groups of three: Three things that are important to the illustration are

_____, _____

_____, and _____.

➤ Question: People ask _____

_____ about this generalization.

➤ Quotation: Someone said "_____
_____" about the topic I
am illustrating.

➤ Try out a title of your own: _____

Feedback Activities

Getting Your Questions Answered by Peer Reviewers

You'll get better feedback from peer reviewers if you ask for specific help with comments and questions like these.

➤ I'm not sure whether or not _____ is working.

➤ Does the example about _____ make sense?

➤ My biggest concern is _____.

Now write the question with which you *most* want your peer reviewers' help.

_____

_____

Asking Reviewers for Feedback about an Illustration Essay

To find out if reviewers are getting the impressions you want to give in your illustration essay, have them answer the following questions.

➤ What is the thesis? Is it interesting?

➤ How clearly do the examples illustrate the thesis? Which example(s) do you like best? Which do you like least?

➤ What questions are not answered that should be answered?

➤ What details work well in the examples? What do you like about them?

➤ Which details are weakest? Which ideas need further development?

➤ Does the essay's organization make sense?

➤ How well does the essay hang together? How effective are the transitions between paragraphs?

➤ How enticing is the introduction? Which parts make you want to keep reading? What is less interesting?

➤ How well does the conclusion end the essay? What works best to bring the essay to an end? What should change?

➤ How effective is the title? Why?

➤ My favorite part of this essay is _____

_____

because _____.

➤ The part that I think needs the most improvement is _____

_____

because _____.

Conducting a Self-Review

Put your draft aside for at least one day. Then, read it again, doing your best to pretend that you have never seen it before. Use the Rubric for Assessing Illustration Essays to see how well you think you have accomplished the essay's objectives in this draft. (Your instructor may use other criteria for assessing student writing, so be sure to check with him or her about expectations.)

Rubric for Assessing Illustration Essays

	Exceeds expectations	Meets expectations	Needs improvement	Does not meet expectations
Focus, purpose, and audience	The thesis addresses a term or concept that is interesting and important to the audience. The introduction indicates how the essay will clarify, explain, or support the thesis by using illustration, and promises an insight or learning experience. Unified body paragraphs have clearly focused topic sentences.	The thesis addresses a claim, term, or concept appropriate to the audience and the assignment. The introduction clearly indicates the intent to clarify or support the thesis by using illustration. Unified body paragraphs include functional topic sentences.	A thesis is evident but is too broad or narrow, or does not meet the assignment's purpose or appeal to the target audience. Body paragraphs are too broadly or too narrowly focused, or lack clearly governing topic sentences. Some irrelevant material may be included.	No clear thesis is evident, or the thesis is inadequate to control the essay or engage the reader's favorable attention. Body paragraphs lack topic sentences, or are too long or too short to effectively develop individual subtopics.

	Exceeds expectations	Meets expectations	Needs improvement	Does not meet expectations
Development	The essay offers well-chosen, authoritative, representative, relevant, and concrete examples to clarify and support the paper's thesis and engage the audience's favorable attention. The writer's extended examples are fully integrated with the paper's explanatory content; personal experience examples are balanced with historical, topical, or other examples that can be authenticated.	Examples are appropriate to the audience and purpose, and sufficient to adequately support the thesis, but may be left to "speak for themselves" without being fully integrated with the paper or paragraph topic. Essay and paragraph content is relevant, with no disruption of essay or paragraph unity and no visible bias.	Examples are offered to support the thesis, but are too broad or too general to fully engage the audience or validate the thesis. Development may be overbalanced with unverifiable personal experience or hypothetical examples.	Few examples are offered, or they distort or confuse the thesis rather than serving to validate or clarify it.
Organization and coherence	Clear, logical organizing principles govern the arrangement of content at both essay and paragraph levels. Forecasting statements are used effectively in the introduction. Smooth, largely unnoticed transitions within and between ideas and paragraphs enhance coherence.	Development is reasonably organized throughout. Sentences within paragraphs are arranged to show the logical sequencing of ideas. Each body paragraph is unified and coherent. Body paragraphs are sequenced effectively for the types(s) of examples that writer employs. Transitions link ideas and paragraphs.	Organization is attempted but is ineffective or unclear. The reader can follow the writer's points only with difficulty. Body paragraph sequencing seems uncontrolled or random, with insufficient or confusing transitional, organizational cues being employed.	The essay has no discernible organization at essay or paragraph level. The reader is unable to follow the writer's train of thought, and the essay employs inadequate or misleading transitional devices or organizational cues.

	Exceeds expectations	Meets expectations	Needs improvement	Does not meet expectations
Style and structure	Introductory, body, and concluding elements engage the audience's attention and guide it through the essay's coherent body paragraphs. A conclusion prompts rethinking of the topic or promotes new insight. The essay achieves variety in sentence pattern and type. If using sources, the writer uses signal phrasing and clearly sets off cited from original material. Tone is skillfully controlled; word choice is apt.	The introduction is relevant and sets the tone, and guides the reader into the body of the paper, which is developed in multiple paragraphs. A functional conclusion is present. Sentences are well constructed if not varied. If used, sources are acknowledged, but signal phrasing or parenthetical elements may be misplaced or confusing. Diction is appropriate, but may be repetitive or imprecise.	Paragraphing is weak. Introductory elements are not controlled, and a separate body and conclusion may not be included. Sentences are vague or ambiguous, with little or no variety in pattern or type. If outside sources are used, no in-text citation is offered, or it is too confusing to clearly distinguish the writer's work from cited material. Tone is inappropriate for the purpose and audience. Diction is faulty or inappropriate.	Paragraphing is absent or insufficient to meet the demands of the writing situation, with no distinct introductory or concluding elements included. Sentences are difficult to interpret; the writer does not demonstrate control of grammar or paragraph structure. Tone and diction are confusing, contradictory, or inappropriate.
Precision and editing	All elements of grammar, usage, and mechanics are mastered. Listed examples are punctuated properly and are parallel. Outside sources, if used, are cited in proper bibliographic form. Formatting conventions are applied appropriately throughout. An attractive page design draws the reader's eye through the page. The writer executes the assignment memorably with no careless errors.	The essay is largely free of errors in grammar, punctuation, and mechanics. Sentences are coherent, and structural errors (where present) do not disrupt the reading. Outside sources, if used, are cited, with minor lapses in form or format. The paper is neat, legible, and clear, with formatting consistently applied. The paper satisfies the assignment with only scattered careless errors.	The essay has frequent errors in grammar, punctuation, and mechanics. Outside sources, when used, are cited, but formatted incorrectly, sometimes leading to ambiguity of source or source type. Errors in manuscript formatting conventions draw unfavorable attention. The writer attempts but fails to fully execute the assignment. Numerous careless errors distract, though perhaps cause little or no confusion.	Verb and pronoun usage, sentence construction, and diction are consistently faulty. Punctuation is arbitrary. Where outside sources are used, bibliographic entries are omitted or incomplete. Careless or illegible writing is confusing. Stains, tears, blots, or printing errors distract the reader and may make parts of the paper unreadable. The writer fails to observe manuscript conventions or to satisfy other demands of the assignment. Errors throughout are serious enough to cause confusion and obscure meaning.

Gathering Responses and Collecting Your Thoughts

Gather all the reviewer responses. Make notes about what you and your reviewers agree and disagree on, moving from most important issues, such as appropriateness of the topic, the effectiveness of the examples, the organization, and the support for ideas, to least important, such as spelling and comma placement. List areas where you agree that improvement is needed, and make a plan about what you need to revise. Think about areas of disagreement, too. You make the final decisions about what changes to make, so determine which comments you need to respond to and which you can ignore.

Revision and Editing Activities

Identifying Options for Revision Planning

After you have gathered revision comments on your early draft from peer reviewers and your instructor (pp. 77–78), choose one of the following strategies to begin making your revision plan.

➤ Create a storyboard. On a sticky note or note card, write the generalization you are illustrating, and put it at the top of your work area. Using separate sticky notes or note cards for each paragraph or example, write down important features such as topic sentences and supporting details. Does your organization make sense? Do the parts work together? Does every paragraph help to advance the story and clarify the point it makes? Using sticky notes or note cards of a different color, add notes to each paragraph about how you will strengthen, change, or delete content based on your reviewers' comments and your own. Take photos of the parts of the storyboard so you'll have a record of what you decide, even if you lose your notes.

➤ Create a graphic organizer. Using either paper and pencil or a digital document, create text boxes representing each introductory paragraph, body paragraph, and conclusion paragraph, and write the main idea of each paragraph in the box. Below it, leave room to revise the main idea. To the right of each main idea box, draw additional boxes for changes, additions, and deletions you have decided to make to supporting details, transitions, and other material in that paragraph.

➤ Make an annotated outline. Using formal complete sentences or informal phrases, make an outline that shows the current main ideas, supporting details, and organization of your draft. Using highlighters, colored pens, different colors of type, or some other method to make your changes clearly visible, annotate your outline to show the changes you plan to make to your thesis, dominant impression, organization, supporting ideas, introduction, conclusion, and so on.

➤ Make a plan of your own. _____

_____

_____

_____

_____

Revising an Illustration Essay

Following the plan you've created, write a complete revised draft. Repeat as needed until you feel that you have a solid draft that is nearly final.

Using Your Common Issues to Focus Editing of Your Illustration Essay

Edit for grammar, punctuation, and other common problems you have.

➤ The two kinds of problems that teachers or peer reviewers point out most often in my writing are _____

and _____.

➤ I know I sometimes struggle with _____.

Review the information in Part 3 (pp. 190–247) about the errors you have identified above. Then reread your draft again, correcting any such errors and other issues that you find.

Proofreading

➤ Run the spell checker and carefully consider every suggestion. Do not automatically accept the suggestions! Remember that spell checkers cannot identify problems with certain kinds of words, such as homonyms and proper nouns (names), so check the spelling of such words yourself. Write the words you have misspelled on a spelling checklist you can use to identify and avoid words that give you trouble.

➤ Read your essay aloud slowly, noting and correcting any issues that you find.

➤ Read your essay aloud backwards, word by word, looking for repeated words and similar mistakes that are easy to miss in work that is very familiar. Correct any problems you see.

When your work is as error-free and professional as you can make it, submit your essay.

8

Process Analysis*

Prewriting Activities

Getting Started with a Process Analysis Topic

Complete the following prompts to start thinking about topics for an essay on how to do something or how something works.

➤ I know better than most people how to _____.

➤ I learned how to _____ when I was young.

➤ I am interested in how _____ because
_____.

➤ Most people think that the best way to _____
is _____, but they are mistaken.

➤ From observing _____, I learned
how _____ works.

Now try one of your own.

_____

_____

_____

*Activities for the Guided Writing Assignment in Chapter 14, *Successful College Writing*, Seventh Edition

Collaborating on Ideas for a Process Analysis Essay

Working with two or three classmates, come up with a familiar task (making a sandwich, completing a homework assignment) and list the steps for the *worst possible* way to accomplish it. Include as many vivid concrete details and specific actions as you can. Share this with the class as a whole.

Freewriting to Come Up with Ideas for an Analysis of How Something Works

Spend five minutes writing without stopping about a system you are familiar with (such as a machine you understand or a process you know well at home, work, or school). When you finish, underline or highlight the most important parts of the process you have described. What needs more explanation? What can you omit? What do you need to add?

Identifying a Useful Preliminary Topic for a Process Analysis Essay

What process or system seems like a good preliminary topic for a process analysis essay? The topic can be one that you started with on p. 83, or it can be an idea that came to you while you were freewriting about something else.

➤ My preliminary topic is _____
_____
_____ .

Finding a Perspective on the Process or System

➤ Thinking about this process or system makes me feel _____
_____ .

➤ I want anyone who reads my essay to know that _____
_____ .

➤ The best way to show my point of view is to include _____ ,
_____ , and _____ .

Identifying the Readers You Want to Reach

➤ My audience includes _____ .

➤ They might be interested in this process or system because _____
_____ .

➤ They probably will not know much about _____
_____ .

➤ I need to tell this audience _____

_____.

so they will understand the process or system.

➤ I need to show this audience _____

_____.

so they will understand the process or system.

➤ When they read my essay, I want them to feel _____

_____.

➤ My purpose for writing is to _____.

Finding Concrete Details to Support a Process Analysis Essay

Brainstorm as many of the following prompts as possible, identifying concrete sensory details that reinforce the ability of your readers to understand a system (in a how-it-works essay) or follow the steps of a process (in a how-to essay). What details will be most helpful in clarifying crucial parts of the system or process?

➤ something seen, observed, watched that is part of the process or system

  EXAMPLES: the blue litmus paper turning pink, the magician's curled fingers disguising the coin in his palm

  _____

  _____

  _____

➤ a sound that is part of the process or system

  EXAMPLES: the whir of sewing machines, the dog trainer's commanding tone

  _____

  _____

  _____

➤ an aroma, smell, or stench that relates to the process or system

  EXAMPLES: the stale smell of socks being loaded into a washer, the scent of earth in a greenhouse full of seedlings ready for transplant

  _____

  _____

  _____

➤ something tangible or textured that is part of the process or system

EXAMPLES: the smooth, elastic texture of dough after kneading, the tiny meshing teeth of the gears in the clock

_____

_____

_____

➤ a flavor or taste that connects to the process or system

EXAMPLES: the mouth-puckering sourness of raw rhubarb, the sweet and salty taste of my favorite lemonade recipe

_____

_____

_____

Finding Figures of Speech to Enliven a Process Analysis

Practice making comparisons to make an unfamiliar process or system clear to readers.

➤ If _____ (process or system) were a living thing,

it would be _____

because _____.

➤ If _____ (process or system) were a _____,

it would be _____

because _____.

➤ _____ (process or system) reminds me of

_____ because

_____.

➤ People say that _____ (process or system) is like

_____, but I don't

think that is true because _____

Now try writing your own comparison.

_____

_____

_____

Illustrating a Process or System

You may find that readers of your process analysis essay need diagrams or other visuals to help them understand the process you are describing. Will your audience need such assistance? If so, where can you find—or how can you create—visuals that will be helpful?

Brainstorming the Steps in a Process

Make a list of every step that readers unfamiliar with the process or system will need to know, and then try one or more of these ideas to figure out what else you will need to include.

➤ Ask a friend or classmate to act out the steps as you read them. What is missing or difficult to follow?

➤ Ask someone to sketch the steps as you read them. Where do the instructions go wrong?

➤ Ask two or three classmates to listen while you read the steps and raise their hands whenever something is not clear. Do they agree on what the problems are?

Thesis Activities

➤ My preliminary topic (from p. 84) is _____.

Narrowing and Focusing a Topic for a Process Analysis Essay

Is your preliminary topic something that you can describe in an essay of the assigned length? Sometimes a narrower topic allows you to create a better process analysis.

➤ To me, the single most important thing about this topic is (pick one and complete the sentence)

- that it made me realize _____.
- that it is unique because _____.
- that it reminds me of _____.
- that understanding it allows me to _____.
- that _____

_____.

➤ If I had five minutes to explain why I have a strong interest in this process or system, I would start with _____

_____.

Moving from Topic to Thesis for a Process Analysis Essay

Fill in the blanks to start thinking about making some kind of assertion about the importance or relevance of your topic to your readers.

➤ Many people are surprised to find out that (the process or system) is

_____.

➤ I used to believe _____ about (the process or system), but now I think _____.

➤ This may sound strange, but (the process or system) reminds me of because

_____.

➤ I did not expect (the process or system) to make much of an impression on me, but _____.

➤ The reason audiences should care about (the process or system) is _____

_____.

➤ An ordinary _____ is like _____, but (this process or system) is different because _____

_____.

➤ Invent your own assertion about your topic.

_____

_____

_____

Creating a Preliminary Thesis Statement for a Process Analysis Essay

Remember that a thesis statement needs a topic—but it also needs to make some kind of assertion about the topic. In a process analysis essay, the thesis should emphasize why readers will benefit from understanding this process or system.

➤ Understanding _____ (the process or system) can make your life better because _____.

➤ _____ (the process or system) is beneficial for _____ (audience) because _____

_____.

Reread the ideas you've come up with about your topic on pp. 83–87, and try writing a thesis statement of your own.

_____

_____

_____

Drafting Activities

Deciding Where to Begin

What part of the draft are you most excited about writing or do you feel best prepared to begin? Start with that part. If you feel confident about the steps in the process but not how you want to introduce or conclude the process analysis, begin with body paragraphs. If you have an idea for a solid jumping-off place that will help you write coherent body paragraphs, begin with an introduction. You don't need to write the draft in the order it will be read; just get started.

Brainstorming Ways to Get Readers' Attention

Keeping your thesis and the steps of your process in mind, try your hand at these effective ways to start an introduction.

➤ a quotation (something you said, something someone said to you, a quotation from a book or film, etc.)

_____

➤ an anecdote or story (something that sheds light on the process you're describing or explains how you came to realize the importance of your topic)

_____

➤ a provocative statement (a surprising or shocking comparison or an unexpected revelation)

_____

➤ a question that prompts readers to think about how they will answer it

_____

➤ a hypothetical situation that invites others to imagine being in someone else's place

_____

➤ a comparison of the process with something more familiar to readers (see p. 84)

_____

Drafting an Introduction

Choose the opening you like most from the examples you've created, and start a new draft that begins with that opening. Then write the preliminary thesis that you created on p. 89. How easily can you move from a catchy opening sentence to your preliminary thesis?

1. Try to connect your opening to your thesis. Can you include background information for your readers and forecast the main idea of your essay in three sentences? Expand your introduction as needed.

2. Copy and paste your opening statement, connecting sentences, and preliminary thesis into a new document. Revising any of the sentences as needed, write a complete introductory paragraph.

Trying Options for Organizing Body Paragraphs

A process analysis essay needs a clear, logical organization. For a process with a fairly small number of steps, chronological organization is a standard approach; it typically uses one paragraph per step.

Chronological order (starting at the beginning and moving forward)

➤ First, _____.

➤ Then, _____.

➤ Next, _____.

➤ After that, _____.

➤ Finally, _____.

If the process is more complicated, try organizing by association. Group categories of steps, using one paragraph per category, with a topic sentence that indicates the overall category.

Associational order (grouping related sets of steps)

➤ One part of the process _____.
- The first step of this part is _____.
- The second step of this part is _____.
- The third step is _____.
- The fourth step is _____.

➤ Another part of the process _____.
- The first step of this part is _____.
- The second step of this part is _____.
- The third step is _____.

➤ A third part of the process _____.

• The first step of this part is _____.

• The second step of this part is _____.

• The third step is _____.

• The fourth step is _____.

Try it yourself!

Topic sentence of first body paragraph: _____

_____

Steps and details to include in the paragraph:

• _____

• _____

• _____

Topic sentence of second body paragraph: _____

_____

Steps and details to include in the paragraph:

• _____

• _____

• _____

Topic sentence of third body paragraph: _____

_____

Steps and details to include in the paragraph:

• _____

• _____

• _____

Continue until you have outlined or sketched a plan for all your body paragraphs.

Drafting a Conclusion

Your conclusion should reinforce the idea that the process is important, remind readers of situations in which the knowledge will be useful, tell a memorable story, or otherwise indicate the value of knowing the information in the essay.

➤ The takeaway for readers about this process or system should be that

_____

➤ A story or detail that reminds readers of the importance of this process is

_____

➤   A reason that I chose to inform readers about this process is that

_____.

Try it yourself!

Draft a conclusion that sells the value of understanding this process.

_____

_____

Creating an Intriguing Title

Your title should indicate your topic and say something about it that will interest read-ers. Try the following ideas to create an intriguing title that your audience will want to read.

➤   Alliteration: The process I am describing is _____

and some words that begin with the same sound and relate to my topic are

_____.

➤   Groups of three: Three things I talk about in the essay are _____

_____, _____, and _____.

➤   Question: People ask _____

_____ about this process.

➤   Quotation: Someone said "_____

_____" about this process.

➤   Try out a title of your own: _____

Feedback Activities

Getting Your Questions Answered by Peer Reviewers

You'll get better feedback from peer reviewers if you ask for specific help with com-ments and questions like these.

➤   I'm not sure whether or not _____ is working.

➤   Does the description of _____ make sense?

➤   My biggest concern is _____.

Now write the question with which you *most* want your peer reviewers' help.

_____

_____

Asking Reviewers for Feedback about a Process Analysis Essay

To find out if reviewers are getting the information they need from your process analysis essay, have them answer the following questions.

➤ What is the thesis? How well does it explain the value of reading this essay?

➤ How well do the topic sentences of the body paragraphs explain what is to follow in the steps of the process?

➤ How well do you understand each step? What, if anything, is unclear?

➤ What important questions do you have that are not answered by the essay?

➤ What details work best for this essay? What do you like about them?

➤ Which details are weakest? Which ideas need further development?

➤ How well does the essay hang together? How effective are the transitions between paragraphs?

➤ How enticing is the introduction? Which parts make you want to keep reading? What is less interesting?

➤ How well does the conclusion end the essay? What works best to bring the essay to an end? What should change?

➤ How effective is the title? Why?

➤ My favorite part of this essay is _____

_____

because _____.

➤ The part that I think needs the most improvement is _____

_____

because _____.

Conducting a Self-Review

Put your draft aside for at least one day. Then, read it again, doing your best to pretend that you have never seen it before. Use the Rubric for Assessing Process Analysis Essays to rate your draft in its current form. (Your instructor may use other criteria for assessing student writing, so be sure to check with him or her about expectations.)

Rubric for Assessing Process Analysis Essays

	Exceeds expectations	Meets expectations	Needs improvement	Does not meet expectations
Focus, purpose, and audience	The essay identifies a specific process from the writer's experience or knowledge. The introduction briefly establishes the process to be analyzed, the kind of process it is, the writer's purpose for analyzing it, and the tone. A clear thesis gives purpose to the analysis and controls all development; body paragraphs analyzing steps in the process are focused by effectively governing topic sentences.	The essay addresses a process that is meaningful to the audience and appropriate to the assignment. The introduction indicates the writer's purpose and establishes a tone, but may not indicate what kind of process will be analyzed or why it might be important or interesting to the target audience. The thesis focuses all or most of the development. Body paragraphs analyze steps in the process, but topic sentences may be too narrow to effectively focus the content.	A topic is apparent but the paper may confuse process analysis with another pattern of development, or it may fail in some other way to satisfy the assignment's requirements. If a thesis is present, it is not analytical or is too broad to clarify the purpose or appeal to the target audience. Body paragraphs may be too short or too long, and their development is not effectively focused by topic sentence reflecting steps in the process being analyzed. Some irrelevant content may be included.	No clear thesis or analytical purpose is evident, or the paper fails to engage the reader's favorable attention. Impressions and vague abstract statements may generally relate to an identified topic but do not constitute analysis. Body paragraphs are either underdeveloped or are undifferentiated, with the paper taking the form of one long paragraph. Irrelevant material may intrude or contradictory material may confuse the reader about the paper's focus or purpose.
Development	The essay offers well-chosen, concrete details that allow audience members to understand how the process is completed or to perform the steps themselves. All materials necessary for completing directional process analysis are listed. Instructive exposition develops each body paragraph, anticipating the readers' questions. Where appropriate, cautions or alternative means of completing each step are included. Exposition and forecasting statements offer helpful context.	Details serve to effectively engage the audience and suffice to explain how the process is completed, accomplishing the composition's analytical purpose. Content is relevant, with no disruption of essay or paragraph unity and no distortion or ambiguity about completion of either the individual steps or the process as a whole. A list of materials necessary for completing the process may be included and will be largely complete; cautions or caveats may also be included if warranted.	Details and specifics are sparse, overbalanced by general statements that tell about the process rather than relating the steps and how they occur or are completed. Descriptive or editorial observations may inappropriately constitute the bulk of the paper's development. Irrelevant observations or opinions may intrude and distract the reader or obscure the point. A list of materials may be incomplete, and steps may be missing.	Few or no details or specifics are included. General statements are vague or they distort or confuse the thesis rather than serving to validate or clarify it. No effort to offer instructions or explain how steps occur is apparent. Commentary or personal opinion is offered, but is not clearly related to an analytical purpose. No lists of materials or conditions are included, so development fails to engage or instruct the reader.

	Exceeds expectations	Meets expectations	Needs improvement	Does not meet expectations
Organization and coherence	A clear chronological sequence governs development of a process at both essay and paragraph levels. Background information and forecasting statements are marked clearly with well-chosen transitional devices. Nonlinear process elements are clearly distinguished and are organized using some appropriate principle. Topic sentences of body paragraphs relate consistently to linking elements in the introduction and conclusion.	Development is reasonably organized throughout, arranged to show the chronological sequencing of elements, but arrangement of nonlinear elements may be misrepresented as occurring in a chronological sequence as well. Background and forecasting statements are signaled with adequate transition. Transitions are adequate but may be used repetitively. Focusing statements in the introduction and conclusion help provide context. Analysis is generally coherent throughout.	Chronological organization is attempted but inconsistent. The reader can discern a sequence of steps but can only follow it with difficulty, as exposition and explanation are inserted with little transition. Transitions are used improperly, randomly, or repetitively. The introduction and conclusion fail to provide coherence or make the analysis fully comprehensible. The writer may include statements such as "I forgot to mention." Coherence is generally weak at both essay and paragraph levels.	The essay has no discernible organization at essay or paragraph level. Disjointed sentences fail to reflect the structure of the process being analyzed. No expository or explanatory content is introduced, and the essay employs inadequate or misleading transitional devices or organizational cues. No contextualizing statements are included in either introduction or conclusion; the analytical purpose is not achieved.
Style and structure	Design of introductory and body elements engage the audience's favorable attention and guide it through the essay's content, arranged in coherent body paragraphs. A conclusion sums up the steps in the process or offers commentary reinforcing the purpose and thesis. The paper achieves variety in sentence pattern and type. Tone is skillfully controlled; word choice is apt and artful.	The introduction identifies the process to be analyzed, establishes an appropriate tone, and guides the reader into the body of the paper, which is developed in multiple separate paragraphs. A functional conclusion is present. The writing employs little variety of pattern or type, but sentence construction is competent. Diction is appropriate to audience or purpose, but may be repetitive or imprecise.	The essay uses spacing or indention, but paragraphing is weak. Introductory and concluding elements may be underdeveloped or absent entirely. Steps are not distinguished from one another by inclusion in separate, distinct paragraphs. Sentences employ faulty or mixed constructions, with little or no variety in pattern or type. Tone and diction are inappropriate for the purpose and audience.	Paragraphing is absent or insufficient to meet the demands of the writing situation, with no distinct introductory or concluding elements included. Body paragraphs are either too short or the body is not organized into separate paragraphs. Sentences are difficult to interpret; the writer does not demonstrate control of grammar or paragraph structure. Tone and diction are contradictory or inappropriate.

	Exceeds expectations	Meets expectations	Needs improvement	Does not meet expectations
Precision and editing	The writer reveals mastery of all elements of grammar, usage, and mechanical conventions. Verb tenses are consistent, with appropriate shifts. Uses of second person perspective and passive voice are absent or appropriate. Items in lists are parallel in construction and punctuated properly. Body paragraphs representing individual steps are also parallel in construction and length. The paper is properly formatted and attractive in appearance, and contains few or no careless errors.	The essay is largely free of errors in grammar, punctuation, and use of mechanical conventions, though occasional lapses occur. Inappropriate shifts in verb tense and person may occasionally be included, but do not create confusion. Listed items are parallel in construction and are generally punctuated correctly, with only minor and infrequent error. The paper is neat and clear, with formatting of manuscript conventions applied consistently. The paper satisfies the assignment with only scattered errors.	The essay is weakened with frequent errors in grammar, punctuation, and the use of mechanical conventions. Punctuation of items in lists includes frequent errors; parallelism is faulty, and shifts in verb tense and perspective are pervasive and distracting. The submission may be crumpled, stained, or torn. Errors in manuscript formatting conventions draw unfavorable attention. Numerous editing errors distract the reader, though perhaps cause little or no confusion.	Verb and pronoun usage, sentence constructions, and diction are consistently faulty. Sentence structure is dysfunctional. Punctuation is inconsistent. Careless or illegible writing is confusing. Stains, rips, blots, or printing errors distract the reader and may make parts of the paper unreadable. The writer fails to observe manuscript conventions or to satisfy other demands of the assignment. Errors throughout are serious enough to cause confusion and misunderstanding of meaning.

Gathering Responses and Collecting Your Thoughts

Gather all the reviewer responses. Make notes about what your reviewers agree and disagree on, moving from most important issues, such as thesis, organization, completeness of coverage of the process, interest, and support for ideas, to least important, such as spelling and comma placement. List areas where you agree that improvement is needed, and make a plan about what you need to revise. Think about areas of disagreement, too. You make the final decisions about what changes to make, so determine which comments you need to respond to and which you can ignore.

Revision and Editing Activities

Identifying Options for Revision Planning

After you have gathered revision comments on your early draft from peer reviewers and your instructor (pp. 92–93), choose one of the following strategies to begin making your revision plan.

➤ Create a storyboard. On a sticky note or note card, write your thesis statement or dominant impression, and put it at the top of your work area. Using separate sticky notes or note cards for each paragraph or example, write down important features such as topic sentences and supporting details. Does your organization make sense? Do the parts work together? Does every paragraph contribute to an understanding of the process? Using sticky notes or note cards of a different color, add notes to each paragraph about how you will strengthen, change, or delete content based on your reviewers' comments and your own. Take photos of the parts of the storyboard so you'll have a record of what you decide, even if you lose your notes.

➤ Create a graphic organizer. Using either paper and pencil or a digital document, create text boxes representing each introductory paragraph, body paragraph, and conclusion paragraph, and write the main idea of each paragraph in the box. Below it, leave room to revise the main idea. To the right of each main idea box, draw additional boxes for changes, additions, and deletions you have decided to make to supporting details, transitions, and other material in that paragraph.

➤ Make an annotated outline. Using formal complete sentences or informal phrases, make an outline that shows the current main ideas, supporting details, and organization of your draft. Using highlighters, colored pens, different colors of type, or some other method to make your changes clearly visible, annotate your outline to show the changes you plan to make to your thesis, dominant impression, organization, supporting ideas, introduction, conclusion, and so on.

➤ Make a plan of your own. _____

_____

_____

_____

_____

Revising a Process Analysis Essay

Following the plan you've created, write a complete revised draft. Repeat as needed until you feel that you have a solid draft that is nearly final.

Using Your Common Issues to Focus Editing of Your Process Analysis Essay

Edit for grammar, punctuation, and other common problems you have.

➤ The two kinds of problems that teachers or peer reviewers point out most often in my writing are _____ and _____

➤ I know I sometimes struggle with _____.

Review the information in Part 3 (pp. 190–247) about the errors you have identified. Then reread your draft again, correcting any such errors and other issues that you find.

Proofreading

➤ Run the spell checker and carefully consider every suggestion. Do not automatically accept the suggestions! Remember that spell checkers cannot identify problems with certain kinds of words, such as homonyms and proper nouns (names), so check the spelling of such words yourself. If you keep track of the words you commonly misspell, you can improve your spelling, so consider a spelling-mistake list based on what you find.

➤ Read your essay aloud slowly, noting and correcting any issues that you find.

➤ Read your essay aloud backwards, word by word, looking for repeated words and similar mistakes that are easy to miss in work that is very familiar. Correct any problems you see.

When your work is as error-free and professional as you can make it, submit your essay.

9

Comparison and Contrast*

Prewriting Activities

Getting Started with a Comparison and Contrast Topic

Complete as many of the following prompts as you can to start thinking about topics for an essay that analyzes the similarities and differences between two objects, activities, places, people, or other comparable things. Comparison focuses on similarities, and contrast focuses on differences. Most comparison and contrast essays will emphasize either similarities or differences rather than discussing both equally.

➤ I need to buy a _____, and I have narrowed the choices down to _____ and _____.

➤ Because I enjoy _____, people often think I will also enjoy _____, but I don't.

➤ Two well-known people I admire who are both _____ are _____ and _____.

➤ The "culture clash" [in my family/among my friends] involves those who _____ and those who _____.

*Activities for the Guided Writing Assignment in Chapter 15, *Successful College Writing*, Seventh Edition

➤ The biggest change in my views on _____ since _____ [time period] is that I used to feel _____, but now I feel _____.

➤ If I could go anywhere I wanted on vacation, it would be difficult for me to choose between _____ and _____.

Now try one of your own.

_____
_____
_____

Brainstorming Ideas for a Comparison and Contrast Essay

Working with two or three classmates, decide on a general category for comparison and contrast (music, films, local restaurants, etc.) and spend five minutes calling out everything that you can think of that fits the category. Write down any ideas that seem interesting. When you finish, select two subjects from the list of ideas you have jotted down, and freewrite for two minutes about the characteristics they have in common, then for two more minutes on ways that they differ.

Identifying a Useful Preliminary Topic for a Comparison and Contrast Essay

Which two places, people, ideas, activities, or things seem like a good preliminary topic for a comparison and contrast essay? The topic can be one that you started with on p. 99, or it can be a different idea.

➤ My preliminary topic is _____
_____
_____.

Finding a Perspective on What You Will Compare and Contrast

Respond to the following prompts to begin thinking about your point of view for the comparison and contrast essay.

➤ Of the two subjects I will compare, I have [a slight/a strong/no] preference for _____.

➤ I want anyone who reads my essay to understand that _____
_____.

➤ The best way to show my point of view is to include _____, _____, and _____.

Identifying the Readers You Want to Reach

➤ My audience includes _____.

➤ They might be interested in this comparison and contrast because _____
_____.

➤ They probably will not know much about _____
_____.

➤ I need to tell this audience _____
_____

so they will understand points of similarity and difference.

➤ When they read my essay, I want them to feel _____
_____.

➤ My purpose for writing is to _____.

Finding Concrete Details to Support a Comparison and Contrast Essay

Brainstorm as many of the following prompts as possible, identifying concrete sensory details that reinforce the ability of your readers to understand the subjects you are comparing and contrasting. What details will be most helpful in clarifying similarities and differences?

➤ something seen, observed, watched that is part of the comparison or contrast

EXAMPLES: Bookman serif typeface and Helvetica sans serif typeface for signage

_____

_____

_____

➤ a sound that relates to one or both of the subjects being compared

EXAMPLES: the garage-band production of the band's first album, the lush, layered studio sound of their second album

_____

_____

_____

➤ an aroma, smell, or stench that is relevant to one or both of the subjects being compared

  EXAMPLES: the new-car smell that may or may not be worth the extra cost of a new car

  _____

  _____

  _____

➤ something tangible or textured that is part of one or both subjects being compared

  EXAMPLES: the hard steel taps on the sole of a tap shoe, the flexible leather sole of a jazz shoe

  _____

  _____

  _____

➤ a flavor or taste that connects to one or both subjects being compared

  EXAMPLES: cumin seeds fried in ghee, mustard seeds fried in oil

  _____

  _____

  _____

Finding Figures of Speech to Enliven a Comparison and Contrast

Using figurative language ("my mother's books are like pristine museum pieces on display, and my father's are worn and bedraggled like a child's favorite toys") can clarify the subjects of your comparison and contrast essay to help readers grasp some ideas more easily.

➤ If _____ [one subject in the comparison and contrast essay] were a living thing, it would be _____

  _____

  because _____ .

➤ If _____ [one subject] is like a _____ , then _____ [other subject] is like a _____ .

➤ People seem to believe that _____ is very much like _____ , but I don't think that is true because _____

  _____

Now try writing your own figure of speech to clarify information about one or both of the subjects in your comparison.

_____

_____

_____

Thesis Activities

➤ My preliminary topic (from p. 100) is _____.

Narrowing and Focusing a Topic for a Comparison and Contrast Essay

Is your preliminary topic something that you can describe in an essay of the assigned length? Sometimes a narrower topic allows you to focus attention more effectively on the most relevant aspects of your comparison.

➤ To me, the single most important thing about this comparison is (pick one and complete the sentence)

- that it made me realize _____.

- that it is meaningful because _____.

- that it helped me decide _____.

- that _____

   _____.

➤ If I had five minutes to explain why I have a strong interest in making this comparison, I would start with _____

   _____.

Moving from Topic to Thesis for a Comparison and Contrast Essay

Fill in the blanks to start thinking about making some kind of assertion about the importance or relevance of your topic to your readers.

➤ Many people are surprised to find out that [some aspect of the comparison] is

   _____.

➤ I used to believe _____ about [the two subjects being compared], but now I think _____

   _____.

➤ This may sound strange, but [one of the subjects being compared] reminds me of

   _____, and the other reminds me of

   _____.

➤ I did not expect [one of the subjects being compared] to make much of an impression on me, but _____.

➤ The reason audiences should care about [the comparison] is _____
_____.

➤ Invent your own assertion about your topic.

_____

_____

_____

Creating a Preliminary Thesis Statement for a Comparison and Contrast Essay

Remember that a thesis statement needs a topic—but it also needs to make some kind of assertion about the topic. In a comparison and contrast essay, the thesis should make a point so readers will understand why you are making this comparison.

➤ Comparing _____ and _____ reveals important differences that matter because _____.

➤ _____ [one subject being compared] is beneficial for _____ [audience] because _____
_____.

Reread the ideas you've come up with about your topic on pp. 99–103, and try writing a thesis statement of your own.

_____

_____

_____

Drafting Activities

Deciding Where to Begin

What part of the draft are you most excited about writing or do you feel best prepared to begin? Start with that part. If you have an idea for a solid jumping-off place, you can begin with an introduction, but you don't need to write the draft in the order it will be read; just get started.

Brainstorming Ways to Get Readers' Attention

Keeping your thesis and the steps of your process in mind, try your hand at these effective ways to start an introduction:

➤ a quotation [something you said, something someone said to you, a quotation from a book or film, etc.]

_____

➤ an anecdote or story [something that sheds light on the comparison you're making or explains how you came to realize the importance of your topic]

_____

➤ a provocative statement [a surprising or shocking fact about the comparison or an unexpected revelation]

_____

➤ a question that prompts readers to think about how they will answer it

_____

➤ a hypothetical situation that invites others to imagine being in someone else's place

_____

➤ a comparison that aligns what you are writing about with something more familiar to readers [see p. 101]

_____

Drafting an Introduction

Choose the opening you like most from the examples you've created, and start a new draft that begins with that opening. Then write the preliminary thesis that you created on p. 104. How easily can you move from a catchy opening sentence to your preliminary thesis?

1. Try to connect your opening to your thesis in four sentences or fewer. Be sure to introduce both things you will compare, and try to indicate a general overview of what your essay will say.

2. Copy and paste your opening statement, connecting sentences, and preliminary thesis into a new document. Revising any of the sentences as needed, write a complete introductory paragraph or paragraphs.

Trying Options for Organizing Body Paragraphs

A comparison and contrast essay is usually organized in one of two ways: either point by point or subject by subject.

A point-by-point organization addresses one aspect of one subject being discussed, then a related aspect of the other subject; another aspect of the first subject, then a related aspect of the second; and so on.

Point-by-point order (comparing an aspect of one subject, then a related aspect of the other subject)

- The first point of comparison for subject A _____
  _____

- The first point of comparison for subject B _____
  _____

- The second point of comparison for subject A _____
  _____

- The second point of comparison for subject B _____
  _____

- The third point of comparison for subject A _____
  _____

- The third point of comparison for subject B _____
  _____

A subject-by-subject comparison and contrast essay covers all aspects of the first subject being discussed before covering all the aspects of the second subject.

Subject-by-subject order (discussing all the points of comparison and contrast for one subject, then all the points for the second subject)

- The first point of comparison for subject A _____
  _____

- The second point of comparison for subject A _____
  _____

- The third point of comparison for subject A _____
  _____

- The first point of comparison for subject B _____
  _____

- The second point of comparison for subject B _____
  _____

- The third point of comparison for subject B _____
  _____

Try it yourself!

Topic sentence of first body paragraph: _____

_____.

Details about the subject and the point of comparison:

- _____

- _____

- _____

Topic sentence of second body paragraph: _____

_____.

Details about the subject and the point of comparison:

- _____

- _____

- _____

Topic sentence of third body paragraph: _____

_____.

Details about the subject and the point of comparison:

- _____

- _____

- _____

Topic sentence of fourth body paragraph: _____

_____.

Details about the subject and the point of comparison:

- _____

- _____

- _____

(Continue until you have outlined or sketched a plan for all your body paragraphs.)

Drafting a Conclusion

Your conclusion should reinforce the idea that you have an important reason for comparing the two subjects and leave readers with a comment on the comparison.

➤ The takeaway for readers about this comparison should be that

_____.

➤ A reason that I chose to compare and contrast these two subjects is

_____.

Try it yourself!

Draft a conclusion that clarifies the importance of your comparison.

_____

_____

_____

Creating an Intriguing Title

Your title should indicate your topic and say something about it that will interest readers. Try the following ideas to create an intriguing title that your audience will want to read:

➤ Alliteration: I can use these words that start with the same sound to refer to the subjects I am comparing or to the idea I am conveying about them: _____.

➤ Groups of three: Three things I talk about in the essay are _____, _____, and _____ _____.

➤ Question: People ask _____ _____ about the subjects of my comparison and contrast essay.

➤ Quotation: Someone said "_____ _____" about the subjects of my comparison and contrast essay.

➤ Try out a title of your own: _____

Feedback Activities

Getting Your Questions Answered by Peer Reviewers

You'll get better feedback from peer reviewers if you ask for specific help with comments and questions like these.

➤ I'm not sure whether or not _____ is working.

➤ Does the description of _____ make sense?

➤ My biggest concern is _____.

Now write the question with which you *most* want your peer reviewers' help:

_____

_____

Asking Reviewers for Feedback about a Comparison and Contrast Essay

To find out if reviewers are getting the information they need from your comparison and contrast essay, have them answer the following questions.

➤ What is the thesis? How well does it explain the value of reading this essay?

➤ Are the subjects similar enough and different enough to make a valuable comparison? Why or why not?

➤ How well does the organization work to convey the aspects of the subjects that I am comparing and contrasting?

➤ How well do you understand the similarities and differences between the subjects? What, if anything, is unclear?

➤ What important questions do you have that are not answered by the essay?

➤ What details work best for this essay? What do you like about them?

➤ Which details are weakest? Which ideas need further development?

➤ How well does the essay hang together? How effective are the transitions between paragraphs?

➤ How enticing is the introduction? Which parts make you want to keep reading? What is less interesting?

➤ How well does the conclusion end the essay? What works best to bring the essay to an end? What should change?

➤ How effective is the title? Why?

➤ My favorite part of this essay is _____

_____

because _____.

➤ The part that I think needs the most improvement is _____

_____

because _____.

Conducting a Self-Review

Put your draft aside for at least one day. Then, read it again, doing your best to pretend that you have never seen it before. Use the Rubric for Assessing Comparison and Contrast Essays to rate your draft in its current form. (Your instructor may use other criteria for assessing student writing, so be sure to check with him or her about expectations.)

Rubric for Assessing Comparison and Contrast Essays

	Exceeds expectations	Meets expectations	Needs improvement	Does not meet expectations
Focus, purpose, and audience	The essay identifies at least two subjects of comparison, establishes a basis of comparison, and identifies specific points of comparison common to each subject; the topic is fresh and unexpected. The essay's purpose determines whether the paper employs comparison, contrast, or both, and the logic behind the choice is clear. The tone reflects the target audience's profile and the introduction forecasts content or conclusions that will engage the reader. A clear thesis statement encompasses the purpose of comparison or contrast and controls all development; body paragraphs are clearly focused by topic sentences addressing points of comparison.	The essay addresses a comparison or contrast topic that is appropriate to the assignment. The introduction identifies subjects and points of comparison, generally indicates the writer's purpose, and establishes an appropriate tone, but may not clearly identify a basis of comparison or suggest why the paper's content or conclusions might be important or interesting to the target audience. A thesis statement focuses all or most of the development, but may not include forecasting elements that would help engage and focus the reader's attention. Body paragraphs develop the same points of comparison for each subject of comparison addressed, but topic sentences may not sharply focus the content.	A topic is apparent but may be trite or obvious. The essay identifies two or more subjects of comparison but does not establish a basis of comparison or identify points of comparison, or it may fail in some other way to satisfy the assignment's requirements. If a thesis is present, it is not clearly comparative, or is too broad to clarify the purpose or focus the reader's attention. The tone does not match the purpose or is not appropriate for the target audience. Body paragraphs may be too short or too long, and their development is not effectively focused by topic sentences addressing points of comparison. The paper may drift off topic in some passages and shift from comparison to contrast, or some other irrelevant content may be included.	No comparative topic is evident in the introduction, although one subject may be addressed in the first paragraph and another identified without prior indication elsewhere in the paper, or the composition may fail to be comparative in nature by addressing different features or characteristics for each subject (strengths and weaknesses, for example). Impressions and vague abstract statements may generally relate to an identified topic but do not constitute comparison. Body paragraphs are underdeveloped or are undifferentiated, with the paper taking the form of one long paragraph. Irrelevant material may intrude or contradictory material may confuse the reader about the paper's focus or purpose.

	Exceeds expectations	Meets expectations	Needs improvement	Does not meet expectations
Development	The paper provides comprehensive development for each point of comparison or contrast and clearly interprets the significance of the content with respect to the identified purpose. Instructive clarifying detail or description develops each body paragraph, anticipating the readers' questions. Where appropriate, supplementary patterns of development are employed to clarify or enrich the reader's understanding of the subjects.	Details serve to effectively engage the audience and support the paper's thesis and topic sentences. The development is sufficient to explain how the subjects are similar or different with respect to each point of comparison, and why their similarity or difference is relevant to the paper's purpose. All content is directly relevant to the thesis, and the development of each body paragraph directly relates to its topic sentence, with no disruption of essay or paragraph unity.	Development lacks specific detail and general statements or claims concerning the subjects and points of comparison are unsubstantiated or unsupported. The paper fails to clearly explain how the subjects of comparison are similar or different with respect to the points of comparison, so the comparative purpose is not fully achieved. Irrelevant observations or opinions may intrude and distract the reader or obscure the point.	If subjects of comparison are identified, few or no details are included to develop them. General statements are vague or they distort or confuse the thesis, if one is present, rather than serving to validate or clarify it. If two subjects of comparison are addressed, the paper does not clarify the ways in which they are similar or different, so fails to achieve the comparative purpose. Body paragraphs are not unified, being largely constituted of impressions or statements of opinion.
Organization and coherence	Subject by subject or point by point organization governs consistently throughout. If both comparison and contrast are included, passages are clearly distinguished. Shifts from one subject or point to the next are marked with well-chosen transitional devices. Forecasting elements in the introduction prepare the reader for shifts or for the inclusion of passages developed around other patterns of development, also effectively organized, so the essay is coherent at essay and paragraph levels.	Development is reasonably organized throughout, using either subject-by-subject or point-by-point organization, but comparison and contrast elements may be mixed without clear transition. Transitions from one subject or one point to the next are appropriately signaled; transitions are adequate but may be used repetitively. Focusing statements in the introduction and conclusion help provide context. The essay is generally coherent throughout.	Organization is attempted but inconsistent, alternating between point by point and subject by subject. Individual sentences are comprehensible, but the reasons governing their sequencing is unclear. Transitions are used improperly, randomly, or repetitively. The introduction and conclusion fail to provide coherence to the progression of body paragraphs. Shifts from one subject or point to the next are not clearly marked. Coherence is generally weak at both essay and paragraph levels.	The essay has no discernible organization at essay or paragraph level. Disjointed sentences fail to reflect systematic development of either the subjects or points of comparison. No explanatory content is introduced, and the essay employs inadequate or misleading transitional devices or organizational cues. Shifts from one subject or point to the next are not signaled. No contextualizing statements are included in either introduction or conclusion; the composition is largely incoherent throughout.

	Exceeds expectations	Meets expectations	Needs improvement	Does not meet expectations
Style and structure	Introductory and body elements establish the subject and points of comparison, engage the audience's favorable attention, and provide a map of the essay's content, arranged in coherent body paragraphs. A conclusion reinforces the purpose and thesis. The essay achieves variety in sentence pattern and type. Tone is skillfully controlled; word choice is apt, varied, and artful.	The introduction identifies subjects and points of comparison, establishes an appropriate tone, and guides the reader into the body of the essay, which is developed in multiple separate paragraphs. A functional conclusion is present. The writing employs little variety of pattern or type, but sentence construction is competent. Diction is generally appropriate to audience and purpose, but phrasing may be repetitive or imprecise.	The essay uses spacing or indention, but paragraphing is weak. Introductory and concluding elements may be underdeveloped or absent entirely. Subjects or points are not distinguished from one another by inclusion in separate, distinct paragraphs. Sentences employ faulty or mixed constructions, with little or no variety in pattern or type. Tone and diction lapse into inappropriate informality or stiffness.	Paragraphing is absent or insufficient to meet the demands of the writing situation, with no distinct introductory or concluding elements included. Body paragraphs are either too short or the body is not organized into separate paragraphs. Sentences are difficult to interpret; the writer does not demonstrate control of grammar or paragraph structure. Tone and diction are contradictory or inappropriate.
Precision and editing	The writer reveals mastery of all elements of grammar, usage, and mechanical conventions. Verb tenses are consistent, with appropriate shifts in passages of transition and forecasting. Uses of second person perspective and passive voice are absent or appropriate. The paper is properly formatted and attractive in appearance, and contains few or no editing errors. Overall, the composition is memorable and exemplary.	The essay is largely free of errors in grammar, punctuation, and use of mechanical conventions, though occasional lapses occur. Inappropriate shifts may occasionally be included, but do not create confusion. Passages are punctuated competently, with only minor and infrequent error. The paper is neat, legible, and clear, with formatting of manuscript conventions applied consistently. The paper satisfies the assignment with only scattered editing errors.	The essay is weakened with frequent errors in grammar, punctuation, and the use of mechanical conventions. Parallelism is faulty, and inappropriate shifts are pervasive and distracting. The submission may be crumpled, stained, or torn. Errors in manuscript formatting conventions draw unfavorable attention. Numerous editing errors distract the reader, though perhaps cause little or no confusion.	Verb and pronoun usage, sentence constructions, and diction are consistently faulty. Sentence structure is dysfunctional. Punctuation does not follow conventions. Unedited or illegible writing is confusing. Stains, rips, blots, or printing errors distract the reader and may make parts of the paper illegible. The writer fails to observe manuscript conventions or to satisfy other demands of the assignment. Errors throughout are serious enough to cause confusion and misunderstanding.

Gathering Responses and Collecting Your Thoughts

Gather all the reviewer responses. Make notes about what your reviewers agree and disagree on, moving from most important issues, such as thesis, organization, completeness of the comparisons and contrasts, interest, and support for ideas, to least important, such as spelling and comma placement. List areas where you agree that improvement is needed, and make a plan about what you need to revise. Think about areas of disagreement, too. You make the final decisions about what changes to make, so determine which comments you need to respond to and which you can ignore.

Revision and Editing Activities

Identifying Options for Revision Planning

After you have gathered revision comments on your early draft from peer reviewers and your instructor (p. 109), choose one of the following strategies to begin making your revision plan.

➤ Create a storyboard. On a sticky note or note card, write the main point you are making as you compare and contrast your subjects, and put it at the top of your work area. Using separate sticky notes or note cards for each paragraph or example, write down important features such as topic sentences and supporting details. Does your organization make sense? Do the parts work together? Does every paragraph help to support the comparison or contrast? Using sticky notes or note cards of a different color, add notes to each paragraph about how you will strengthen, change, or delete content based on your reviewers' comments and your own. Take photos of the parts of the storyboard so you'll have a record of what you decide, even if you lose your notes.

➤ Create a graphic organizer. Using either paper and pencil or a digital document, create text boxes representing each introductory paragraph, body paragraph, and conclusion paragraph, and write the main idea of each paragraph in the box. Below it, leave room to revise the main idea. To the right of each main idea box, draw additional boxes for changes, additions, and deletions you have decided to make to supporting details, transitions, and other material in that paragraph.

➤ Make an annotated outline. Using formal complete sentences or informal phrases, make an outline that shows the current main ideas, supporting details, and organization of your draft. Using highlighters, colored pens, different colors of type, or some other method to make your changes clearly visible, annotate your outline to show the changes you plan to make to your thesis, dominant impression, organization, supporting ideas, introduction, conclusion, and so on.

➤ Make a plan of your own. _____

_____

_____

_____

_____

Revising a Comparison and Contrast Essay

Following the plan you've created, write a complete revised draft. Repeat as needed until you feel that you have a solid draft that is nearly final.

Using Your Common Issues to Focus Editing of Your Comparison and Contrast Essay

Edit for grammar, punctuation, and other common problems you have.

➤ The two kinds of problems that teachers or peer reviewers point out most often in my writing are _____ and _____

_____.

➤ I know I sometimes struggle with _____.

Review the information in Part 3 (pp. 190–247) about the errors you have identified above. Then reread your draft again, correcting any such errors and any other issues that you find.

Proofreading

➤ Run the spell checker and carefully consider every suggestion. Do not automatically accept the suggestions! Remember that spell checkers cannot identify problems with certain kinds of words, such as homonyms and proper nouns (names), so check the spelling of such words yourself. If you keep track of the words you commonly misspell, you can improve your spelling, so consider a spelling-mistake list based on what you find.

➤ Read your essay aloud slowly, noting and correcting any issues that you find.

➤ Read your essay aloud backwards, word by word, looking for repeated words and similar mistakes that are easy to miss in work that is very familiar. Correct any problems you see.

When your work is as error-free and professional as you can make it, submit your essay.

10

Classification and Division*

Prewriting Activities

Getting Started with a Classification and Division Topic

Complete as many of the following prompts as you can to start thinking about topics for an essay that analyzes the parts that make up a whole, or the categories into which members of a group may be divided.

➤ Every _____ is either _____, _____, or _____.

➤ The class is made up of the following kinds of students: _____, _____, _____, and _____. Which one are you?

➤ The idea of _____ can seem overwhelming until you realize that you can break it down into manageable parts.

➤ There are [two/three/four] types of _____: _____, _____, and _____.

*Activities for the Guided Writing Assignment in Chapter 16, *Successful College Writing*, Seventh Edition

Now try one of your own:

_____

_____

_____

Freewriting to Generate Ideas for a Classification and Division Essay

Work with a classmate to decide on a broad general category (Internet memes, movies featuring a particular star, restaurants near campus, classes or majors, and so on). Then spend five minutes brainstorming to name everything that you can think of that fits into the category, writing down all the responses. When you finish, freewrite for two minutes about ways to classify and group the elements you have named, aiming to avoid overlap between groups. Have you covered every group that is part of the category you chose?

Using Social Media to Brainstorm Classification Options

Start with a search engine such as Google and enter a phrase such as "four types of" or "three kinds of" into the search bar. Scroll through the first two pages of results. Make notes about interesting or amusing content you find that suggests ideas for your own classification and division essay.

Identifying a Useful Preliminary Topic for a Classification and Division Essay

Which category or parts of a whole seem like a good preliminary topic for a classification and division essay? The topic can be one that you started with on p. 115, or it can be a different idea.

➤ My preliminary topic is _____

_____

_____.

Finding a Perspective on What You Will Compare and Contrast

Respond to the following prompts to begin thinking about your point of view for the classification and division essay.

➤ I am interested in this topic because it _____.

➤ This topic could be amusing if _____.

➤ I want anyone who reads my essay to understand that _____

_____.

➤ The best way to show my point of view is to include _____,

_____, and _____.

Identifying the Readers You Want to Reach

➤ My audience includes _____.

➤ They might be interested in this classification and division topic because

_____

➤ They probably will not know much about _____

_____

➤ I need to tell this audience _____
so they will understand what I am discussing.

➤ When they read my essay, I want them to feel _____

_____

➤ My purpose for writing is to _____.

Finding Concrete Details to Support a Classification and Division Essay

Brainstorm as many of the following prompts as possible, identifying concrete sensory details that reinforce the ability of your readers to understand the subgroups you are classifying or the whole that is made up of the parts. What details will be most helpful?

➤ something seen, observed, watched that is part of the class or group

EXAMPLES: the clothing styles of the 1980s

_____

_____

_____

➤ a sound that relates to the class as a whole or to a part or subgroup

EXAMPLES: the rattle of the dice rolled by Dungeons and Dragons players

_____

_____

_____

➤ an aroma, smell, or stench that is relevant to the class or a subgroup

EXAMPLES: the multiple aromas wafted around the food court by competing fast-food restaurants

_____

_____

_____

➤ something tangible or textured that is part of the class as a whole or a subgroup

   EXAMPLES: venetian blinds, sheer gauzy curtains, vinyl roller shades, and heavy, lined drapes that cover windows in public areas of the residence hall

   _____

   _____

   _____

➤ a flavor or taste that connects to the class or a subgroup

   EXAMPLES: the sweet, salty, sour, bitter, and umami taste receptors on the tongue

   _____

   _____

   _____

Finding Figures of Speech to Enliven a Classification and Division Essay

Using figurative language that makes comparisons can help to clarify the categories and subgroups for readers of your classification and division essay.

➤ If _____ [a class] were a living thing, it would be

   _____

   because _____.

➤ If _____ [the subgroups that the class is made up of] are like [types of cars/food groups/sports], [one subgroup] would be like _____, [another subgroup] would be like _____, and [another subgroup] would be like _____.

➤ People say that _____ [a category] is like

   _____,

   but I don't think that is true because _____

   _____.

Now try writing your own figure of speech to clarify information about the category you are describing or the subgroups of which it is composed:

_____

_____

_____

Thesis Activities

➤ My preliminary topic [from p. 116] is _____.

Narrowing and Focusing a Topic for a Classification and Division Essay

Is your preliminary topic something that you can describe in an essay of the assigned length? Sometimes a narrower topic allows you to focus attention more effectively on the most relevant aspects of your classification.

➤ To me, the single most important thing about this class and the subgroups of which it is composed is (pick one and complete the sentence)

- that it made me realize _____.
- that it is meaningful because _____.
- that it helped me decide _____.
- that _____

_____.

➤ If I had five minutes to explain why I have a strong interest in making this comparison, I would start with _____

_____.

Moving from Topic to Thesis for a Classification and Division Essay

Fill in the blanks to start thinking about making some kind of assertion about the importance or relevance of your topic to your readers.

➤ Many people are surprised to find out that [some part of the overall class] is

_____.

➤ I used to believe _____ about [the class or one or more subgroups], but now I think _____.

➤ This may sound strange, but [the class or one or more subgroups] reminds me of

_____.

➤ I did not expect [the class or subgroup] to make much of an impression on me, but _____.

➤ The reason audiences should care about [the classification] is _____

_____.

Invent your own assertion about your topic:

_____

_____

_____

Creating a Preliminary Thesis Statement for a Classification and Division Essay

Remember that a thesis statement needs a topic — but it also needs to make some kind of assertion about the topic. In a classification and division essay, the thesis should make a point about the importance of the topic so readers will understand why you are creating your essay.

➤ Classifying how _____ [category] is made up of _____ _____ [subcategories] reveals important ways that the class as a whole is _____ _____.

➤ Understanding the types of _____ [the parts that make up the whole] is useful because _____ _____.

Reread the ideas you've come up with about your topic on pp. 115–19, and try writing a thesis statement of your own.

_____

_____

_____

Drafting Activities

Deciding Where to Begin

What part of the draft are you most excited about writing or do you feel best prepared to begin? Start with that part. If you feel confident talking about the points you want to make about the class as a whole but not about the parts, start with the section about which you have more to say. If you have an idea for a solid jumping-off place, you can begin with an introduction. You don't need to write the draft in the order it will be read; just get started.

Brainstorming Ways to Get Readers' Attention

Keeping your thesis and the steps of your process in mind, try your hand at these effective ways to start an introduction.

➤ a quotation (something you said, something someone said to you, a quotation from a book or film, etc.)

_____

➤ an anecdote or story (something that sheds light on the classification you're addressing or explains how you came to realize the importance of your topic)

_____

➤ a provocative statement (a surprising or shocking fact about the classification or division or an unexpected revelation)

_____

➤ a question that prompts readers to think about how they will answer it

_____

➤ a hypothetical situation that invites others to imagine being in someone else's place

_____

➤ a comparison that aligns what you are writing about with something more familiar to readers (see p. 117)

_____

Drafting an Introduction

Choose the opening you like most from the examples you've created, and start a new draft that begins with that opening. Then write the preliminary thesis that you created on p. 120. How easily can you move from a catchy opening sentence to your preliminary thesis?

1. Try to connect your opening to your thesis in four sentences or fewer. Be sure to introduce the class of subjects and give an overview of the subdivisions that you will discuss. Clarify whether you will focus on the category as a whole or on the subcategories.

2. Copy and paste your opening statement, connecting sentences, and preliminary thesis into a new document. Revising any of the sentences as needed, write a complete introductory paragraph or paragraphs.

Trying Options for Organizing Body Paragraphs

If you aren't certain what organization makes sense for the examples that will support your thesis, try completing any of the following options that seems viable. Use the option you choose as the basis for an outline or graphic organizer that you can follow as you draft.

By Time

Chronological order (starting at the beginning and moving forward)

➤ First, _____.

➤ Then, _____.

➤ Finally, _____.

Out of order (flashback or arrangement by association)

➤ A little while ago, _____.

➤ Before that, _____.

➤ Now, _____.

In Order of Importance, Familiarity, or Interest

Least to most important, familiar, or interesting (saving the best for last)

➤ Least _____.

➤ More _____.

➤ Most _____.

Most to least important, familiar, or interesting (starting strong)

➤ Most _____.

➤ Less _____.

➤ Least _____.

In Spatial Order

Moving around an object or a physical space

➤ On the right, _____.

➤ At the front, _____.

➤ On the left, _____.

➤ At the back, _____.

Try it yourself!

Topic sentence of first body paragraph: _____

Details to include in the paragraph:

- _____
- _____
- _____

Topic sentence of second body paragraph: _____

Details to include in the paragraph:

- _____
- _____
- _____

Topic sentence of third body paragraph: _____

Details to include in the paragraph:

- _____
- _____
- _____

(Continue until you have outlined or sketched a plan for all your body paragraphs.)

Drafting a Conclusion

Your conclusion should reinforce the idea that you have an important reason for writing the essay.

➤ The takeaway for readers should be that _____
_____

➤ The new perspective I am offering is that _____
_____.

Try it yourself!

Draft a conclusion that clarifies the importance of your classification.

_____

_____

_____

Creating an Intriguing Title

Your title should indicate your topic and say something about it that will interest readers. Try the following ideas to create an intriguing title that your audience will want to read.

➤ Alliteration: Words that start with the same sound and that relate to the classification or the subgroups are _____

_____

➤ Groups of three: Three things I talk about in the essay are _____

_____, _____

_____, and _____.

➤ Question: People ask _____

_____ about the

subjects of my classification and division essay.

➤ Quotation: Someone said "_____

_____" about

the subjects of my classification and division essay.

➤ Try out a title of your own: _____

Feedback Activities

Getting Your Questions Answered by Peer Reviewers

You'll get better feedback from peer reviewers if you ask for specific help with comments and questions like these.

➤ I'm not sure whether or not _____ is working.

➤ Does the description of _____ make sense?

➤ My biggest concern is _____.

Now write the question with which you *most* want your peer reviewers' help.

_____

_____

Asking Reviewers for Feedback about a Classification and Division Essay

To find out if reviewers are getting the information they need from your classification and division essay, have them answer the following questions.

➤ What is the thesis? How well does it explain the value of reading this essay?

➤ Is the subject interesting and compelling? Why or why not?

➤ How well does the organization work to convey the aspects of the subjects that are being classified and divided?

➤ What, if anything, is unclear? What important questions do you have that are not answered by the essay?

➤ What details work best for this essay? What do you like about them?

➤ Which details are weakest? Which ideas need further development?

➤ How well does the essay hang together? How effective are the transitions between paragraphs?

➤ How enticing is the introduction? Which parts make you want to keep reading? What is less interesting?

➤ How well does the conclusion end the essay? What works best to bring the essay to an end? What should change?

➤ How effective is the title? Why?

➤ My favorite part of this essay is _____

_____

because _____.

➤ The part that I think needs the most improvement is _____

_____

because _____.

Conducting a Self-Review

Put your draft aside for at least one day. Then, read it again, doing your best to pretend that you have never seen it before. Use the Rubric for Assessing Classification and Division Essays to rate your draft in its current form. (Your instructor may use other criteria for assessing student writing, so be sure to check with him or her about expectations.)

Rubric for Assessing Classification and Division Essays

	Exceeds expectations	Meets expectations	Needs improvement	Does not meet expectations
Focus, purpose, and audience	The essay identifies a subject of classification or division, establishes a classifying or dividing principle, and identifies categories or parts that result from applying the principle to the subject. The essay demonstrates how the system can be useful for sorting or for identifying the subject's component parts. The writer's purpose for employing this mode of development is clear. The tone reflects the target audience's profile and the introduction forecasts content or conclusions that will engage the reader. A clear thesis statement controls all development; body paragraphs are clearly focused by topic sentences addressing classes or components.	The essay addresses a classification or division topic that is appropriate to the assignment. The introduction clearly indicates whether the essay will classify, divide, or both. It also identifies the subject's principle and categories or parts, generally indicates the writer's purpose, and establishes an appropriate tone, but may not clearly indicate how the classification or division system is useful or important, or suggest why the content or conclusions might be interesting to the target audience. A thesis statement focuses all or most of the development, but may not engage and focus the reader's attention. Body paragraphs illustrate the contents of the categories or describe the component parts, but topic sentences may not sharply focus the content.	The essay addresses a subject of classification or division, but it may be too familiar or obvious to the audience to be engaging. The introduction may list categories or parts but does not clearly state the classifying or dividing principle, or it may fail in some other way to satisfy the assignment's requirements. If a thesis is present, it fails to clarify the purpose of either the system or the essay, or both, or in some other way fails to clearly focus the reader's attention. The tone does not match the purpose or is not appropriate for the target audience. Body paragraphs may not be effectively focused by topic sentences describing the contents of the categories or the component elements the subject. The writing may drift off topic.	Although a subject suitable to the assignment may be addressed in the first paragraph, no classifying or dividing principle is identified and categories or component parts are not listed systematically, or the composition may be comparative in nature instead of classifying or dividing as stipulated by the assignment. Impressions and vague abstract statements may generally relate to an identified topic but do not list or describe categories or components. Body paragraphs are unfocused and may be undifferentiated, with the paper taking the form of one long paragraph. Irrelevant material may intrude or contradictory material may confuse the reader about the paper's focus or purpose.

	Exceeds expectations	Meets expectations	Needs improvement	Does not meet expectations
Development	The essay provides comprehensive development for each category or component of the subject and clearly interprets the significance of the content with respect to the identified purpose. Instructive clarifying detail or description develops each body paragraph, anticipating the readers' questions. Where appropriate, supplementary modes of development are employed to clarify or enrich the reader's understanding of the subjects.	Details engage the audience and support the thesis and topic sentences. The development is sufficient to show how the categories or components are distinguished according to the classifying or dividing principle, but may not show how the system is useful or why it is relevant to the writer's purpose or to the reader. All content is directly relevant to the thesis, and the development of each body paragraph relates to its topic sentence, with no disruption of essay or paragraph unity.	Development lacks specific detail, and general statements or claims concerning the subject of classification or division and its classes or component parts are unsupported. Although it may imply a principle, the essay fails to clearly explain how the system is useful or why an understanding of it is relevant to the reader, so the purpose is not fully achieved. Irrelevant observations or opinions may intrude and distract the reader or obscure the point.	If a subject of classification is identified, few or no details are included to develop categories or describe components. General statements are vague or they confuse the thesis, if one is present, rather than serving to validate or clarify it. No classification or division principle is identified, and the paper does not explain how the system works or is useful, or how it is relevant to the audience, so it fails to achieve any meaningful purpose. Body paragraphs are not unified, being largely constituted of impressions or statements of opinion.
Organization and coherence	Development is logically organized, following the sequence indicated in a thesis statement. The order in which categories or components are addressed is organized for emphasis or according to some other discernible organizing principle. If both classification and division elements are included, passages are clearly distinguished. Shifts are clearly marked with well-chosen transitions. Passages developed around supplementary modes of development are also organized appropriately, so the writing is fully coherent at essay and paragraph levels.	Development is reasonably organized, generally following the sequence of categories or components indicated in a governing thesis statement, but no discernible organizing principle informs the sequencing of body paragraphs. Classification and division elements are generally distinguishable from one another, if both are present. Transitions from one category or component to the next are appropriately signaled; transitional expressions are employed effectively but may be used repetitively. The essay is generally coherent throughout.	Organization is attempted but inconsistent. An ineffective thesis statement fails to clearly signal the order in which body content will be presented. Individual sentences are comprehensible, but their sequencing is not governed by a discernible organizing principle. Transitions are used improperly, randomly, or repetitively. Classification and division elements are not distinguished if both are present, leading to confusion. Shifts from one category or component to the next are not clearly marked. Coherence is generally weak at both essay and paragraph levels.	The essay has no discernible organization at essay or paragraph level. Disjointed sentences reflect failure to systematically arrange any elements of the essay. An introduction offers no indication of the order in which body content will be introduced, and the essay employs inadequate or misleading transitional devices or organizational cues. Shifts from one category or component to the next are unsignaled. Classification and division elements are mixed indiscriminately if both are present. The composition is largely incoherent throughout.

	Exceeds expectations	Meets expectations	Needs improvement	Does not meet expectations
Style and structure	Design of introductory and body elements establish and fully develop the subject, principle, and categories of classification or division, engage the audience's favorable attention, and provide a map of essay's content, arranged in coherent body paragraphs. A conclusion sums up the purpose, function, and significance of the system, and reinforces the writer's purpose and thesis. The paper achieves variety in sentence pattern and type. Tone is skillfully controlled; word choice is apt, varied, and artful.	The introduction identifies a subject, principle, and categories or components of classification or division, establishes an appropriate tone, and guides the reader into the body of the paper, which is developed in multiple separate paragraphs. A functional conclusion is present. The writing employs little variety of pattern or type, but sentence construction is competent. Diction is generally appropriate to audience and purpose, but phrasing may be repetitive or imprecise.	The essay uses spacing or indention, but paragraphing is weak. Introductory and concluding elements may be underdeveloped or absent entirely. Categories or components are not distinguished from one another by inclusion in separate, distinct paragraphs. Sentences employ faulty or mixed constructions, with little or no variety in pattern or type. Tone and diction lapse into inappropriate informality or stiffness.	Paragraphing is absent or insufficient to meet the demands of the writing situation, with no distinct introductory or concluding elements included. Body paragraphs are either too short or the body is not organized into separate paragraphs. Sentences are difficult to interpret; the writer does not demonstrate control of grammar or paragraph structure. Tone and diction are contradictory or inappropriate.
Precision and editing	The writer reveals mastery of all elements of grammar, usage, and mechanical conventions. Verb tenses are consistent, with appropriate shifts in passages of transition and forecasting. Uses of second person perspective and passive voice are absent or appropriate. Paragraphs treating parallel categories or components are parallel in construction and length. The paper is properly formatted and attractive in appearance, and contains few or no careless errors. Overall the composition is memorable and exemplary.	The essay is largely free of errors in grammar, punctuation, and use of mechanical conventions, though occasional lapses occur. Inappropriate shifts may occasionally occur but do not create confusion. Passages are punctuated competently, with only minor and infrequent error. The paper is neat, legible, and clear, with formatting of manuscript conventions applied consistently. The paper satisfies the assignment with only scattered editing errors.	The essay is weakened with frequent errors in grammar, punctuation, and the use of mechanical conventions. Parallelism is faulty, and inappropriate shifts in verb tense and perspective are pervasive and distracting. The submission may be crumpled, stained, or torn. Errors in manuscript formatting conventions draw unfavorable attention. Numerous careless errors distract the reader, though perhaps cause little or no confusion.	Verb and pronoun usage, sentence constructions, and diction are consistently faulty. Sentence structure is dysfunctional. Punctuation is not consistent with established conventions. Careless or illegible writing is confusing. Stains, rips, blots, or printing errors distract the reader and may make parts of the paper illegible. The writer fails to observe manuscript conventions or to satisfy other demands of the assignment. Errors throughout are serious enough to cause confusion and misunderstanding.

Gathering Responses and Collecting Your Thoughts

Gather all the reviewer responses. Make notes about what your reviewers agree and disagree on, moving from most important issues, such as thesis, organization, completeness of the groupings, interest, and support for ideas, to least important, such as spelling and comma placement. List areas where you agree that improvement is needed, and make a plan about what you need to revise. Think about areas of disagreement, too. You make the final decisions about what changes to make, so determine which comments you need to respond to and which you can ignore.

Revision and Editing Activities

Identifying Options for Revision Planning

After you have gathered revision comments on your early draft from peer reviewers and your instructor (pp. 124–25), choose one of the following strategies to begin making your revision plan.

➤ Create a storyboard. On a sticky note or note card, write the main point you are making as you classify and divide your subjects, and put it at the top of your work area. Using separate sticky notes or note cards for each paragraph or example, write down important features such as topic sentences and supporting details. Does your organization make sense? Do the parts work together? Does every paragraph help to support the classification or division? Using sticky notes or note cards of a different color, add notes to each paragraph about how you will strengthen, change, or delete content based on your reviewers' comments and your own. Take photos of the parts of the storyboard so you'll have a record of what you decide, even if you lose your notes.

➤ Create a graphic organizer. Using either paper and pencil or a digital document, create text boxes representing each introductory paragraph, body paragraph, and conclusion paragraph, and write the main idea of each paragraph in the box. Below it, leave room to revise the main idea. To the right of each main idea box, draw additional boxes for changes, additions, and deletions you have decided to make to supporting details, transitions, and other material in that paragraph.

➤ Make an annotated outline. Using formal complete sentences or informal phrases, make an outline that shows the current main ideas, supporting details, and organization of your draft. Using highlighters, colored pens, different colors of type, or some other method to make your changes clearly visible, annotate your outline to show the changes you plan to make to your thesis, dominant impression, organization, supporting ideas, introduction, conclusion, and so on.

➤   Make a plan of your own. _____

_____

_____

_____

Revising a Classification and Division Essay

Following the plan you've created, write a complete revised draft. Repeat as needed until you feel that you have a solid draft that is nearly final.

Using Your Common Issues to Focus Editing of Your Classification and Division Essay

Edit for grammar, punctuation, and other common problems you have.

➤   The two kinds of problems that teachers or peer reviewers point out most often in my writing are _____ and

_____

_____.

➤   I know I sometimes struggle with _____.

Review the information in Part 3 (pp. 190–247) about the errors you have identified above. Then reread your draft again, correcting any such errors and any other issues that you find.

Proofreading

➤   Run the spell checker and carefully consider every suggestion. Do not automatically accept the suggestions! Remember that spell checkers cannot identify problems with certain kinds of words, such as homonyms and proper nouns (names), so check the spelling of such words yourself. If you keep track of the words you commonly misspell, you can improve your spelling, so consider a spelling-mistake list based on what you find.

➤   Read your essay aloud slowly, noting and correcting any issues that you find.

➤   Read your essay aloud backwards, word by word, looking for repeated words and similar mistakes that are easy to miss in work that is very familiar. Correct any problems you see.

When your work is as error-free and professional as you can make it, submit your essay.

11

Definition[*]

Prewriting Activities

Finding Ideas for a Definition Essay Topic

An extended definition essay is a detailed explanation of the meaning of an unfamiliar term, often including multiple patterns of development and addressing misconceptions about what is being defined. To identify a concept that can serve as the topic for your definition essay, try the following prompts.

➤ Recently, several people have asked me what _____

_____ means.

➤ An unfamiliar term I have encountered over and over in my _____

class is _____.

➤ Older people probably do not know the meaning of _____

_____.

➤ I call myself a _____, but that term means different

things to different people. To me, it means _____.

Try it yourself!

Identify a word or phrase that you can define for an audience that is likely to be unfamiliar with it.

_____

_____

_____

*Activities for the Guided Writing Assignment in Chapter 17, *Successful College Writing*, Seventh Edition

Browsing for Ideas for a Definition Essay Topic

To generate ideas for the topic of a definition essay, browse for topics directly, and also keep an eye out for ideas as you do your coursework and go about your daily life.

➤   Browse online, starting with topics that interest you and following links and resources where they take you. Keep a running list of concepts that are new to you or that you think will probably be unfamiliar to an audience you want to reach.

➤   Look at dictionary Web sites. The aggregator site onelook.com features a "word of the day" on its home page, and Merriam Webster's online site has a sidebar for "trending words," often with links to short articles about those hot topics.

➤   Review your notes from other classes, and consider whether terms you learn in history or psychology might make good choices for a definition essay.

Identifying a Preliminary Topic for a Definition Essay

What general statement or concept will you define in your essay? The topic can be one that you started with on p. 131, or it can be an idea that came to you while you were exploring something else in one of the activities above.

➤   My preliminary topic is _____
_____
_____ .

Finding a Perspective on the Preliminary Topic for Your Definition Essay

In order to find examples that will work well for your definition, you should consider your point of view of the topic.

➤   This topic makes me feel _____
_____ .

➤   I want anyone who reads my definition essay to know that _____
_____

➤   The best way to show my point of view is to include _____ ,
_____ , and _____ .

Identifying the Readers I Want to Reach in My Definition Essay

Figuring out what your audience already knows and does not know about the topic will be extremely important. If you consider what they already believe or actually know, you will be able to identify information that will make your definition more compelling. Complete the following prompts to analyze the audience you expect to reach.

➤ My audience includes _____.

➤ They may already know _____
about this topic, but they may not know _____
_____.

➤ I need to tell this audience about _____
_____ so they
will understand my perspective on the topic.

➤ When they read my essay, I want them to feel _____
_____.

➤ My purpose for writing is to _____.

Exploring Ideas for a Definition Essay

What do you need to explain so that your definition is clear, and do you need to seek additional information? Respond to any of the following prompts that are appropriate for your definition essay:

➤ I (already have/do not yet have) the information I need to complete a definition essay.

➤ Other resources for information for my definition essay might include _____
_____.

➤ A mistaken idea that people may associate with this topic is _____
_____.

➤ A visual that would clarify the topic is _____.
My plan for including a visual is _____
_____.

➤ My own experience with _____
can help me explain it to others because _____
_____.

Identifying Strong, Vivid Examples for a Definition Essay

Specific details make a definition come alive. Brainstorm as many of the following prompts as possible to try out other patterns of development that can add interest to your definition essay.

➤ narrative examples

    EXAMPLE: a story about the people who originally called themselves "mugwumps"

    _____

    _____

    _____

➤ descriptive examples

    EXAMPLE: a detailed description of the setting for a meditation retreat

    _____

    _____

    _____

➤ process analysis examples

    EXAMPLES: a definition of multitasking that identifies the steps in completing a reading assignment while texting and listening to music

    _____

    _____

    _____

➤ causal analysis examples

    EXAMPLES: an examination of the effects of single-payer healthcare systems on patients' treatment in Canada and France

    _____

    _____

    _____

➤ Try creating an example from any pattern of development that seems useful.

    _____

    _____

    _____

Choosing Visuals or Other Media to Enliven a Definition Essay

If you have access to photos or other media that will help create a vivid impression of the concept you are defining, consider including one or more of them in your essay. Video and audio files can be used in an essay that you will post online.

Thesis Activities

➤ My preliminary topic [p. 132] is _____.

Narrowing and Focusing a Topic for a Definition Essay

Will you be able to define the concept adequately in an essay of the assigned length? Sometimes a narrower, more focused topic may allow you to create a better definition essay.

➤ If I had five minutes to define the idea to people who are not familiar with it, I would start with _____
_____.

Identifying a Point for Your Definition Essay

To me, the single most important thing about the topic I am trying to define is (pick one and complete the sentence)

- that it clarifies _____.
- that it helps people understand _____.
- that it proves _____.
- that it is exciting because _____.
- that it is important because _____.
- that _____
_____.

Moving from Topic to Preliminary Thesis for a Definition Essay

Fill in the blanks to start thinking about the point you want to make in your definition essay.

1. Many people will be surprised to find out that _____

2. I used to believe _____, but now I think _____

3. This may sound strange, but [the topic] makes me think about _____
_____ because _____

4. At first I did not understand [the topic], but now I think of it as _____
_____

5. A new insight my readers should have about [the topic] is _____
_____

Now, write your own generalization that can serve as a preliminary thesis.

_____

_____

_____

Testing Your Thesis

In a sentence or two, explain your proposed thesis for your definition essay to a class-mate or friend who is part of your audience. Ask for responses to these questions.

➤ How much do you understand about the concept being defined?

_____

_____

➤ How does the plan for this definition essay seem likely to expand your under-standing of the concept?

_____

_____

➤ What interests you most about this topic? Why? _____

_____

Do the reviewer's responses suggest that you are on the right track? If not, consider whether you should rethink your topic, review your assumptions about what your audience knows and cares about, or reconsider the examples you will use.

Drafting Activities

Deciding Where to Begin

Begin at the easiest point for you to get started. If starting with the dictionary defi-nition will help you get your draft underway, begin there. If you know you want to include an image or video clip as an example, begin with that. You can start with the introduction, of course, but you do not have to begin at the beginning; you can draft the introduction and conclusion after the body of your essay if you like.

Brainstorming Ways to Get Readers' Attention

Keeping your preliminary thesis in mind, try your hand at these effective ways to start an introduction:

➤ a quotation (something you said, something someone said to you, a relevant snip-pet of dialogue that will be part of one of your examples)

_____

_____

➤ an anecdote or story (something that sheds light on the subject you are defining or explains how you came to realize the importance of your topic)

_____

_____

➤ a provocative statement (a surprising or shocking announcement or an unexpected revelation)

_____

_____

➤ a question that prompts readers to think about how they will answer it

_____

_____

➤ a hypothetical situation that invites others to imagine being in someone else's place

_____

_____

➤ a comparison that shows how your unfamiliar concept is like something more familiar to your readers

_____

_____

Drafting an Introduction

Choose the opening you like most from the examples you've created, and start a new draft that begins with that opening. How can you move from this catchy opening to your first example?

Trying Options for Organizing Body Paragraphs

If you aren't certain what organization makes sense for the examples that will support your thesis, try completing any of the following options that seem viable. Use the option you choose as the basis for an outline or graphic organizer that you can follow as you draft.

By Time

➤ Chronological order: start at the beginning and move forward in time

➤ Reverse chronological order: move from most recent time to earliest

In Order of Importance, Familiarity, or Interest

➤ Least to most important, familiar, or interesting: save the best for last

➤ Most to least important, familiar, or interesting: start strong

Try it yourself!

➤ Organization plan for examples: _____

Topic of first body paragraph: _____

➤ I will develop the example(s) using the _____ pattern.
   Details to include in the paragraph:

   • _____

   • _____

   • _____

Topic of second body paragraph: _____

➤ I will develop the example(s) using the _____ pattern.
   Details to include in the paragraph:

   • _____

   • _____

   • _____

Topic of third body paragraph: _____

➤ I will develop the example(s) using the _____ pattern.
   Details to include in the paragraph:

   • _____

   • _____

   • _____

(Continue until you have outlined or sketched a plan for all your body paragraphs.)

Drafting a Conclusion

Your conclusion should reinforce the way you have defined your concept and make a final statement.

➤ This definition is important because _____.

➤ Readers should feel _____ _____.

Try it yourself!
Draft a conclusion that reinforces your thesis and ties the whole essay together.

_____

_____

_____

Creating an Intriguing Title

Your title should indicate the topic of your definition essay and say something about it that will interest readers. Try the following ideas to create an intriguing title that your audience will want to read:

➤ Alliteration: My definition relates to _____,
and some words that begin with the same sound and relate to my examples are
_____

➤ Groups of three: Three things that are important to the definition are
_____, _____
_____, and _____.

➤ Question: People ask _____
_____ about this definition.

➤ Quotation: Someone said "_____
_____" about the topic I am defining.

➤ Try out a title of your own: _____

Feedback Activities

Getting Your Questions Answered by Peer Reviewers

You'll get better feedback from peer reviewers if you ask for specific help with comments and questions like these.

➤ I'm not sure whether or not _____ is working.

➤ Does the example about _____ make sense?

➤ My biggest concern is _____.

Now write the question with which you *most* want your peer reviewers' help.

_____

_____

_____

Asking Reviewers for Feedback about a Definition Essay

To find out if reviewers are getting the impressions you want to give in your definition essay, have them answer the following questions.

➤ What is the thesis? Is it interesting?

➤ How clearly do the examples illustrate the thesis? Which example(s) do you like best? Which do you like least?

➤ What questions are not answered that should be answered?

➤ What details work well? What do you like about them?

➤ Which details are weakest? Which ideas need further development?

➤ Does the essay's organization make sense?

➤ How well does the essay hang together? How effective are the transitions between paragraphs?

➤ How enticing is the introduction? Which parts make you want to keep reading? What is less interesting?

➤ How well does the conclusion end the essay? What works best to bring the essay to an end? What should change?

➤ How effective is the title? Why?

➤ My favorite part of this essay is _____

_____

because _____.

➤ The part that I think needs the most improvement is _____

_____

because _____.

Conducting a Self-Review

Put your draft aside for at least one day. Then, read it again, doing your best to pretend that you have never seen it before. Use the Rubric for Assessing Definition Essays to see how well you think you have accomplished the essay's objectives in this draft. (Your instructor may use other criteria for assessing student writing, so be sure to check with him or her about expectations.)

Rubric for Assessing Definition Essays

	Exceeds expectations	Meets expectations	Needs improvement	Does not meet expectations
Focus, purpose, and audience	The essay identifies a term to serve as the subject of definition, indicates the class to which it belongs (what it is a type of), and identifies the feature(s) that distinguish it from other members of its class. The writer's purpose for employing this pattern is clear. The introduction forecasts the supplementary modes of development that will be used to develop an extended definition. The tone is engaging to an academic audience. A clear thesis statement controls all development; body paragraphs are clearly focused by topic sentences.	The essay defines a term or concept appropriate to the assignment. The introduction clearly indicates the term, its class, and its distinguishing features, generally indicates the writer's purpose, and establishes an appropriate tone, but may not clearly establish why the paper's content or conclusions might be important or interesting to an academic audience. A thesis statement focuses all or most of the development. Body paragraphs describe the distinguishing features, but topic sentences may not sharply focus the content.	The essay addresses a subject of definition, but it may be too familiar or obvious to the audience to be engaging. The introduction may list distinguishing features but does not clearly state the class to which the subject of definition belongs. If a thesis is present, it fails to clarify the purpose, or in some other way fails to focus the reader's attention. The tone does not match the purpose or is not appropriate for an academic audience. Body paragraphs may be too short or too long, and their development is not effectively focused by topic sentences. No supplementary modes of development are employed to create an extended definition.	Although a subject suitable to the assignment may be addressed in the first paragraph, no class or distinguishing features are identified, or the composition may be descriptive in nature instead of establishing a definition. Vague general statements may relate to an identified topic but do not indicate a purpose. The essay may seem to have been written to fulfill a requirement rather than to benefit a reader. Body paragraphs are underdeveloped or are undifferentiated, taking the form of one long paragraph. Irrelevant material may intrude or contradictory material may confuse the reader about the focus or purpose.

	Exceeds expectations	Meets expectations	Needs improvement	Does not meet expectations
Development	The essay provides authoritative development for each distinguishing feature and each component of the extended definition, and clearly interprets the significance of the content with respect to the identified purpose. Instructive clarifying detail or description develops each body paragraph, anticipating the readers' questions. Supplementary modes of development (i.e., description, illustration, or classification) are employed to clarify or enrich the reader's understanding of the subject of definition.	Corroborative details serve to effectively engage the audience and support the paper's thesis and topic sentences. The development is sufficient to show how the features described distinguish the subject from other members of its class, but may not show why the information is relevant to the writer's purpose or to an academic audience. All content is directly relevant to the thesis, and the development of each body paragraph clarifies the distinguishing features or contributes to the extended definition, with no disruption of essay or paragraph unity.	Development lacks specific detail and general statements or claims concerning the subject of definition and its class or distinguishing features are unsupported. Although the paper may offer a thesis statement, it fails to clearly explain how the information is useful or why an understanding of it is relevant to an academic audience, so the purpose of the essay is not fully achieved. Irrelevant observations or opinions may intrude and distract the reader or obscure the point.	If an appropriate subject of definition is identified, few or no details are included to develop the basic definition, and no extended definition is developed. General statements are vague or they distort or confuse the thesis, if one is present, rather than serving to validate or clarify it. The essay does not explain or suggest how an understanding of the subject of definition is useful or relevant to the audience, so fails to achieve any meaningful purpose. Body paragraphs are not unified, being largely comprised of impressions or statements of opinion.
Organization and coherence	Development is logically organized, following the sequence of distinguishing features indicated in a governing thesis statement. Those features are sequenced for emphasis or according to a logical principle. Shifts from one feature to the next are clearly marked with well-chosen and artfully varied transitional expressions or brief transition paragraphs. Elements of an extended definition developed around supplementary modes of development (such as contrast, description, or process analysis) are also clearly and logically organized, so the essay is fully coherent at essay and paragraph levels.	Development is reasonably organized, generally following the sequence of distinguishing features indicated in a governing thesis statement, but no discernible organizing principle informs the sequencing of features. Elements of an extended definition are generally distinguishable from one another, if present. Transitions from one distinguishing feature or extension strategy to the next are appropriately signaled; transitional expressions are employed effectively but may be used repetitively. The essay is generally coherent throughout.	Organization is attempted but inconsistent. An ineffective thesis statement fails to clearly signal the order in which body content will be presented. Individual sentences are comprehensible, but their sequencing is not clearly governed by a discernible organizing principle. Transitions are used improperly, randomly, or repetitively. Elements developing distinguishing features or extending the definition are not adequately distinguished if present, leading to some confusion. Shifts from one feature or extension component to the next are not clearly marked. Coherence is generally weak at both essay and paragraph levels.	The essay has no discernible organization at essay or paragraph level. Disjointed sentences reflect failure to systematically arrange any elements of the essay. An introduction offers no indication of the order in which body content will be introduced, and the essay employs inadequate or misleading transitional devices or organizational cues. Shifts from one distinguishing feature to the next are random. No elements of an extended definition are included, or are mixed indiscriminately if present. The composition is largely incoherent throughout.

	Exceeds expectations	Meets expectations	Needs improvement	Does not meet expectations
Style and structure	Design of introductory, body, and concluding elements establish and fully develop the subject, class, and distinguishing features, engage the audience's favorable attention, and provide a map of the essay's content, arranged in coherent body paragraphs. A conclusion sums up the purpose, function, and significance of the definition offered, and reinforces the writer's purpose and thesis. The paper achieves variety in sentence pattern and type. Tone is skillfully controlled; word choice is apt, varied, and artful.	The introduction identifies a subject, class, and distinguishing features, establishes an appropriate tone, and guides the reader into the body of the paper, which is developed in multiple separate paragraphs. A functional conclusion is present. The writing employs little variety of pattern or type, but sentence construction is competent. Diction is generally appropriate to audience and purpose, but phrasing may be repetitive or imprecise.	The essay uses spacing or indention, but paragraphing is weak. Introductory and concluding elements may be underdeveloped or absent entirely. Development of distinguishing features is delineated in separate, distinct paragraphs. Sentences employ faulty or mixed constructions, with little or no variety in pattern or type. Tone and diction lapse into inappropriate informality or stiffness.	Paragraphing is absent or insufficient to meet the demands of the writing situation, with no distinct introductory or concluding elements included. Body paragraphs are either too short or the body is not organized into separate paragraphs. Sentences are difficult to interpret; the writer does not demonstrate control of grammar or paragraph structure. Tone and diction are contradictory or inappropriate.
Precision and editing	The writer reveals mastery of all elements of grammar, usage, and mechanical conventions. Verb tenses are consistent, with appropriate shifts in passages of transition and forecasting. Uses of second person perspective and passive voice are appropriate if present. The paper is properly formatted and attractive in appearance, and contains few or no careless errors. Overall the composition is memorable and exemplary.	The essay is largely free of errors in grammar, punctuation, and use of mechanical conventions, though occasional lapses occur. Verb tenses may shift, and inappropriate shifts in person may occasionally be included, but do not create confusion. The paper is neat, legible, and clear, with formatting of manuscript conventions applied consistently. The paper satisfies the assignment with only scattered careless errors.	The essay is weakened with frequent errors in grammar, punctuation, and the use of mechanical conventions. Shifts in verb tense and perspective are pervasive and distracting. The submission may be crumpled, stained, or torn. Errors in manuscript formatting conventions draw unfavorable attention. Numerous careless errors distract the reader, though perhaps cause little or no confusion.	Verb and pronoun usage, sentence constructions, and diction are consistently faulty. Sentence structure is dysfunctional. Punctuation is arbitrary. Careless or illegible writing is confusing. Stains, rips, blots, or printing errors distract the reader and may make parts of the paper illegible. The writer fails to observe manuscript conventions or to satisfy other demands of the assignment. Errors throughout are serious enough to cause confusion and misunderstanding.

Gathering Responses and Collecting Your Thoughts

Gather all the reviewer responses. Make notes about what you and your reviewers agree and disagree on, moving from most important issues, such as appropriateness of the topic, the effectiveness of the examples, the organization, and the support for ideas, to least important, such as spelling and comma placement. List areas where you agree that improvement is needed, and make a plan about what you need to revise. Think about areas of disagreement, too. You make the final decisions about what changes to make, so determine which comments you need to respond to and which you can ignore.

Revision and Editing Activities

Identifying Options for Revision Planning

After you have gathered revision comments on your early draft from peer reviewers and your instructor (pp. 139–40), choose one of the following strategies to begin making your revision plan.

➤ Create a storyboard. On a sticky note or note card, write the term you are defining, and put it at the top of your work area. Using separate sticky notes or note cards for each paragraph or example, write down important features such as topic sentences and supporting details. Does your organization make sense? Do the parts work together? Does every paragraph help to advance the definition and clarify the point the essay makes? Using sticky notes or note cards of a different color, add notes to each paragraph about how you will strengthen, change, or delete content based on your reviewers' comments and your own. Take photos of the parts of the storyboard so you'll have a record of what you decide, even if you lose your notes.

➤ Create a graphic organizer. Using either paper and pencil or a digital document, create text boxes representing each introductory paragraph, body paragraph, and conclusion paragraph, and write the main idea of each paragraph in the box. Below it, leave room to revise the main idea. To the right of each main idea box, draw additional boxes for changes, additions, and deletions you have decided to make to supporting details, transitions, and other material in that paragraph.

➤ Make an annotated outline. Using formal complete sentences or informal phrases, make an outline that shows the current main ideas, supporting details, and organization of your draft. Using highlighters, colored pens, different colors of type, or some other method to make your changes clearly visible, annotate your outline to show the changes you plan to make to your thesis, dominant impression, organization, supporting ideas, introduction, conclusion, and so on.

➤ Make a plan of your own. _____

_____

_____

_____

_____

Revising a Definition Essay

Following the plan you've created, write a complete revised draft. Repeat as needed until you feel that you have a solid draft that is nearly final.

Using Your Common Issues to Focus Editing of Your Definition Essay

Edit for grammar, punctuation, and other common problems you have.

➤ The two kinds of problems that teachers or peer reviewers point out most often in my writing are _____ and

_____.

➤ I know I sometimes struggle with _____.

Review the information in Part 3 (pp. 190–247) about the errors you have identified above. Then reread your draft again, correcting any such errors and other issues that you find.

Proofreading

➤ Run the spell checker and carefully consider every suggestion. Do not automatically accept the suggestions! Remember that spell checkers cannot identify problems with certain kinds of words, such as homonyms and proper nouns (names), so check the spelling of such words yourself. Write the words you have misspelled on a spelling checklist you can use to identify and avoid words that give you trouble.

➤ Read your essay aloud slowly, noting and correcting any issues that you find.

➤ Read your essay aloud backwards, word by word, looking for repeated words and similar mistakes that are easy to miss in work that is very familiar. Correct any problems you see.

When your work is as error-free and professional as you can make it, submit your essay.

12

Cause and Effect*

Prewriting Activities

Finding Ideas for a Cause and Effect Essay Topic

A cause and effect essay analyzes the causes that bring about one or more effects, traces an effect back to one or more causes, or both. To identify causes or effects that can serve as the starting point for your cause and effect essay, try the following prompts.

➤ I am lucky that _____ happened so that
I _____.

➤ If _____ is not stopped, the
terrible results could include _____
or even _____.

➤ We wanted to find out why _____
happened and ensure that it would be [more likely/less likely] to happen again.

➤ Surprisingly, an important reason for _____
is _____.

Try it yourself!

Identify one or more causes for which you will identify effects or work backward from one or more effects to identify causes.

_____

_____

_____

_____

*Activities for the Guided Writing Assignment in Chapter 18, *Successful College Writing*, Seventh Edition

Clustering to Find Ideas for a Cause and Effect Essay Topic

To generate ideas for the topic of a cause and effect essay, try clustering. Write an idea, either for an event that you see as causing effects or for a result for which you will identify causes, in the middle of a sheet of paper and circle it. Then, write causes or effects of the central idea around it, circling each and joining it to the central circle. If you are certain that there is a causal connection, use a solid line to connect the circles, but use a dotted line if you need to find out more about whether the events are linked. Keep going, generating ideas related to circled concepts as you think of them, until the paper is filled. (You can also use software for digital clustering diagrams if you prefer.)

➤ What ideas were most productive for you, prompting the largest clusters of circled words and phrases?

➤ Which connections are most surprising? Will any require evidence?

➤ Are any ideas unexpectedly unproductive, going nowhere on your diagram? Pay attention to what doesn't work as well as to what does.

➤ What connections seem most likely to interest you and your readers?

Identifying a Preliminary Topic for a Cause and Effect Essay

What causal relationship will you talk about in your essay? The topic can be one that you started with on p. 146, or it can be an idea that came to you while you were exploring something else in one of the previous activities.

➤ My preliminary topic is _____
_____
_____ .

Finding a Perspective on the Preliminary Topic for Your Cause and Effect Essay

In order to find examples that will work well for your cause and effect essay, you should consider your point of view of the topic.

➤ This topic makes me feel _____
_____ .

➤ I want anyone who reads my cause and effect essay to know that _____
_____ .

➤ The best way to show my point of view is to include _____ ,
_____ , and _____ .

Identifying the Readers for Your Cause and Effect Essay

Figuring out what your audience already knows and does not know about the topic will be extremely important. If you consider what they already believe or know, you will be able to determine what you need to prove and what kinds of evidence will be most convincing. Complete the following prompts to analyze the audience you expect to reach.

➤ My audience includes _____.

➤ They may already know _____

about this topic, but they may not know _____

_____.

➤ I need to tell this audience about _____

_____ so they will

understand my perspective on the topic.

➤ When they read my essay, I want them to feel _____

_____.

➤ My purpose for writing is to _____.

Exploring Logical Ideas for a Cause and Effect Essay

What are some logical, persuasive, and interesting points you will need to make to clarify the chain of causes and effects? Respond to any of the following prompts that are appropriate for your cause and effect essay.

➤ A cause that everyone associates with this effect is _____

_____. It is [useful/not

useful] for my cause and effect essay because _____

_____

➤ An effect that people assume comes from this cause is _____

_____. It is

[useful/not useful] for my cause and effect essay because _____

_____.

➤ A visual that would clarify the causes and effects is _____

_____.

➤ My own experience with _____

could be used as [a cause/an effect] in the causal chain I am writing about because

_____.

➤ I [need/do not need] to use sources from research.

➤ Additional sources I could use include _____
_____, and
I can find them _____.

Identifying Strong, Vivid Examples for a Cause and Effect Essay

Sensory details can make a cause and effect essay come alive. Brainstorm as many of the following prompts as possible to try out different details to enliven the information you will include.

➤ something seen, observed, or watched that is part of a causal connection

EXAMPLES: fewer songbirds at my backyard feeder since the neighbors began letting their cat go outside

_____

_____

_____

➤ a sound that relates to causes or effects

EXAMPLES: the wall of sound rumbling from the stack of Marshall amplifiers that stood behind the guitarist, who now has difficulty hearing certain frequencies

_____

_____

➤ an aroma, smell, or stench that is relevant to the causal connection

EXAMPLES: the smell of cinnamon that contributed to the nausea I felt while waiting for my flight to depart

_____

_____

_____

➤ something tangible or textured that relates to a cause or an effect

EXAMPLES: the solid thunk of the bag connecting with the heel of my hand as I dove into second base

_____

_____

_____

➤ a flavor or taste that connects to a cause or effect

> EXAMPLES: the creamy taste of the high-fat chocolate ice cream I enjoyed every day that summer before I found that my back-to-school wardrobe was too small

_____

_____

➤ Try creating an example from any pattern of development that seems useful.

_____

_____

Choosing Visuals or Other Media to Enliven a Cause and Effect Essay

If you have access to photos or other media that will help create a vivid impression of one or more of the causes or effects you are discussing, consider including one or more of them in your essay. Video and audio files can be used in an essay that you will post online.

Thesis Activities

➤ My preliminary topic [p. 147] is _____.

Narrowing and Focusing a Topic for a Cause and Effect Essay

Will you be able to clarify all of the causes and effects you will need to make your case in an essay of the assigned length? Sometimes a narrower topic may allow you to create a better cause and effect essay.

➤ If I had five minutes to explain the most important cause-and-effect relationship

to people who are not familiar with it, I would start with _____

_____

_____

Identifying a Main Point for Your Cause and Effect Essay

To me, the single most important thing about the topic I am trying to illustrate is (pick one and complete the sentence)

- that it explains _____.
- that it helps people understand _____.
- that it proves _____.

- that it is exciting because _____.
- that it is important because _____.
- that _____

_____.

Moving from Topic to Preliminary Thesis for a Cause and Effect Essay

Fill in the blanks to start thinking about the point you want to make in your cause and effect essay.

➤ Many people will be surprised to find out that _____ [causes/affects] _____.

➤ I used to believe _____ about the cause or effect I am describing, but I have changed my mind. Now I think _____

_____

➤ This may sound strange, but [the causal relationship] makes me think about _____ because

_____.

➤ At first I did not understand [the relationship between cause and effect], but now I think of it as _____

_____.

➤ A new insight my readers should have about [the causal relationship] is

_____.

Now, write your statement about the cause and effect relationship that can serve as a preliminary thesis.

_____

_____

_____

Testing Your Thesis

In a sentence or two, explain your proposed thesis for your cause and effect essay to a classmate or friend who is part of your audience, and briefly tell him or her about how you propose to support the thesis. Ask for responses to these questions.

➤ How much do you understand about the relationship between the cause(s) and effect(s) I'm describing?

_____

_____

➤   How convincing is my plan to demonstrate the relationship between the cause(s) and effect(s) in my essay? Why? _____

_____

➤   What interests you most about this topic? Why? _____

_____

Do the reviewer's responses suggest that you are on the right track? If not, consider whether you should rethink your topic, review your assumptions about what your audience knows and cares about, or find better evidence to show the relationship between the causes and effects.

Drafting Activities

Deciding Where to Begin

Begin at the easiest point for you to get started. If starting with the cause will help you get your draft underway, begin there; if the effect is more interesting or easier to write about, begin with that. You may want to begin with ideas you know your readers will accept and then turn later to proving less clear connections. You can start with the introduction, of course, but you do not have to begin at the beginning; you can draft the introduction and conclusion after the body of your essay if that will help you get started.

Brainstorming Ways to Get Readers' Attention

Keeping your preliminary thesis in mind, try your hand at these effective ways to start an introduction.

➤   a quotation (something you said, something someone said to you, a relevant snippet of dialogue that will be part of one of your examples)

_____

_____

➤   an anecdote or story (something that sheds light on the subject you are discussing or explains how you came to realize the connection between causes and effects)

_____

_____

➤   a provocative statement (a surprising or shocking announcement or an unexpected revelation)

_____

_____

➤ a question that prompts readers to think about how they will answer it

_____

_____

➤ a hypothetical situation that invites others to imagine being in someone else's place

_____

_____

➤ a comparison that shows how your unfamiliar concept is like something more familiar to your readers

_____

_____

Drafting an Introduction

Choose the opening you like most from the examples you've created, and start a new draft that begins with that opening. How can you move from this catchy opening to your first example?

➤ State the cause and effect relationship clearly rather than asking readers to guess.

➤ What background information will readers need right up front to make sense of your thesis? How can you incorporate it smoothly?

➤ How will you help readers get a sense of the scope of the information you will provide? How can you make yourself seem trustworthy?

Trying Options for Organizing Body Paragraphs

If you aren't certain what organization makes sense for the examples that will support your thesis, try completing any of the following options that seems viable. Use the option you choose as the basis for an outline or graphic organizer that you can follow as you draft.

By Time

➤ Chronological order: start with the earliest cause(s) and move forward in time to the most recent effect(s)

➤ Reverse chronological order: start with most recent effect(s) and move backward to the earliest cause(s)

Point by Point or Subject by Subject (for Multiple Causes and Effects)

➤ Start with the first cause and first effect, then give the second cause and second effect, then the third cause and third effect, and so on

➤ Present the first cause, second cause, and third cause together; then present the first effect, second effect, third effect, and so on

As a Causal Chain

➤ Start with the first cause and effect; then use the first effect as the second cause that leads to a new effect; then use the second effect as a third cause, and so on.

Try it yourself!

➤ Organization plan for examples: _____

Topic of first body paragraph: _____

➤ Causes and/or effects to discuss: _____
   Details and evidence to include in the paragraph:

   • _____

   • _____

   • _____

Topic of second body paragraph: _____

➤ Causes and/or effects to discuss: _____
   Details and evidence to include in the paragraph:

   • _____

   • _____

   • _____

Topic of third body paragraph: _____

➤ Causes and/or effects to discuss: _____
   Details and evidence to include in the paragraph:

   • _____

   • _____

   • _____

(Continue until you have outlined or sketched a plan for all your body paragraphs.)

Drafting a Conclusion

Your conclusion should reinforce the point you are making by presenting the causes and effects you have discussed. It should also make a memorable final statement.

➤ The point of this cause and effect analysis is _____

_____.

➤ Thinking about these causes and effects is important because _____

_____.

➤ Readers should feel _____.

Try it yourself!

Draft a conclusion that reinforces your thesis and ties the whole essay together:

_____

_____

_____

Creating an Intriguing Title

Your title should indicate the topic of your cause and effect essay and say something about it that will interest readers. Try the following ideas to create an intriguing title that your audience will want to read.

➤ Alliteration: My causes and effects relate mainly to _____

_____, and some words that begin with the

same sound and relate to my examples are _____

_____.

➤ Groups of three: Three things that are important to the cause and effect

relationship I'm discussing are _____,

_____, and _____.

➤ Question: People wonder _____

_____ about this

cause and effect relationship.

➤ Quotation: Someone said "_____

_____" about this

causal relationship.

➤ Try out a title of your own: _____.

Feedback Activities

Getting Your Questions Answered by Peer Reviewers

You'll get better feedback from peer reviewers if you ask for specific help with comments and questions like these.

➤ I'm not sure whether or not _____ is working.

➤ Is the evidence for a cause and effect relationship between _____ _____ and _____ convincing?

➤ My biggest concern is _____.

Now write the question with which you *most* want your peer reviewers' help.

_____

_____

Asking Reviewers for Feedback about a Cause and Effect Essay

To find out if reviewers are getting the impression you want to give in your cause and effect essay, have them answer the following questions.

➤ What is the thesis? Is it interesting?

➤ How persuasively does the essay explain the relationship between the causes and the effects? What evidence is most and least convincing?

➤ What questions are not answered that should be answered?

➤ What details work well? What do you like about them?

➤ Which details are weakest? Which ideas need further development?

➤ Does the essay's organization make sense?

➤ How well does the essay hang together? How effective are the transitions between paragraphs?

➤ How enticing is the introduction? Which parts make you want to keep reading? What is less interesting?

➤ How well does the conclusion end the essay? What works best to bring the essay to an end? What should change?

➤ How effective is the title? Why?

➤ My favorite part of this essay is _____

_____

because _____.

➤ The part that I think needs the most improvement is _____

_____

because _____.

Conducting a Self-Review

Put your draft aside for at least one day. Then, read it again, doing your best to pretend that you have never seen it before. Use the Rubric for Assessing Cause and Effect Essays to see how well you think you have accomplished the essay's objectives in this draft. (Your instructor may use other criteria for assessing student writing, so be sure to check with him or her about expectations.)

Rubric for Assessing Cause and Effect Essays

	Exceeds expectations	Meets expectations	Needs improvement	Does not meet expectations
Focus, purpose, and audience	The thesis addresses a term or concept that is interesting and important to the audience. The introduction indicates how the essay will clarify, explain, or support the thesis by using cause and effect, and promises an insight or learning experience. Unified body paragraphs have clearly focused topic sentences.	The thesis addresses a claim, term, or concept appropriate to the audience and the assignment. The introduction clearly indicates the intent to clarify or support the thesis by using cause and effect. Unified body paragraphs include functional topic sentences.	A thesis is evident but is too broad or narrow, or does not meet the assignment's purpose or appeal to the target audience. Body paragraphs are too broadly or too narrowly focused, or lack clearly governing topic sentences. Some irrelevant material may be included.	No clear thesis is evident, or the thesis is inadequate to control the essay or engage the reader's favorable attention. Body paragraphs lack topic sentences, or are too long or too short to effectively develop individual subtopics.

	Exceeds expectations	Meets expectations	Needs improvement	Does not meet expectations
Development	The essay offers well-chosen, authoritative, representative, relevant, and concrete examples to clarify and support the paper's thesis and engage the audience's favorable attention. Extended examples are fully integrated with the explanatory content; personal experience examples are balanced with historical, topical, or other examples that can be authenticated.	Examples are appropriate to the audience and purpose, and sufficient to adequately support the thesis, but may be left to "speak for themselves" without being fully integrated with the paper or paragraph topic. Essay and paragraph content is relevant, with no disruption of essay or paragraph unity and no visible bias.	Examples are offered to support the thesis, but are too broad or too general to fully engage the audience or validate the thesis. Development may be overbalanced with unverifiable personal experience or hypothetical examples.	Few examples are offered, or they distort or confuse the thesis rather than serving to validate or clarify it.
Organization and coherence	Clear, logical organizing principles govern the arrangement of content at both essay and paragraph levels. Forecasting statements are used effectively in the introduction. Smooth, largely unnoticed transitions within and between ideas and paragraphs enhance coherence.	Development is reasonably organized throughout. Sentences within paragraphs are arranged to show the logical sequencing of ideas. Each body paragraph is unified and coherent. Body paragraphs are sequenced effectively for the types(s) of examples employed. Transitions link ideas and paragraphs.	Organization is attempted but is ineffective or unclear. The reader can follow the writer's points with difficulty. Body paragraph sequencing seems uncontrolled or random, with insufficient or confusing transitional, organizational cues being employed.	The essay has no discernible organization at essay or paragraph level. The reader is unable to follow the writer's train of thought, and the essay employs inadequate or misleading transitional devices or organizational cues.
Style and structure	Design of introductory, body, and concluding elements engage the audience's favorable attention and guide it through the essay's content, arranged in coherent body paragraphs. A conclusion prompts rethinking of the topic or promotes new insight. The essay achieves variety in sentence pattern and type. If using sources, the writer uses signal phrasing and clearly sets off cited from original material. Tone is skillfully controlled; word choice is apt.	The introduction addresses the topic, sets the tone, and guides the reader into the body of the paper, which is developed in multiple separate paragraphs. A functional conclusion is present. The writing employs little variety, but sentence construction is competent. If used, sources are acknowledged, but signal phrasing or parenthetical elements may be misplaced or confusing. Diction is appropriate, but may be repetitive or imprecise.	The essay uses spacing or indention, but paragraphing is weak. Introductory elements are not controlled, and a separate body and conclusion may not be included. Sentences are vague or ambiguous, with little or no variety in pattern or type. If outside sources are used, no in-text citation is offered, or it is too confusing to clearly distinguish the writer's work from cited material. Tone is inappropriate for the purpose and audience. Diction is faulty or inappropriate.	Paragraphing is absent or insufficient to meet the demands of the writing situation, with no distinct introductory or concluding elements included. Sentences are difficult to interpret; the writer does not demonstrate control of grammar or paragraph structure. Tone and diction are confusing, contradictory, or inappropriate.

	Exceeds expectations	Meets expectations	Needs improvement	Does not meet expectations
Precision and editing	The writer reveals mastery of all elements of grammar, usage, and mechanical conventions. Listed examples are punctuated properly and are parallel in construction. Where outside sources are used, they are cited in proper bibliographic form. Formatting conventions for use of font and line spacing, use of headings, headers and footers, are applied appropriately throughout. An attractive page design draws the reader's eye through the page. The writer executes the assignment memorably with no careless errors.	The essay is largely free of errors in grammar, punctuation, and use of mechanical conventions, though occasional lapses occur. Sentences are coherent, and structural errors (where present) do not disrupt the reading. Where outside sources are used, proper bibliographic form and mechanical conventions are employed, with minor lapses in form or format. The paper is neat, legible, and clear, with formatting of manuscript conventions applied consistently. The paper satisfies the assignment with only scattered careless errors.	The essay has frequent errors in grammar, punctuation, and the use of mechanical conventions. Where outside sources are used, the bibliographic information is included but is formatted incorrectly, sometimes leading to ambiguity of source or source type. The submission may be crumpled, stained, or torn. Errors in manuscript formatting conventions draw unfavorable attention. The writer attempts but fails to fully execute the assignment. Numerous careless errors distract, though perhaps cause little or no confusion.	Verb and pronoun usage, sentence constructions, and diction are consistently faulty. Sentence structure is dysfunctional. Punctuation is arbitrary. Where outside sources are used, bibliographic entries are omitted or incomplete. Careless or illegible writing is confusing. Stains, tears, blots, or printing errors distract the reader and may make parts of the paper unreadable. The writer fails to observe manuscript conventions or to satisfy other demands of the assignment. Errors throughout are serious enough to cause confusion and misunderstanding of meaning.

Gathering Responses and Collecting Your Thoughts

Gather all the reviewer responses. Make notes about what you and your reviewers agree and disagree on, moving from most important issues, such as appropriateness of the topic, the effectiveness of the examples, the organization, and the support for ideas, to least important, such as spelling and comma placement. List areas where you agree that improvement is needed, and make a plan about what you need to revise. Think about areas of disagreement, too. You make the final decisions about what changes to make, so determine which comments you need to respond to and which you can ignore.

Revision and Editing Activities

Identifying Options for Revision Planning

After you have gathered revision comments on your early draft from peer reviewers and your instructor (pp. 156–57), choose one of the following strategies to begin making your revision plan.

➤ Create a storyboard. On a sticky note or note card, write the main point you are making about cause and effect, and put it at the top of your work area. Using separate sticky notes or note cards for each paragraph or example, write down important features such as topic sentences and supporting details. Does your organization make sense? Do the parts work together? Does every paragraph help to advance the story and clarify the point it makes? Using sticky notes or note cards of a different color, add notes to each paragraph about how you will strengthen, change, or delete content based on your reviewers' comments and your own. Take photos of the parts of the storyboard so you'll have a record of what you decide, even if you lose your notes.

➤ Create a graphic organizer. Using either paper and pencil or a digital document, create text boxes representing each introductory paragraph, body paragraph, and conclusion paragraph, and write the main idea of each paragraph in the box. Below it, leave room to revise the main idea. To the right of each main idea box, draw additional boxes for changes, additions, and deletions you have decided to make to supporting details, transitions, and other material in that paragraph.

➤ Make an annotated outline. Using either formal complete sentences or informal phrases, make an outline that shows the current main ideas, supporting details, and organization of your draft. Using highlighters, colored pens, different colors of type, or some other method to make your changes clearly visible, annotate your outline to show the changes you plan to make to your thesis, dominant impression, organization, supporting ideas, introduction, conclusion, and so on.

➤ Make a plan of your own. _____

_____

_____

_____

_____

Revising a Cause and Effect Essay

Following the plan you've created, write a complete revised draft. Repeat as needed until you feel that you have a solid draft that is nearly final.

Using Your Common Issues to Focus Editing of Your Cause and Effect Essay

Edit for grammar, punctuation, and other common problems you have.

➤ The two kinds of problems that teachers or peer reviewers point out most often in my writing are _____ and
_____.

➤ I know I sometimes struggle with _____.

Review the information in Part 3 (pp. 190–247) about the errors you have identified above. Then reread your draft again, correcting any such errors and other issues that you find.

Proofreading

➤ Run the spell checker and carefully consider every suggestion. Do not automatically accept the suggestions! Remember that spell checkers cannot identify problems with certain kinds of words, such as homonyms and proper nouns (names), so check the spelling of such words yourself. Write the words you have misspelled on a spelling checklist you can use to identify and avoid words that give you trouble.

➤ Read your essay aloud slowly, noting and correcting any issues that you find.

➤ Read your essay aloud backwards, word by word, looking for repeated words and similar mistakes that are easy to miss in work that is very familiar. Correct any problems you see.

When your work is as error-free and professional as you can make it, submit your essay.

13

Argument*

Prewriting Activities

Finding Issues for an Argument Essay

An argument essay makes a logical, persuasive claim on an issue about which people can reasonably disagree. To identify arguable claims that can serve as the starting point for your argument essay, try the following prompts.

➤ I recently had a heated discussion with [a friend/an acquaintance/a family member] about _____ because [she/he] believes _____ and I believe _____.

➤ When I read about _____, it makes me [angry/unhappy/inspired/hopeful].

➤ People who want _____ should _____ and not _____.

➤ Individuals can make a difference in my community by _____, but few people are willing to make the effort.

➤ _____ is a problem because _____, and one way to make it better is _____.

*Activities for the Guided Writing Assignment in Chapter 20, *Successful College Writing*, Seventh Edition

Try it yourself!

Identify one or more topics you might be interested in tackling in an argument essay.

_____

_____

_____

Freewriting to Find Arguable Issues for a Persuasive Essay

To generate ideas for an argument essay, try starting with freewriting to discover what you know, what you need to find out, and how you feel about an issue. Set a timer for five minutes and write without stopping, putting down every thought about your argument that comes to mind. If a new thought derails your initial idea, can you find ways to use that idea persuasively? Keep going, generating as many ideas and comments as you can, until the time is up.

➤ Read over what you wrote, and highlight or underline words, phrases, and sentences that strike you as interesting or useful in some way.

➤ In a new document, write (or copy and paste) the most interesting words or phrases you called out from the first round of freewriting. Set the timer for another five minutes and use your initial freewriting prompt to generate more ideas.

➤ Keep going until you have some ideas to get started on your persuasive essay.

Identifying a Tentative Claim for an Argument Essay

What issue will you talk about in your essay, and what position do you intend to argue? The topic can be one that you started with on p. 162, or it can be an idea that came to you while you were exploring something else in one of the activities above.

➤ My tentative claim is _____

_____

_____.

Collaborating to Identify Opposing Arguments

Now that you have a tentative claim for a topic for your argument essay, make sure that it is arguable. Jot down as much supporting evidence as you can for the topic, and then write down all the opposing evidence you can think of. Working with a partner, take turns reading your points, both pro and con, and asking the partner to identify any weaknesses in either the supporting or the opposing argument and to identify the strongest and most persuasive points on both sides of the issue. Take notes of points your partner brings up so you can determine how to address them.

Finding a Perspective on the Preliminary Topic for Your Argument Essay

In order to find examples that will work well for your argument essay, you should consider your point of view of the topic.

➤ My perspective on this topic is _____
_____ .

➤ I want anyone who reads my argument essay to know that _____
_____ .

➤ The best way to show my point of view is to include _____ ,
_____ , and _____ .

Identifying the Readers for Your Argument Essay

Figuring out what your audience already knows and does not know about the topic will be extremely important. If you consider what they already believe or know, you will be able to determine what you need to prove and what kinds of evidence will be most convincing. Complete the following prompts to analyze the audience you expect to reach.

➤ My audience includes _____ .

➤ Some of them probably agree with me about _____ .

➤ I may convince those who do not agree with my perspective on the topic to take my argument seriously if _____ .

➤ The kind of evidence that this audience will find convincing is most likely
_____ .

➤ I need to tell this audience about _____
_____ so they
will understand my perspective on the topic.

➤ When they read my argument essay, I want them to feel _____
_____ .

➤ When they read my argument essay, I would ideally like them to do _____
_____ .

➤ My purpose for writing is to _____ .

Exploring the Library to Find Logical and Persuasive Evidence for an Argument

To find the most persuasive evidence to support your ideas and refute opposing ideas for an argument, you will probably need to do library research. A preliminary visit to the library to look for books and articles is a good place to begin. List your responses to the prompts below and then talk with reference librarians about how to find useful sources; a librarian's advice will probably save you time and produce better results.

➤ Types of evidence that may change the minds of people who don't agree with me yet: _____

_____

➤ Types of evidence I need to find to prove what I already believe to be true:

_____

_____

➤ Other information I need to make my case: _____

_____

_____

➤ Possible sources for the most persuasive opposing viewpoints that I will need to address:

_____

_____

_____

Collaborating to Explore Opposing Viewpoints

After doing library research and talking with a partner about the pros and cons of the issue, you should have a sense of the most important opposing arguments that your argument essay will need to address. Jot down information about each opposing argument (and the source, if you are quoting or paraphrasing someone else's words) on a note card. Working with a group of classmates, read the information, and then discuss with the group whether the argument has any of the following issues.

➤ Credibility: Is the source an expert? Is there evidence that the source is biased? Are there other reasons to question the accuracy of the argument?

➤ Relevance here and now: When was the argument made — recently, or long ago? Has anything changed significantly since then? Is the argument still valid? Does the argument address the same situation in the same place that you are talking about?

➤ Counterexamples: Can you identify examples, anecdotes, or stories to refute the points in the argument?

Identifying Good Reasons for Your Argument

After you've looked at ways to argue against opposing claims, brainstorm reasons in support of the tentative claim you are making. (For help making claims based on sources, see Chapter 14, "Sentence Guides for Academic Writers," on pp. 181–89.)

➤ Experts say _____

_____

_____.

➤ My experience shows _____

_____

_____.

➤ Facts and statistics demonstrate _____

_____

_____.

➤ A convincing visual that would support my point is _____

_____.

Thesis Activities

➤ My tentative claim [p. 163] is _____.

Narrowing and Focusing a Topic for an Argument Essay

Will you be able to argue this claim effectively in an essay of the assigned length? Sometimes a narrower topic may allow you to create a better argument essay.

➤ If I had five minutes to explain the essence of my argument to people who are not familiar with it, I would start with _____

_____.

Identifying a Main Point for Your Argument Essay

To me, the single most important thing about my tentative claim is (pick one and complete the sentence)

- that it would help _____.
- that it would improve understanding of _____.
- that it could prove _____.
- that _____
  _____.

Moving from Tentative Claim to Preliminary Thesis for an Argument Essay

If you still need to strengthen your tentative claim, fill in the blanks to start thinking about the point you want to make in your argument essay.

➤ Many people will be surprised to find out that _____
_____

➤ I used to believe _____, but I have changed my mind. Now I think _____
_____

➤ At first I did not understand _____
but now _____.

➤ A new insight I want my readers to gain from reading my essay is _____
_____.

Now, write your statement about the argument relationship that can serve as a preliminary thesis.

_____
_____
_____
_____

Testing Your Thesis

In a sentence or two, explain your proposed thesis for your argument essay to a class-mate or friend who is part of your audience, and briefly tell him or her about how you propose to support the thesis. Ask for responses to these questions.

➤ Does the thesis make a claim that a reasonable person could disagree with?

_____
_____

➤ How easily could this claim be refuted? Is it too absolute? _____
_____

➤   What interests you most about this topic? Why? _____

_____

Do the reviewer's responses suggest that you are on the right track? If not, consider whether you should rethink your thesis, review your assumptions about what your audience knows and cares about, or find better evidence to support your claim.

Drafting Activities

Deciding Where to Begin

Begin at the easiest point for you to get started. If starting with an opposing argument will help you get underway, start there; if you want to begin by making your own case, do so. You can start with the introduction, of course, but you do not have to begin at the beginning; you can draft the introduction and conclusion after you have completed the body of your essay if that will help you get started.

Brainstorming Ways to Get Readers' Attention

Keeping your preliminary thesis in mind, try your hand at these effective ways to start an introduction.

➤   a quotation (something you said, something someone said to you, a relevant snippet of dialogue that will be part of one of your examples)

_____

_____

➤   an anecdote or story (something that sheds light on the subject you are discussing or explains how you came to realize the connection between causes and effects)

_____

➤   a provocative piece of information (a surprising or shocking fact from your research or an unexpected revelation)

_____

➤   a question that prompts readers to think about how they will answer it

_____

➤   a hypothetical situation that invites others to imagine being in someone else's place

_____

_____

➤ a comparison that shows how your unfamiliar concept is like something more familiar to your readers

_____

_____

Drafting an Introduction

Choose the opening you like most from the examples you've created, and start a new draft that begins with that opening. How can you move from this catchy opening to your thesis? Complete the relevant prompts to brainstorm ways to provide everything your readers need from you.

➤ I should present the issue by _____

_____.

➤ Background information my readers may not know includes _____

_____.

➤ Terms I may need to define include _____

_____.

➤ To make readers feel that I am trustworthy and likable, I will _____

_____.

Trying Options for Organizing Body Paragraphs

If you aren't certain what organization makes sense for the evidence that will support your thesis, try different options. You can begin with strongest claims or build up from weaker claims to stronger ones, or you may move from more to less familiar or less to more familiar claims.

Deductive Methods

➤ Present your claim, then the reasons and evidence, and then present and refute opposing views.

➤ Present your claim, then present and refute opposing views, and finally, present your reasons and evidence.

Inductive Methods

➤ Present your reasons and evidence, then present and refute opposing views, and finally, present your claim.

➤ Present opposing views, present your reasons and evidence, and finally, present your claim.

Try it yourself!

➤ Use graphic organizers or outlines to try different possibilities.

Topic of first body paragraph: _____

Information and evidence to include in the paragraph:

- _____
- _____
- _____

Topic of second body paragraph: _____

Information and evidence to include in the paragraph:

- _____
- _____
- _____

Topic of third body paragraph: _____

Information and evidence to include in the paragraph:

- _____
- _____
- _____

(Continue until you have outlined or sketched a plan for all your body paragraphs.)

Drafting a Conclusion

Your conclusion should reinforce the point you are making in your thesis. It should also make a memorable final statement, appeal to readers' values, and perhaps ask them to take action.

➤ The takeaway from my argument essay should be _____

_____.

➤ Readers should feel _____

and do _____.

Try it yourself!

Draft a conclusion that reinforces your thesis and ties the whole essay together.

_____

_____

_____

Creating an Intriguing Title

Your title should indicate the topic of your argument essay and say something about it that will interest readers. Try the following ideas to create an intriguing title that your audience will want to read.

➤ Alliteration: My issue relates mainly to _____
_____, and some words that begin with
the same sound and relate to my argument are _____
_____.

➤ Groups of three: Three things that are important to the argument I'm making are
_____, _____
_____, and _____.

➤ Question: People wonder _____
_____
about this argument.

➤ Quotation: Someone said "_____
_____" about this argument.

➤ Try out a title of your own: _____

Feedback Activities

Getting Your Questions Answered by Peer Reviewers

You'll get better feedback from peer reviewers if you ask for specific help with comments and questions like these.

➤ I'm not sure whether or not _____ is
working.

➤ Is the evidence for my claim convincing? Why or why not?

➤ My biggest concern is _____.

Now write the question with which you *most* want your peer reviewers' help.

_____
_____

Asking Reviewers for Feedback about an Argument Essay

To find out if reviewers are getting the impressions you want to give in your argument essay, have them answer the following questions.

➤ What is the thesis? Is it interesting?

➤ How persuasively does the essay make its case? What evidence is most and least convincing?

➤ What questions are not answered that should be answered?

➤ What sources are most useful (if the essay includes research)? How effectively are they included? Does the essay include a works-cited page or list of references?

➤ What details work well? What do you like about them?

➤ Which details are weakest? Which ideas need further development?

➤ Does the essay's organization make sense?

➤ How well does the essay hang together? How effective are the transitions between paragraphs?

➤ How enticing is the introduction? Which parts make you want to keep reading? What is less interesting?

➤ How well does the conclusion end the essay? What works best to bring the essay to an end? What should change?

➤ How effective is the title? Why?

➤ My favorite part of this essay is _____
_____

because _____.

➤ The part that I think needs the most improvement is _____
_____

because _____.

Conducting a Self-Review

Put your draft aside for at least one day. Then, read it again, doing your best to pretend that you have never seen it before. Use the Rubric for Assessing Argument Essays to see how well you think you have accomplished the essay's objectives in this draft. (Your instructor may use other criteria for assessing student writing, so be sure to check with him or her about expectations.)

Rubric for Assessing Argument Essays

	Exceeds expectations	Meets expectations	Needs improvement	Does not meet expectations
Focus, purpose, and audience	The thesis challenges an open-minded but skeptical audience by addressing an important, current subject of public debate or controversy. The introduction engages the audience's favorable attention, briefly addresses the key perspectives, defines relevant terms, and identifies shared values or uses Rogerian strategy to minimize tension and establish goodwill. The essay indicates what the writer wants the audience to think, believe, or do after reading the paper, and this purpose is appropriate given the target audience. Body paragraphs focus individually on each key point or reason for each perspective, effectively supporting one position and refuting the other(s).	The thesis addresses an academic audience on a topic of public discussion, but the topic may be too overworked to effectively engage the readers' favorable attention. The introduction briefly addresses the key perspectives and defines relevant terms, and attempts to establish goodwill, but may not fully alleviate tension generated by conflicting viewpoints. The paper generally suggests what the writer wants to achieve—what he or she wants the audience to think, believe, or do after reading—but this purpose may be unrealistic, given the target audience. Body paragraphs focus on key points informing each perspective, supporting one position and attempting to refute the other(s).	A thesis is evident but may be more analytical than persuasive, failing to address a subject with multiple valid perspectives, or it may not clearly meet the assignment's persuasive requirement, identify the purpose it will attempt to serve, or appeal to an academic audience. The introduction fails to address multiple perspectives and is ineffective in attempts to establish goodwill or convince the reader to continue reading. Body paragraphs are too broadly or too narrowly focused, or lack clearly governing topic sentences. The paper does not develop arguments for both perspectives or fails to adequately support one and refute the other. Some irrelevant material may be included.	No clear thesis is evident, or the thesis is inadequate to control the essay or engage the reader's favorable attention. The introduction, if present, fails to address a subject of argument appropriate to the assignment or indicate a purpose. If a subject of debate is identified, the introduction fails to address the perspectives adequately. Content may not be organized into separate body paragraphs. If present, body paragraphs lack topic sentences, or are too long or too short to effectively develop individual subtopics. The paper takes no position on the subject of argument, or acknowledges only one perspective. Irrelevant or inappropriately subjective personal commentary distorts the focus.

	Exceeds expectations	Meets expectations	Needs improvement	Does not meet expectations
Development	The paper offers an interesting balance of general statement and concrete supporting detail and is ample and authoritative, fully illustrating each point in each perspective's argument. The development in each body paragraph is directly relevant to its topic sentence and is appropriate to the mode of development employed at the paragraph level to develop the points of argument for each perspective and refutation. Counterevidence is acknowledged and addressed without distortion.	Content at the essay level is appropriate to the audience and purpose, and sufficient to adequately support the thesis, but may lack specific or explicit detail. Paragraph development is relevant to topic sentences, with no extraneous material to disrupt unity. Both perspectives are developed with relevant evidence taken from valid research. Counterevidence is acknowledged and the writer's argument attempts to accommodate it with little or no evident bias.	Development offered to support the thesis is limited to generalization or is insufficient to fully engage the audience or validate the thesis. Vagueness, inaccuracy, or unclear reasoning may confuse the audience or leave the reader unconvinced of the thesis' validity. Body paragraphs do not clearly correlate to individual points developing each perspective and are not informed by authoritative research. Bias is evident throughout.	Vague claims are unsubstantiated. Reasoning is distorted or unclear. If a thesis is discernible, attempts to develop it are limited to statements of personal opinion or conjecture. Content is not always directly relevant to the essay's subject. Body paragraphs are either too underdeveloped to support each subtopic, or are undifferentiated and form one long, unfocused paragraph lacking unity. The paper is too subjective to function as academic writing.
Organization and coherence	Clear, logical inductive or deductive organizing principles appropriate to the purpose and audience are employed at both essay and paragraph levels. The introduction offers a brief "essay map" forecasting the sequencing of subtopics. Each body paragraph uses an organizing approach appropriate to its role in developing the argument. Transitions effectively clarify relationships between ideas and subtopics throughout.	Development is reasonably organized throughout, primarily according to deductive order. Subtopics follow a sequence suggested by forecasting elements in the introduction. Each body paragraph uses an organizing approach appropriate to its mode of development. Body paragraphs are sequenced effectively, leading to coherence of the essay as a whole. Transitions effectively link ideas and paragraphs.	Organization is attempted but is ineffective or unclear. The reader can follow the writer's points with difficulty. The introduction offers no forecasting elements to govern sequencing of subtopics, so body paragraph sequencing seems uncontrolled or random, with insufficient or confusing transitional, organizational cues being employed.	The essay has no discernible organization at essay or paragraph level. The reader is unable to follow the writer's train of thought, and the essay employs inadequate or misleading transitional devices or organizational cues.

	Exceeds expectations	Meets expectations	Needs improvement	Does not meet expectations
Style and structure	Design of introductory, body, and concluding elements engage the audience's favorable attention and guide it through the essay's content, arranged in coherent body paragraphs that fully frame each perspective, clearly establish and support the writer's perspective, and refute opposing views and counterevidence. A conclusion reinforces the writer's position on the topic or promotes new insight. The paper achieves variety in sentence pattern and type. If using sources, the writer uses signal phrasing and clearly sets off cited from original material. Tone is skillfully controlled; word choice is apt, establishing the writer's credibility.	The introduction addresses the topic, sets the tone, and guides the reader into the body of the paper, which is developed in multiple separate paragraphs. A functional conclusion is present. The writing employs some variety of sentence pattern, and sentence construction is competent. Sources used are acknowledged, but signal phrasing or parenthetical elements may be misplaced or lead to confusion. Diction is appropriate to audience or purpose, so the writer establishes credibility, but it may be eroded by repetitive or imprecise word choice.	The essay uses spacing or indention, but paragraphs are not built around sound paragraphing principles and lack unity and coherence. A separate body and conclusion may not be included. Sentences are unclear, employing faulty or mixed constructions, with little or no variety in pattern or type. No in-text citations are used to reference outside material, or they do not clearly distinguish the original work from cited material. Tone and diction are uncontrolled or inappropriate for the purpose and audience, so the writer's credibility is not fully established.	Paragraphing is absent with sentences placed together without a discernible strategy. Introductory or concluding elements are inadequate, misleading, or omitted altogether. Sentences are difficult to interpret; grammar and paragraph structure are uncontrolled. Sources, if used, are unacknowledged, resulting in plagiarism. Tone and diction are confusing, contradictory, or inappropriate, so the writer fails to establish credibility.
Precision and editing	The essay reveals mastery of all elements of grammar, usage, and mechanical conventions. Any outside sources are cited using proper bibliographic form. Formatting conventions for use of font and line spacing, use of headings, headers and footers, are applied appropriately throughout. Design elements direct the reader through each page. The writer executes the assignment memorably with no careless errors.	The essay is largely but not entirely free of grammatical, punctuation, and mechanical errors. Sentences are coherent, and structural errors (where present) do not disrupt the reading. Proper bibliographic form and mechanical conventions are employed to cite sources, with only minor lapses in form or format. The paper is neat, legible, and clear, with formatting of manuscript conventions applied consistently. The paper satisfies the assignment with only scattered careless errors.	The essay is weakened with frequent errors in grammar, punctuation, and the use of mechanical conventions. References to outside sources are formatted incorrectly, sometimes leading to ambiguity of source or source type. The submission may be crumpled, stained, or torn. Errors in manuscript formatting conventions draw unfavorable attention. The writer attempts but fails to fully execute the assignment. Numerous editing errors distract, though perhaps cause only minor confusion.	Sentence structure is not adequately controlled. Punctuation does not follow established convention. Bibliographic entries for outside sources are omitted or incomplete, and formatting conventions for citing sources are not followed. Illegible writing is confusing. Stains, rips, blots, or printing errors may make parts of the paper unreadable. The writer fails to observe manuscript conventions or to satisfy other demands of the assignment. Errors throughout are serious enough to cause confusion and misunderstanding of meaning.

Gathering Responses and Collecting Your Thoughts

Gather all the reviewer responses. Make notes about what you and your reviewers agree and disagree on, moving from most important issues, such as appropriateness of the topic, the persuasiveness of evidence and examples, the organization, and the support for ideas, to least important, such as spelling and comma placement. List areas where you agree that improvement is needed, and make a plan about what you need to revise. Think about areas of disagreement, too. You make the final decisions about what changes to make, so determine which comments you need to respond to and which you can ignore.

Revision and Editing Activities

Identifying Options for Revision Planning

After you have gathered revision comments on your early draft from peer reviewers and your instructor (pp. 171–72), choose one of the following strategies to begin making your revision plan.

➤ Create a storyboard. On a sticky note or note card, write your argumentative thesis and put it at the top of your work area. Using separate sticky notes or note cards for each paragraph or example, write down important features such as topic sentences, research sources, and supporting details. Does your organization make sense? Do the parts work together? Does every paragraph help to advance the story and clarify the point it makes? Using sticky notes or note cards of a different color, add notes to each paragraph about how you will strengthen, change, or delete content based on your reviewers' comments and your own. Take photos of the parts of the storyboard so you'll have a record of what you decide, even if you lose your notes.

➤ Create a graphic organizer. Using either paper and pencil or a digital document, create text boxes representing each introductory paragraph, body paragraph, and conclusion paragraph, and write the main idea of each paragraph in the box. Below it, leave room to revise the main idea. To the right of each main idea box, draw additional boxes for changes, additions, and deletions you have decided to make to supporting details, transitions, and other material in that paragraph.

➤ Make an annotated outline. Using formal complete sentences or informal phrases, make an outline that shows the current main ideas, supporting details, and organization of your draft. Using highlighters, colored pens, different colors of type, or some other method to make your changes clearly visible, annotate your outline to show the changes you plan to make to your thesis, dominant impression, organization, supporting ideas, introduction, conclusion, references, and so on.

➤ Make a plan of your own. _____

_____

_____

_____

_____

Revising an Argument Essay

Following the plan you've created, write a complete revised draft. Repeat as needed until you feel that you have a solid draft that is nearly final.

Using Your Common Issues to Focus Editing of Your Argument Essay

Edit for grammar, punctuation, and other common problems you have.

➤ The two kinds of problems that teachers or peer reviewers point out most often in my writing are _____ and

_____.

➤ I know I sometimes struggle with _____.

➤ The citation issues I notice most often include _____

_____.

Review the information in Part 3 (pp. 190–247) about the errors you have identified above. Then reread your draft again, correcting any such errors and other issues that you find.

Proofreading

➤ Run the spell checker and carefully consider every suggestion. Do not automatically accept the suggestions! Remember that spell checkers cannot identify problems with certain kinds of words, such as homonyms and proper nouns (names), so check the spelling of such words yourself. Write the words you have misspelled on a spelling checklist you can use to identify and avoid words that give you trouble.

➤ Read your essay aloud slowly, noting and correcting any issues that you find.

➤ Read your essay aloud backwards, word by word, looking for repeated words and similar mistakes that are easy to miss in work that is very familiar. Correct any problems you see.

When your work is as error-free and professional as you can make it, submit your essay.

PART THREE

Additional Tools and Practice

Sentence Guides for Academic Writers

Being a college student means being a college writer. No matter what field you are studying, your instructors will ask you to make sense of what you are learning through writing. When you work on writing assignments in college, you are, in most cases, being asked to write for an academic audience.

Writing academically means thinking academically—asking a lot of questions, digging into the ideas of others, and entering into scholarly debates and academic conversations. As a college writer, you will be asked to read different kinds of texts; understand and evaluate authors' ideas, arguments, and methods; and contribute your own ideas. In this way, you present yourself as a participant in an academic conversation.

What does it mean to be part of an *academic conversation*? Well, think of it this way: You and your friends may have an ongoing debate about the best film trilogy of all time. During your conversations with one another, you analyze the details of the films, introduce points you want your friends to consider, listen to their ideas, and perhaps cite what the critics have said about a particular trilogy. This kind of conversation is not unlike what happens among scholars in academic writing—except they could be debating the best public policy for a social problem or the most promising new theory in treating disease.

If you are uncertain about what academic writing *sounds like* or if you're not sure you're any good at it, this chapter offers guidance for you at the sentence level. It helps answer questions such as these:

How can I present the ideas of others in a way that demonstrates my understanding of the debate?

How can I agree with someone, but add a new idea?

How can I disagree with a scholar without seeming, well, rude?

How can I make clear in my writing which ideas are mine and which ideas are someone else's?

The following sections offer sentence guides for you to use and adapt to your own writing situations. As in all writing that you do, you will have to think about your purpose (reason for writing) and your audience (readers) before knowing which guides will be most appropriate for a particular piece of writing or for a certain part of your essay.

The guides are organized to help you present background information, the views and claims of others, and your own views and claims—all in the context of your purpose and audience.

Academic Writers Present Information and Others' Views

When you write in academic situations, you may be asked to spend some time giving background information for or setting a context for your main idea or argument. This often requires you to present or summarize what is known or what has already been said in relation to the question you are asking in your writing.

Presenting What Is Known or Assumed

When you write, you will find that you occasionally need to present something that is known, such as a specific fact or a statistic. The following structures are useful when you are providing background information.

➤ As we know from history, _____.

➤ X has shown that _____.

➤ Research by X and Y suggests that _____.

➤ According to X, _____ percent of
   are/favor _____.

In other situations, you may have the need to present information that is assumed or that is conventional wisdom.

➤ People often believe that _____.

➤ Conventional wisdom leads us to believe _____.

➤ Many Americans share the idea that _____.

➤ _____ is a widely held belief.

In order to challenge an assumption or a widely held belief, you have to acknowledge it first. Doing so lets your readers believe that you are placing your ideas in an appropriate context.

➤ Although many people are led to believe X, there is significant benefit to
   considering the merits of Y.

➤ College students tend to believe that _____ when, in
   fact, the opposite is much more likely the case.

Presenting Others' Views

As a writer, you build your own *ethos,* or credibility, by being able to fairly and accurately represent the views of others. As an academic writer, you will be expected to demonstrate your understanding of a text by summarizing the views or arguments of its author(s). To do so, you will use language such as the following.

➤ X argues that _____.

➤ X emphasizes the need for _____.

➤ In this important article, X and Y claim _____
_____.

➤ X endorses _____ because _____.

➤ X and Y have recently criticized the idea that _____.

➤ _____, according to X, is the most critical cause of _____.

Although you will create your own variations of these sentences as you draft and revise, the guides can be useful tools for thinking through how best to present another writer's claim or finding clearly and concisely.

Presenting Direct Quotations

When the exact words of a source are important for accuracy, authority, emphasis, or flavor, you will want to use a direct quotation. Ordinarily, you will present direct quotations with language of your own that suggests how you are using the source.

➤ X characterizes the problem this way: " . . . "

➤ According to X, _____ is defined as " . . . "

➤ " . . . ," explains X.

➤ X argues strongly in favor of the policy, pointing out that " . . . "

NOTE: You will generally cite direct quotations according to the documentation style your readers expect. MLA style, often used in English and in other humanities courses, recommends using the author name paired with a page number, if there is one. APA style, used in most social sciences, requires the year of publication generally after the mention of the source, with page numbers after the quoted material. In *Chicago* style, used in history and in some humanities courses, writers use superscript numbers (like this[6]) to refer readers to footnotes or endnotes. In-text citations, like the ones shown below, refer readers to entries in the works cited or reference list.

MLA   Lazarín argues that our overreliance on testing in K-12 schools "does not put students first" (20).

APA   Lazarín (2014) argues that our overreliance on testing in K-12 schools "does not put students first." (p. 20)

Chicago   Lazarín argues that our overreliance on testing in K-12 schools "does not put students first."[6]

Many writers use direct quotations to advance an argument of their own:

Student writer's idea

Source's idea

Standardized testing makes it easier for administrators to measure student performance, but it may not be the best way to measure it. Too much testing wears students out and communicates the idea that recall is the most important skill we want them to develop. Even education policy advisor Melissa Lazarín argues that our overreliance on testing in K-12 schools "does not put students first" (20).

Presenting Alternative Views

Most debates, whether they are scholarly or popular, are complex — often with more than two sides to an issue. Sometimes you will have to synthesize the views of multiple participants in the debate before you introduce your own ideas.

➤ On the one hand, X reports that _____, but on the other hand, Y insists that _____.

➤ Even though X endorses the policy, Y refers to it as " . . . "

➤ X, however, isn't convinced and instead argues _____.

➤ X and Y have supported the theory in the past, but new research by Z suggests that _____.

Academic Writers Present Their Own Views

When you write for an academic audience, you will indeed have to demonstrate that you are familiar with the views of others who are asking the same kinds of questions as you are. Much writing that is done for academic purposes asks you to put your arguments in the context of existing arguments — in a way asking you to connect the known to the new.

When you are asked to write a summary or an informative text, your own views and arguments are generally not called for. However, much of the writing you will be assigned to do in college asks you to take a persuasive stance and present a reasoned argument — at times in response to a single text, and at other times in response to multiple texts.

Presenting Your Own Views: Agreement and Extension

Sometimes you agree with the author of a source.

➤ X's argument is convincing because _____.

➤ Because X's approach is so _____, it is the best way to _____.

➤ X makes an important point when she says _____.

Other times you find you agree with the author of a source, but you want to extend the point or go a bit deeper in your own investigation. In a way, you acknowledge the source for getting you so far in the conversation, but then you move the conversation along with a related comment or finding.

➤ X's proposal for _____ is indeed worth considering. Going one step further, _____.

➤ X makes the claim that _____. By extension, isn't it also true, then, that _____?

➤ _____ has been adequately explained by X. Now, let's move beyond that idea and ask whether _____.

Presenting Your Own Views: Queries and Skepticism

You may be intimidated when you're asked to talk back to a source, especially if the source is a well-known scholar or expert or even just a frequent voice in a particular debate. College-level writing asks you to be skeptical, however, and approach academic questions with the mind of an investigator. It is acceptable to doubt, to question, to challenge—as the result is often new knowledge or understanding about a subject.

➤ Couldn't it also be argued that _____?

➤ But is everyone willing to agree that this is the case?

➤ While X insists that _____ is so, he is perhaps asking the wrong question to begin with.

➤ The claims that X and Y have made, while intelligent and well-meaning, leave many unconvinced because they have failed to consider _____.

Presenting Your Own Views: Disagreement or Correction

You may find that at times the only response you have to a text or to an author is complete disagreement.

➤ X's claims about _____ are completely misguided.

➤ X presents a long metaphor comparing _____ to _____; in the end, the comparison is unconvincing because _____.

It can be tempting to disregard a source completely if you detect a piece of information that strikes you as false or that you know to be untrue.

➤ Although X reports that _____, recent studies indicate that is not the case.

A NOTE ABOUT USING THE FIRST PERSON ("I")

Some disciplines look favorably upon the use of the first person "I" in academic writing. Others do not and instead stick to using third person. If you are given a writing assignment for a class, you are better off asking your instructor what he or she prefers or reading through any samples given than *guessing* what might be expected.

First person (I, me, my, we, us, our)

I question Heddinger's methods and small sample size.

Harnessing children's technology obsession in the classroom is, I believe, the key to improving learning.

Lanza's interpretation focuses on circle imagery as symbolic of the family; my analysis leads me in a different direction entirely.

We would, in fact, benefit from looser laws about farming on our personal property.

Third person (names and other nouns)

Heddinger's methods and small sample size are questionable.

Harnessing children's technology obsession in the classroom is the key to improving learning.

Lanza's interpretation focuses on circle imagery as symbolic of the family; other readers' analyses may point in a different direction entirely.

Many Americans would, in fact, benefit from looser laws about farming on personal property.

You may feel that not being able to use "I" in an essay in which you present your ideas about a topic is unfair or will lead to weaker statements. Know that you can make a strong argument even if you write in the third person.

➤ While X and Y insist that _____ is so, an examination of their figures shows that they have made an important miscalculation.

Presenting and Countering Objections to Your Argument

Effective college writers know that their arguments are stronger when they can anticipate objections that others might make.

➤ Some will object to this proposal on the grounds that _____.

➤ Not everyone will embrace _____; they may argue instead that _____.

Countering, or responding to, opposing voices fairly and respectfully strengthens your writing and your *ethos,* or credibility.

➤ X and Y might contend that this interpretation is faulty; however, _____.

➤ Most _____ believe that there is too much risk in this approach. But what they have failed to take into consideration is _____.

Academic Writers Persuade by Putting It All Together

Readers of academic writing often want to know what's at stake in a particular debate or text. They want to know why it is that they should care and that they should keep reading. Aside from crafting individual sentences, you must, of course, keep the bigger picture in mind as you attempt to persuade, inform, evaluate, or review.

Presenting Stakeholders

When you write, you may be doing so as a member of a group affected by the research conversation you have entered. For example, you may be among the thousands of students in your state whose level of debt may change as a result of new laws about financing a college education. In this case, you are a *stakeholder* in the matter. In other words, you have an interest in the matter as a person who could be impacted by the outcome of a decision. On the other hand, you may be writing as an investigator of a topic that interests you but that you aren't directly connected with. You may be persuading your audience on behalf of a group of interested stakeholders—a group of which you yourself are not a member.

You can give your writing some teeth if you make it clear who is being affected by the discussion of the issue and the decisions that have been or will be made about the issue. The groups of stakeholders are highlighted in the following sentences.

➤ Viewers of Kurosawa's films may not agree with X that _____.

➤ The research will come as a surprise to parents of children with Type 1 diabetes.

➤ X's claims have the power to offend potentially every low-wage earner in the state.

➤ Marathoners might want to reconsider their training regimen if stories such as those told by X and Y are validated by the medical community.

Presenting the "So What"

For readers to be motivated to read your writing, they have to feel as if you're addressing something that matters to them, addressing something that matters very much to you, or addressing something that should matter to us all. Good academic writing often hooks readers with a sense of urgency—a serious response to a reader's "So what?"

➤ Having a frank discussion about _____ now will put us in a far better position to deal with _____ in the future. If we are unwilling or unable to do so, we risk _____.

➤ Such a breakthrough will affect _____ in three significant ways.

➤ It is easy to believe that the stakes aren't high enough to be alarming; in fact, _____ will be affected by _____.

➤ Widespread disapproval of and censorship of such fiction/films/art will mean
_____ for us in the future. Culture should represent _____.

➤ _____ could bring about unprecedented opportunities for _____
to participate in _____, something never seen before.

➤ New experimentation in _____ could allow scientists to investigate
_____ in ways they couldn't have imagined _____ years ago.

Presenting the Players and Positions in a Debate

Some disciplines ask writers to compose a review of the literature as a part of a larger
project—or sometimes as a free-standing assignment. In a review of the literature, the
writer sets forth a research question, summarizes the key sources that have addressed
the question, puts the current research in the context of other voices in the research
conversation, and identifies any gaps in the research.

Writing that presents a debate, its players, and their positions can often be lengthy.
What follows, however, can give you the sense of the flow of ideas and turns in such a
piece of writing.

Student writer states the problem.

_____ affects more than 30% of children in America, and signs point to a
worsening situation in years to come because of A, B, and C. Solutions to the problem have
eluded even the sharpest policy minds and brightest researchers. In an important 2003 study,

Student writer summarizes the views of others on the topic.

W found that _____, which pointed to more problems than solutions. [. . .] Research
by X and Y made strides in our understanding of _____ but still didn't offer specific
strategies for children and families struggling to _____. [. . .] When Z rejected both the
methods and the findings of X and Y, arguing that _____, policymakers and health care

Student writer presents her view in the context of current research.

experts were optimistic. [. . .] Too much discussion of _____, however, and too little
discussion of _____, may lead us to solutions that are ultimately too expensive to sustain.

Using Appropriate Signal Verbs

Verbs matter   Using a variety of verbs in your sentences can add strength and clarity as
you present others' views and your own views.

WHEN YOU WANT TO PRESENT A VIEW FAIRLY NEUTRALLY

acknowledges	observes
adds	points out
admits	reports
comments	suggests
contends	writes
notes	

➤ X points out that the plan had unintended outcomes.

WHEN YOU WANT TO PRESENT A STRONGER VIEW

argues   emphasizes

asserts   insists

declares

➤   Y argues in favor of a ban on _____; but Z insists the plan is misguided.

WHEN YOU WANT TO SHOW AGREEMENT

agree

confirms

endorses

➤   An endorsement of X's position is smart for a number of reasons.

WHEN YOU WANT TO SHOW CONTRAST OR DISAGREEMENT

compares   refutes

denies   rejects

disputes

➤   The town must come together and reject X's claims that _____ is in the best interest of the citizens.

WHEN YOU WANT TO ANTICIPATE AN OBJECTION

admits

acknowledges

concedes

➤   Y admits that closer study of _____, with a much larger sample size, is necessary for _____.

15

Editing Practice

Editing Paragraphs

Exercise P.1   Topic Sentences

Read the following sentences and determine which make effective topic sentences and which make poor or unfocused topic sentences. If the topic sentence is effective, write *effective*. If the topic sentence is poor or unfocused, rewrite the sentence so that it is an effective topic sentence for a paragraph.

For help with this exercise, see Chapter 6 in *Successful College Writing*.

EXAMPLE:

➤ Many Americans spend more than they earn.

The widespread availability of credit cards allows many Americans to spend more than they earn and accumulate a lot of high-interest debt.

1. Americans often wonder why obesity is not such a big problem in other countries.

   _____

   _____

2. Every Thursday, I take my dog Buster to the children's hospital to visit the patients.

   _____

   _____

3. The Boston Marathon is a very tough race that requires a lot of training.

   _____

   _____

190

4. People who choose high-stress jobs they do not enjoy in order to make a lot of money often find themselves unhappy and unsatisfied later in life.

_____

_____

5. Online dating is a popular way to meet people.

_____

_____

6. In the interest of closing the digital divide, several companies are currently developing inexpensive laptops to distribute to underprivileged school-children around the world.

_____

_____

7. Celebrities are given far too much attention in our culture.

_____

_____

8. Many Hollywood movies stereotype minorities and perpetuate limited, biased views of them.

_____

_____

9. I can no longer afford to visit national parks on my summer vacations because it's too expensive.

_____

_____

10. Because many drugs that children now take for depression and other mental illnesses have not been tested on children, we have no way of knowing whether their benefits outweigh their possible side effects.

_____

_____

Exercise P.2   Topic Sentences

Each of the following paragraphs contains only supporting sentences. The paragraph may also contain a transitional sentence. Write an appropriate topic sentence in the space provided within each paragraph. (The thesis of the essay from which the paragraph is taken is provided for you.)

For help with this exercise, see Chapter 6 in *Successful College Writing*.

1. **Thesis:** A balanced-budget amendment to the U.S. Constitution is unnecessary and inappropriate.

    Proponents like to argue that a balanced-budget amendment would force the government to be more frugal, like ordinary citizens. _____

_____

If everyone who bought a house had to come up with the full price in cash, very few Americans would be homeowners. The same is true of cars, which are often financed through banks or automobile companies. Most people can't come up with $40,000 for a new sport-utility vehicle, so to get one, they borrow. In addition, keeping up with the Joneses is a time-honored tradition in this country. If our neighbors have a pool, we want a pool, too — and how do we pay for it? We use loans, credit cards, or other buy-now-pay-later financing.

2. **Thesis:** The lifestyle that many Americans enjoy contributes to poor health.

    Medical science has proved that people need exercise if they are to look and feel their best. _____

_____

Many people's parents and grandparents earned a living through physical labor. Today, most workers in this country don't have to exert themselves. In the past, people had to leave the house for entertainment. Now everyone has a television and a remote control, so no one has to get off the couch. When modern Americans do go out, they almost always drive to their destinations. Then, when they arrive, convenient parking and the increasing availability of elevators ensure that people walk no more than a few steps unless they choose to exert themselves.

3. **Thesis:** Parents should give their children the best possible start in life.

    A child is capable of hearing sounds even before it is born. By the time a fetus is a few months old, it can respond to noises it hears. At birth, babies know the sound of their mothers' voices. But voices are   not the only sounds infants can distinguish. Many parents also tell anecdotes about their children recognizing music that the parents played frequently before the children were born. While scientists do not yet know much about the way human brains learn before birth, they do know that when schoolchildren listen to music, especially classical music, their mathematical abilities often improve. Some neurologists speculate that exposure to music might affect the developing brain of a fetus as well.

_____

_____

_____

Exercise P.3   Relevant Details

In each of the following paragraphs, underline any sentences containing details that do not support the topic sentence.

For help with this exercise, see Chapter 6 in *Successful College Writing*.

1.   (1) The long and interesting history of pinball spans a period from ancient times to the present. (2) The first game on record that can be considered an ancestor of modern pinball was an ancient Greek sport in which players rolled balls down a hill, trying to drop them in holes. (3) During the Renaissance, a tabletop version of the game, then called *bagatelle,* was invented. (4) A stick propelled the bagatelle balls up a tilted board filled with holes. (5) Interestingly, the word *bagatelle* can also refer to a short poem or piece of music. (6) In 1930, David Gottlieb designed a bagatelle board with a plunger, and modern pinball was born. (7) Later improvements included the "tilt" alarm, in 1933, and bumpers, in 1936. (8) Pinball was outlawed in some places during World War II because authorities likened it to gambling. (9) When the flipper was added to the game in 1947, pinball became more decidedly a game of skill, and eventually it became a legal, if not always reputable, sport across the country. (10) Pinball remains a common arcade game today, but more people probably play it as a computer game than in any other form.

2.   (1) Although big-budget disaster movies have depicted this scenario, the possibility that a meteor will strike the earth and cause significant damage and loss of human life is very remote. (2) Most meteors are relatively small, some (known as *micrometeors*) only the size of a grain of rice. (3) These meteors burn up as soon as they enter the earth's atmosphere. (4) According to folklore, when observers see one of these "shooting stars," they should make a wish. (5) Vaporized matter from burned-out meteors adds about ten tons to the mass

of the earth every day. (6) About 150 meteors per year actually do survive the trip to earth and strike it. (7) Most of these do no damage even if they hit a spot where people live. (8) Since most of the earth is covered with water, however, meteors are much more likely to land in the ocean. (9) Scientists estimate that a deadly meteor strike — one large enough to kill a hundred people and positioned to strike a populated area — would occur no more often than once every 100,000 years, so the average person doesn't need to worry much about such an event.

3.   (1) Working on a custom cutting crew is a difficult way to make a living, and it's getting harder all the time. (2) First of all, custom cutters — traveling workers who supply the machinery and labor to harvest farmers' crops as they ripen — are able to work only seasonally. (3) Running a family farm has never been easy. (4) Grain crops in the South begin to ripen in the spring, and cutting crews follow the harvest north as the weather warms throughout the summer; when the harvest is finished in August, the work is over for the year. (5) Nor is custom cutting an easy task: The work is hot, dirty, and difficult, and the hours are long. (6) To make matters worse, the machines needed to harvest grain are very expensive, so start-up costs for a custom cutting crew are prohibitive. (7) The expense of new harvesting machines, called combines, and the need to get the harvest in as quickly as possible are major reasons farmers hire custom cutters rather than doing the work themselves. (8) In addition, the amount of work available, and the wages to be earned from it, depend on the success of the farmer's crop. (9) This success, in turn, is dependent on factors beyond human control, such as the weather. (10) Finally, as small farmers become an increasingly rare breed, there is less and less need for custom cutting.

Exercise P.4   Paragraph Unity

For help with this exercise, see Chapter 6 in *Successful College Writing*.

Read through the following paragraphs and decide whether the paragraph is unified or not unified. If the paragraph is unified, write *unified* on the line following the paragraph. If the paragraph is not unified, write *not unified* and then eliminate the sentences that are off-topic.

EXAMPLE:

➤   Most people believe that you can never drink too much water, but studies are now showing that drinking too much water can be very dangerous to your health. In fact, being overhydrated is much more dangerous than being dehydrated. ~~I try to drink eight glasses of water a day.~~ Overhydrating reduces the sodium levels in your blood and can cause confusion, seizures, and even death. ~~On very hot days, many people are in danger of becoming dehydrated.~~ ~~Dehydration is one of the factors that can contribute to heat stroke.~~ Athletes are actually better off waiting until they are thirsty and drinking only what their bodies can absorb. _____*not unified*_____

1.   One alternative to drugs for treating depression is the controversial Eye Movement Desensitization and Reprocessing or EMDR. This treatment is particularly useful for people who are depressed as a result of a traumatic event. Prozac is also useful for treating depression. For those who don't respond to Prozac, doctors often recommend Zoloft. In an EMDR session, the therapist makes hand motions or flashes a light in front of the patient's face while he or she talks about an upsetting experience. People who have experienced trauma often need a lot of support. Many people have found this nontraditional therapy to be very helpful in processing their experiences, though no one knows for sure why EMDR works. _____

2.   The advertisements that now appear before the movie are not effective because they only make moviegoers irritable. Coke is one of the most frequently advertised products and one of the most recognized American brands. People often drink Coke or other soft drinks when they go to the movies. Ads take away from the otherwise enjoyable experience of seeing a movie in the theater. These days, you have to sit through ten minutes of commercials before the previews start. Advertisers also use product placement as a way to increase their product's visibility. By the time the movie begins, you may already have been in your seat for half an hour. Because of this inconvenience, people may decide that it's worthwhile to wait for the DVD and skip the ads. Movie-theater owners would be wise to remember their paying audience and reconsider this partnership with advertisers. _____

3. Contrary to what a person might expect, training to become a clown takes a lot of hard work and dedication. Many clowns-in-training spend significant amounts of time learning their art at one of the many clown schools around the world. These schools teach gesture, expression, and movement in addition to make-up technique and costume design. Some schools specialize in training certain types of clowns, like the "character" clown or the "white-face" clown, and require that students focus on one style of clowning. In addition to choosing a focus and going to school, clowns must be disciplined in order to remain playful, curious, and physically limber. Goofiness is not as easy as it looks. _____

4. One of America's most well-known and important court cases is the Scopes "Monkey Trial." Students should learn their country's history at an early age. Knowing the past can help us predict the future. In 1925, John Scopes, a high school biology teacher, was charged with violating state law by teaching the theory of evolution to his students. He believed he was teaching an important scientific theory, but others believed that evolution contradicted the story of creation told in the Bible. The trial became famous because so many people had such strong feelings on both sides. It has also remained relevant because we haven't come to a definitive conclusion about which ideas students should or should not learn in school. There are many old conflicts that remain unresolved. For instance, people have been arguing for decades over whether or not abortion should be legal.

    _____

5. More animal shelters should adopt a "no kill" policy. Controlling the stray animal population by euthanizing is not the best solution. Killing unwanted pets solves the problem of overpopulation only temporarily, and it creates a bigger problem because it teaches people that animals are disposable. Many people don't consider snakes, iguanas, and other reptiles as pets. When I was seven, I adopted a snake from our local shelter, and he turned out to be a wonderful pet. We need to learn to be kinder and more responsible when it comes to animals. We need to have pets fixed and accept them even when they have special needs. We need to accept humans with special needs as well. Many

of the animals in shelters are there because they were neglected or mistreated. If we change our own behavior, fewer animals will end up abused and unwanted.

_____

6.   Buying a house is not always a good investment. People who sell their houses after owning them for only a couple of years often lose money. Spending money on a computer is not always a good investment either. Computers lose their value very quickly. Unless the buyer uses the computer for work, money spent on a computer is money lost. People who don't buy enough insurance for their homes can lose money if there is a fire, flood, or other disaster. Houses also require a lot of maintenance. When people sell their houses, often they find it difficult to make back the money they spent fixing up the house. Sometimes people are better off investing their money in something that does not cost so much.

_____

7.   Keeping up with all the new developments in communications technology has become nearly impossible. Just knowing what is available takes many hours of research. A new cell phone with better reception and more features may be convenient in the long run, but finding out about it can be time-consuming and inconvenient. It's important to draw a line somewhere to avoid becoming overwhelmed by all the new technology. When drawing the line, it's often best to let necessity be your guide. _____

8.   Hilary Swank is a positive role model for young actresses. Beyoncé Knowles is a good role model for future dancers and singers. Many girls look up to their mothers as well. Unlike many successful women in the movie industry, Swank is not afraid to challenge herself when choosing roles. In both *Boys Don't Cry* and *Million Dollar Baby,* Swank focuses not on looking pretty but on inhabiting her characters and their difficult lives. Her determination and willingness to take these risks may come in part from her background. She was not born into a rich or privileged family and, like some of the characters she plays, has had to work very hard to achieve her goals. Many famous people have rough starts. Beyoncé Knowles did not come from a rich family. It's important for young girls to see a successful movie star who has dedication, integrity, and a real love of acting.

_____

For help with this exercise, see Chapter 6 in *Successful College Writing*.

Exercise P.5   Specific Details

Rewrite each of the following vague, general paragraphs to include concrete, specific details. You may add new information and new sentences.

1. A family gathering is supposed to be a happy occasion, but it may not be. Getting together for a family event can produce negative emotions just as often as positive ones. Just because people are related to each other doesn't mean they understand or like each other especially well. People usually try to be on their best behavior, but the strain of trying to be nice can make them tense. At a big gathering, there are bound to be relatives present who don't get along. Finally, if one of them snaps and an argument ensues, everyone else has bad feelings about the conflict.

2. A movie can't be good unless all of the pieces come together successfully. Sometimes I see a film and think that the concept is great, but the script is just awful. I've seen other films with good scripts but bad acting. Then there are times when the pace is all wrong, and I wonder what the director was thinking. The music, too, can make or break a film. With so many variables, it's a wonder that any good movies exist. They do, of course; I could name two or three recent ones that did almost everything right.

3. Children should have a pet. Taking care of a pet is a good experience for any child. For one thing, having a pet teaches children to assume responsibility. Additionally, pet care can teach children about loving and protecting a creature weaker than themselves. Both of these lessons are valuable for a child. Finally, a pet returns affection and can actually make a child's life happier. Most adults who had a pet in childhood believe that it was a positive experience.

For help with this exercise, see Chapter 6 in *Successful College Writing*.

Exercise P.6   Paragraph Development

Read the following paragraphs and decide whether they are well developed or underdeveloped. On the line after each paragraph write *well developed* if the paragraph is well developed and *underdeveloped* if it is underdeveloped. If you determine that the paragraph is underdeveloped, write three questions or suggestions that might help the writer develop his or her ideas more fully.

EXAMPLES:

➤   The number of children suffering from asthma has reached epidemic proportions over the last three decades. According to the Centers for Disease Control, 6.2 million American children have been diagnosed with this chronic respiratory disease. Several factors have been blamed for this growing problem, though no clear cause is known. Air pollutants, such as ozone and sulfur dioxide, may play a role in the development of asthma. Indoor pollutants, such as dust mites, molds, animal dander, and tobacco smoke, may play an even bigger role. Some experts believe that the increased incidence of asthma is the direct result of children spending more time indoors exposed to these allergens. Whatever the cause, it is clear that children's developing lungs are particularly at risk. The number of asthma-related deaths in America has decreased every year since 2000, but until we know how to stop the epidemic completely, the best we can do is try to minimize exposure to dangerous environments and treat the life-threatening symptoms aggressively.

well developed
_____

1. *If the paragraph is well developed, leave these lines blank.* _____

2. _____

3. _____

➤   Many developing countries are finding it easier to join the developed world by way of technological leapfrogging. Leapfrogging helps developing countries improve their technologies. This entails skipping the intermediate steps of technological development and starting instead with the most current technologies. For instance, an area that has never had phone service might decide it's more efficient to build cell phone towers rather than old-fashioned phone lines. Other areas might decide to install a wi-fi Internet connection, rather than running telephone lines for dial-up service. There are problems with leapfrogging, too, of course. It isn't the right solution for every agricultural economy looking to get up to speed. Sometimes, the old tried-and-true technologies have advantages.

underdeveloped
_____

1. *Which countries are finding success with leapfrogging?* _____

2. *Identify several reasons why a country might choose to leapfrog.* _____

3. *Describe a situation in which leapfrogging would not be advisable and explain why not.* _____

1.   Children's museums are growing faster than any other kind of museum in the country. Parents like museums where their children are allowed to touch and interact with the exhibits. Other museums rely on seeing objects and reading information, which can become tiresome for children. Children's museums are usually educational as well. They introduce kids to many different things, as

well as allowing them a fun, safe place to play. Museums are a great place for children to learn about anatomy, geology, and astronomy. Some of the best children's museums are in big cities like Boston and Cleveland. It's interesting that children's museums are growing faster than natural history museums or aquariums, places that also specialize in children's exhibits.

_____

1. _____

2. _____

3. _____

2.   Though the methods have improved somewhat over the last century, coal mining is still a very dangerous way to make a living. Coal miners are more likely to die on the job than workers in nearly any other occupation, the obvious exception being soldiers in the military. Even the well-organized coal miners' union cannot protect workers from some of the industry's unavoidable hazards. Some people wonder why anyone would do this kind of work. Many people work in coal mines because it's what their fathers and their fathers' fathers did. It's tradition. Some would even argue that the danger of the job is part of the coal miner's tradition. Tradition or not, the government should do more to protect workers from society's necessary but hazardous jobs.

_____

1. _____

2. _____

3. _____

3.   Starting with her debut single "Tim McGraw" and the release of a self-titled album, Taylor Swift brought country music back onto the playlist of American pop. Country music as a genre has rarely made it onto the mainstream music charts, which in recent years have favored the metallic sounds of rock and the lively rhythms of pop. Swift incorporates these elements into her songs, but remains a country musician at heart. Alongside electric bass lines and pop style beats, Swift recalls her Nashville roots with twanging banjos and soaring fiddle parts. This artful melding of genres and styles gives her music mainstream appeal as well as uniqueness. Critics praise Swift also for her barefaced honesty in her lyrics, which address topics such as love and heartbreak with refreshing frankness — all sung in Swift's signature country accent. Swift's beautiful musical blending has earned her multiple Grammy Awards, including the honor of being the only solo country act ever to win Best Album of the Year.

_____

1. _____

2. _____

3. _____

4.   Soap making is a fun and fascinating process. People have been making soap in one way or another for thousands of years. Because most people these days buy their soap at the store, very few of us know how soap is made. In fact, the process hasn't changed much over the years. The basic principles are the same. Most soaps are made by combining two or three things that are easy to get. By adding a few extra ingredients like eggs, you can even make a decent shampoo. It's strange to think that egg could be used to clean your hair. Unfortunately, soap making has gained a somewhat sinister reputation because of movies like *Fight Club*. This reputation is completely undeserved, as any investigation into the subject and the product would quickly reveal. Perhaps if more people took the time to learn how to make soap, they would realize how enjoyable and useful it can be.

   _____

   1. _____

   2. _____

   3. _____

5.   It is unlikely that any baseball team will ever match the comeback that the Boston Red Sox achieved in the 2004 American League Championship Series. Behind three games to zero, the Red Sox came back to win four straight games and beat the seemingly unbeatable New York Yankees. No team in the history of baseball had ever come back from being three games behind to win a postseason series. The fact that the Red Sox achieved this while playing their archrivals only made the victory more memorable. What most baseball fans will remember most, though, is how the Red Sox rode the wave of their playoff comeback. They went on to win the World Series for the first time in eighty-six years. That's a comeback story that will be hard to beat.

   _____

   1. _____

   2. _____

   3. _____

6.   In the past couple of decades, political discourse has gotten so ugly that some Americans have taken to calling it the "inCivil War." YourDictionary .com even named "inCivility" the Word of the Year in 2004. The problem with incivility is that it usually sparks a chain reaction. The chain reaction leads to an escalation of the conflict, making mountains out of molehills. People have a difficult time responding politely to uncivil comments and thus spark more uncivil comments. As a result, public discourse has taken on a

shrill, adversarial tone. This tone is not constructive and just results in more conflict. Unfortunately, we seem to pay more attention to those speakers who are confrontational and offensive.

_____

1. _____

2. _____

3. _____

7.   "The New Black" may be the most overused phrase in the fashion industry. Every color, at one point or another, has taken its turn being the new black. Even black has been the new black. The question that no one seems to be asking is, Why does black need to be replaced, anyway? Black is for more than just funerals. Urban working women, in particular, have found black to be very useful. They have discovered that wearing black is a good way to look formal and chic without a lot of effort. Also, owning a lot of black clothes reduces the amount of time a person has to spend worrying about whether or not her clothes match.

_____

1. _____

2. _____

3. _____

8.   Teenagers who ride their skateboards on city sidewalks create a hazard for everyone. Many passersby are injured every year by skateboarders who are riding in prohibited areas and/or riding too fast. I know several people who have collided or nearly collided with a skateboarder in a pedestrian zone. This can be very dangerous. Several of these incidents resulted in minor injuries to both the skateboarder and the pedestrian. Often, skateboarders are looking to practice their skills and are not simply trying to get from one point to another. They should find other places to practice so that the sidewalks are safe for the rest of us.

_____

1. _____

2. _____

3. _____

For help with this exercise, see Chapter 6 in *Successful College Writing.*

Exercise P.7   Transitions and Repeated Words

Add transitions, repeat key words, or add synonyms as necessary to make the following paragraphs coherent and connected.

1.   The French may still have the international reputation of being the people most interested in gourmet food. Americans are quickly gaining an interest in gourmet food. "American food" meant fast foods like hamburgers and hot dogs. People around the world still associate these foods with American culture. U.S. food lovers may seek out the best burgers, fries, and barbecue foods. They also want to sample foods from ethnic cultures within the United States and other countries. People want the best of what American produce has to offer and will go far to find fresh, local ingredients that are expertly prepared.

2.   Modern conceptions of timekeeping owe a lot to the ancient Babylonians. The ancient Babylonians gave people today the twelve-month year, the twenty-four-hour day, the sixty-minute hour, and the sixty-second minute. The number *twelve* was significant to the ancient Babylonians. They noticed that there were usually twelve full moons in a year. The Babylonian calendar contained twelve months of thirty days each. Five days were left over each year; every six years they had to add an extra month to the year. They divided the day and night into twelve hours each. The number *sixty* was important to the Babylonians. The number *sixty* can be evenly divided by many integers — two, three, four, five, six, ten, twelve, fifteen, twenty, and thirty. They divided each hour into sixty minutes and each minute into sixty seconds. The Romans changed the length of some Babylonian months from thirty to thirty-one or twenty-eight days. The Babylonians' other time measurements survive to this day.

3.   The Restoration period in England, which began with the return of the monarchy in 1660, was marked by the kind of public behavior on the part of aristocrats and courtiers that would still provoke a shocked reaction today. King Charles II served as the model of moral — or immoral — behavior for members of his court. There were no children by his wife. He had a large number of children by his several mistresses. Young male courtiers boasted of numerous love affairs. Court poets and dramatists composed bawdy, amoral literary works. Many contained words and suggestions that even modern newspapers would not print. The public loved to attend performances of plays. Simply being seen at a theater could give a person a questionable reputation. The clergy and other representatives of moral authority protested the literary, theatrical, and personal misbehavior of the aristocrats. Bawdiness became less fashionable. A much more conservative age followed the Restoration.

Exercise P.8   Outlining

Read through the partially completed outline below. Then read through the list of missing notes/phrases that follow. Identify which note or phrase goes in which blank in order to best complete the outline. There are ten phrases and ten blanks, so you will need to use all ten phrases in order to complete the outline.

For help with this exercise, see Chapter 7 in *Successful College Writing*.

Title	**More Than Just a Place to Sleep**
Introduction	*Thesis:* Though it requires some preparation and adaptability, staying at a traditional Japanese hotel, or *ryokan,* is an enjoyable and worthwhile way for a Western visitor to learn about Japanese culture.

Body Paragraph 1 Finding a *ryokan*

- _____
- determine your price range
- _____
- make advance reservations

Body Paragraph 2 Apparel etiquette in a *ryokan*

- take off your shoes when you enter the *ryokan* and put on slippers
- _____
- wear *geta* (wooden clogs) if you stroll around the *ryokan* grounds
- _____
- _____
- wear a *tanzen* (outer robe) over your *yukata* if you get cold

Body Paragraph 3 Japanese bath etiquette

- the Japanese often bathe before dinner
- in changing room, put *yukata* in basket provided
- _____
- do not drain the water from the tub when finished
- _____

Body Paragraph 4 Engaging with your host or hosts

- learn a few key phrases in Japanese
- ask about the building and garden
- _____

Body Paragraph 5 A day in the life of a different culture

- _____
- enjoy the serenity of life without television
- try meditating
- _____

Conclusion   While staying in a familiar Western-style hotel might feel easier, after a night or two in a *ryokan* you'll find yourself more mindful of Japanese culture and traditions, and remarkably refreshed.

1. be willing to try unusual breakfast foods, like cold squid and miso soup
2. decide how formal or informal a *ryokan* you'd like
3. take off the slippers when walking on the tatami mats
4. wear your *yukata* (robe provided by the *ryokan*) when in the *ryokan*
5. ask about the best sights to see in their town
6. locate Web sites that list *ryokans*
7. *yukatas* should be worn left side over right; right side over left is for funerals
8. dry yourself thoroughly before returning to the changing room
9. wash yourself in the bathing area using shower or basin before entering the public bath
10. adjust to the firmness of a futon mattress

Editing Sentences and Words

Exercise E.1   Wordy Sentences

Revise the following sentences to make them as concise as possible.

EXAMPLE:

> ~~At some point in time~~ every year, a list of the most popular names ~~for children~~ in the United States is published.
>
> *E* (above "every") *children's* (above "names")

1. It seems likely that American parents choose really carefully when naming their children.
2. Making comparisons between popular names of today and the names that were popular in the past shows how much our ideas about naming children have changed.
3. The names chosen for girls have undergone the most changes.
4. Forty years ago, the majority of baby girls received names that sounded traditional rather than being considered unusual.

For help with this exercise, see Chapter 9 in *Successful College Writing*.

5. Some of the older names gradually became less popular over a period of time, and newer names, like Jennifer, now a perennial favorite year after year, took their place.

6. In these modern times, parents often give their daughters names that were once considered masculine, like Sidney or Taylor.

7. It is also true that some parents try to make their daughters' names seem quite unusual by spelling a traditional name in a way that is not considered traditional.

8. Boys' names, however, have really changed very little and not as noticeably.

9. For decades the most popular of the names parents have given to boys has been Michael.

10. It may perhaps be true, as the results of a recent poll suggest, that parents think having an unusual name is helpful to girls and having an unusual name is harmful to boys.

For help with this exercise, see Chapter 9 in *Successful College Writing.*

Exercise E.2   Combining Sentences

Combine each of the following pairs of sentences to create a compound or complex sentence.

EXAMPLE:

➤ Many people start smoking as teenagers, ~~They~~ *because they* think it makes them look mature.

1. Nicotine is an ingredient in cigarettes. It is an addictive drug.

2. No smoker sets out to become addicted to cigarettes. Most people have difficulty stopping once they start smoking.

3. Movies can affect young people profoundly. Movies often portray smokers as glamorous and sexy.

4. Many thirty-year-old people do not smoke. They are unlikely to begin smoking.

5. The tobacco companies need new customers. They are more apt to find such customers among the younger generations.

6. Some teenagers take up smoking. They don't consider the possible consequences.

7. The Joe Camel cartoon advertisements were controversial. Cartoons often appeal to children.

8. The Joe Camel advertising campaign was withdrawn. New restrictions have been placed on tobacco ads.

9. Smoking can be unsightly and unhealthy. It is legal.

10. The number of lawsuits against tobacco companies has risen recently. Families have argued that tobacco companies are to blame for the deaths of their loved ones.

Exercise E.3   Adding Modifiers

Revise each sentence by adding the modifiers in any appropriate place.

EXAMPLE:

➤ Scientists have studied criminal behavior.

[*Modifiers:* hoping to find ways to prevent crime; for many years]

Revised: For many years, scientists have studied criminal behavior, hoping to find ways to prevent crime.

For help with this exercise, see Chapter 9 in *Successful College Writing*.

1. Criminal tendencies were thought to be related to physical traits. [*Modifiers:* in the nineteenth century; mistakenly]

2. Phrenologists mapped the human head. [*Modifiers:* who studied bumps on the skull; for antisocial protrusions]

3. They hoped. [*Modifiers:* before crimes occurred; that they could identify potential criminals]

4. Other researchers measured the proportions of the human head. [*Modifiers:* followers of a pseudoscience called craniometry; carefully recording their findings]

5. Craniometrists inferred conclusions. [*Modifiers:* using measurements of skull circumference; about brain size and intelligence as well as criminality]

6. These scientists' studies were fatally flawed. [*Modifiers:* from the beginning; because they found what they expected to find]

7. Researchers have been focusing on psychology. [*Modifiers:* since these "sciences" fell out of favor in the mid-twentieth century; as a means of understanding criminal actions]

8. The debate continues. [*Modifiers:* over which influence is stronger, heredity or environment; among social scientists]

9. The issue may never be resolved. [*Modifiers:* one of the key controversies among scientists; to everyone's satisfaction]

10. Important questions generate useful research. [*Modifiers:* In scientific inquiry; as well as theories that are later discredited; however]

For help with this exercise, see Chapter 9 in *Successful College Writing.*

Exercise E.4   Parallelism

Correct any errors in parallelism in the following sentences.

EXAMPLE:

➤ Americans should investigate renewable energy sources, including solar heat and
   wind power.
   ~~power from the wind.~~
   ^

1. The United States uses large amounts of energy, is depending heavily on oil, and imports much of that oil.

2. Burning oil for energy pollutes the air, causes global warming, destroys an irreplaceable commodity, and is wasting resources.

3. During the 1970s, an embargo made oil expensive and it was not easy to get.

4. The oil crisis led to a wider interest in alternative energy sources that would be renewable, environmentally sound, and would cost less than oil.

5. Some new homes used solar heating, although it was expensive to install and despite its being still relatively untested.

6. Many Americans expected electric cars to be perfected and that they would be widely available by the end of the twentieth century.

7. Instead, the embargo ended, the cost of oil dropped, and there were declining gasoline prices.

8. At the same time, money to invent alternative energy technologies, to develop new products, and for marketing the products dried up.

9. Scientists and those who study the environment hope that there will be plentiful renewable energy sources someday.

10. It would be better to have alternative energy possibilities soon than waiting for the world's oil reserves to run dry.

Exercise E.5   Strong, Active Verbs

Revise the following sentences by using strong, active verbs.

For help with this exercise, see Chapter 9 in *Successful College Writing*.

EXAMPLE:

> ~~There are major fashion shows~~ every year in cities like Paris, Milan, and New York.
>
> *Fashion designers parade their wares*
> ^

1. Big crowds are drawn to annual "Fashion Week" events in American and European cities.

2. Shows by new and established designers are attended by photographers, journalists, models, and celebrities.

3. Many people in the audience have model-thin bodies and photogenic faces.

4. Often, *haute couture* shows with their expensive, trend-setting fashions are the highlight of the event.

5. *Haute couture* garments are not expected to be worn by ordinary people.

6. *Haute couture* creations are frequently more like works of art than mere outfits.

7. Such clothing can be worn in public only by runway models.

8. Other people seem ridiculous in *haute couture* clothes.

9. Clothes can be draped more easily on models who have very thin bodies.

10. Some people are more impressed by the spectacle than by the clothes.

Exercise E.6   Word Choice

Edit the following paragraph for appropriate diction and connotation.

For help with this exercise, see Chapter 9 in *Successful College Writing*.

EXAMPLE:

> *wealthy*
> From middle-class to ~~rich~~ American communities, the disease known as anorexia is on the rise.
> ^

Americans have recently had their noses rubbed in the fact that anorexia nervosa, a disease of self-starvation, is becoming more widespread. Anorexia sufferers are overwhelmingly made up of teenage girls and young women. Most of them are white and come from middle-class or upper-class families. They are also usually sharp. They seem to other people to have pretty much every advantage. Their families and comrades ordinarily have a rough time comprehending why they will not eat. Because anorexia is a psychological disorder, the sufferers themselves may not catch on to what caused the onset of their illness. Anorexics have a weird body image. They often believe they are totally overweight unless they are dangerously slender. The disease is notoriously difficult to treat, even if the patient tries to go along with her doctors.

For help with this exercise, see Chapter 9 in *Successful College Writing.*

Exercise E.7   Concrete, Specific Detail

Revise the following sentences by adding concrete, specific details.

EXAMPLE:

the types of questions featured on standardized tests such as the SAT and ACT

➤ Learning about ~~standardized tests~~ may improve a student's performance on them.

1. Every year, a large number of high school students take standardized tests.
2. A good test score can help a student.
3. Test-preparation courses are becoming popular.
4. These courses are expensive.
5. Experts disagree about the value of such courses.
6. Many students get better scores after taking a course.
7. The amount of improvement is not always significant.
8. Opponents argue that the courses are unfair.
9. Others say that the courses make no real difference.
10. Many people continue to pay for test preparation.

For help with this exercise, see Chapter 9 in *Successful College Writing.*

Exercise E.8   Figures of Speech

Edit the following sentences to eliminate clichéd words and expressions.

EXAMPLE:

marathon runner heading uphill

➤ A woman athlete may have to work like a ~~mule~~ to earn her share of recognition.

1. For generations, women were considered to be delicate flowers too fragile for sports.
2. Many people thought that women would die like an old tree if they were too physically active.
3. Even though these mistaken beliefs were widespread, women athletes have moved forward by leaps and bounds.

4. Individual women athletes, like the track and golf star Babe Didrikson Zaharias, had to be as strong as an ox.

5. During World War II, a women's baseball league drew spectators like a snake in the grass when a shortage of male players depleted men's teams.

6. The end of the war nipped the women's league in the bud.

7. The American women's movement of the 1970s was the dawn of a new era for women in sports.

8. A "battle of the sexes" took place in tennis during that decade, when Billie Jean King, a star female player, made Bobby Riggs, an avowed "male chauvinist" who had challenged her, look as weak as the ocean tides.

9. In the following decades, some individual women became sports heroes, like Florence Griffith Joyner, who could run like the wind.

10. Finally, in the 1990s, the popularity of women's basketball and soccer spread like a disease in a crowded city.

Exercise E.9   Weak Verb/Noun Combinations

Edit the following sentences to eliminate weak verb/noun combinations.

For help with this exercise, see Chapter 9 in *Successful College Writing.*

EXAMPLE:

➤ For many years, mentally ill people were ~~given the same treatment~~ *treated the same* as criminals.

1. The treatment of mental illness has been troublesome to societies throughout history.

2. A thousand years ago, observers thought mental disturbance offered proof that the sufferer was possessed by demons.

3. Many mentally ill people suffered death in the course of treatment for demonic possession.

4. Belief in demonic possession eventually underwent a decrease in much of the world.

5. Instead, doctors and others made a classification of mental illness as a kind of disease.

6. Sufferers were frequently put into confinement and, often, forgotten.

7. Officials made the decision that mentally ill people were antisocial, not sick.

8. Most healthy people rarely gave any consideration to the mentally ill.

9. In the nineteenth century, a reformer, Dorothea Dix, made an investigation into the treatment of the mentally ill in Massachusetts.

10. Her report shocked people so much that Massachusetts, and soon other states, passed legislation requiring humane treatment for sufferers of mental illness.

Addressing Issues with Parts of Speech

Exercise 1.1   Nouns, Pronouns, and Verbs

Identify the underlined word as a noun, a pronoun, or a verb.

EXAMPLE:

For help with this exercise, see handbook sections 1a–1c in *Successful College Writing*.

                                                          pronoun
➤ Many Americans don't realize how much <u>their</u> ignorance of number concepts affects their lives.

1. The mathematician John Allen Paulos <u>claims</u> that too many Americans do not understand basic mathematical ideas.

2. Paulos calls this <u>lack</u> of understanding "innumeracy."

3. Innumerates may not <u>grasp</u> the idea of probability.

4. <u>Failing</u> to understand the likelihood of an event may cause poor judgment.

5. Unreasonable fears—for example, of being killed in a terrorist attack—may paralyze citizens <u>who</u> don't appreciate how unlikely such an event is.

6. A related misunderstanding is the failure to realize how common coincidences <u>are</u>.

7. For instance, the chance of two strangers on an airplane having <u>acquaintances</u> in common is surprisingly high.

8. In addition, probability shows that in any random group of twenty-three people, there is a 50 percent chance that two of <u>them</u> share a birthday.

9. People unfamiliar with rules of probability <u>may</u> be dangerously gullible.

10. Educational reforms and a systematic <u>attempt</u> to show the fun side of math could help Americans overcome their number resistance.

For help with this exercise, see handbook section 1c in *Successful College Writing*.

Exercise 1.2   Verb Form

Correct any errors in verb form in the following sentences. Some sentences may be correct as written.

EXAMPLE:

➤ In recent years, the study of detective stories ~~have~~ *has* become a legitimate academic pursuit.

1. Parents in the early twentieth century was warned that detective magazines could warp children's minds.

2. Pulp fiction about crime did indeed became rather lurid.

3. The detective story does, however, boast a literary past.

4. Many scholars have gave Edgar Allan Poe credit for being the first author to write detective fiction in English.

5. Poe's story "The Murders in the Rue Morgue" features an almost supernaturally clever detective.

6. Poe's detective clearly laid the foundation for the most famous literary sleuth, Sherlock Holmes.

7. In dozens of stories, Holmes, assisted by his friend Dr. Watson, uncovers the truth by careful observation.

8. Arthur Conan Doyle, the creator of Holmes and Watson, were amazed at the popularity of his fictional characters.

9. Some of the best-known writers of detective fiction in the twentieth century have been women.

10. While not all detective stories are worthy of serious study, the best ones are consider by scholars to be very rewarding.

Exercise 1.3   Verb Tense

Identify the tense of each underlined verb.

EXAMPLE:

past perfect progressive

➤ By the spring of 1999, Wayne Gretzky <u>had been playing</u> professional hockey for over twenty years.

1. Wayne Gretzky <u>began playing</u> hockey in his native Canada at the age of three.

2. When he was five, he was frequently <u>scoring</u> goals against players several years older than he was.

3. Hockey fans <u>have known</u> Gretzky's name since his record-setting seasons with the Edmonton Oilers.

4. Before the Oilers traded him to Los Angeles, Gretzky <u>had acquired</u> his nickname, the "Great One."

For help with this exercise, see handbook section 1c in *Successful College Writing.*

5. Gretzky <u>holds</u> or shares more than sixty hockey records, an unprecedented number.

6. Several of his scoring records <u>will</u> probably always <u>stand</u>.

7. Gretzky's decision to retire in 1999 disappointed his fans, although they had perhaps <u>expected</u> the news.

8. When he retired, most of his fans <u>had been watching</u> him play for most of their lives.

9. Gretzky has said that he <u>will be spending</u> more time with his family now that his playing days are over.

10. In recognition of his achievements, the National Hockey League will never again <u>assign</u> a player Gretzky's number, 99.

Exercise 1.4   Verb Mood

For help with this exercise, see handbook section 1c in *Successful College Writing.*

Identify the mood—indicative, imperative, or subjunctive—of the underlined verb or verb phrase in each of the following sentences.

EXAMPLE:

indicative

➤ Charles Darwin's *The Origin of Species* <u>has inspired</u> considerable discussion since its publication in 1859.

1. The study of biology <u>would be</u> very different today if Darwin had never written.

2. Although the mechanics of evolution <u>are</u> still <u>debated</u>, biologists all over the world accept Darwin's ideas.

3. Readers of Darwin's work in the nineteenth and early twentieth centuries <u>were</u> not easily <u>convinced</u>.

4. Many people wish that Darwin's theory <u>were</u> not widely accepted among scientists.

5. In the United States in 1925, a court of law told a Darwinian, "<u>Stop teaching</u> evolution."

6. In that famous trial, the Tennessee teacher J. T. Scopes <u>was tried</u> for telling his students to read about Darwin's theory.

7. Darrow argued that students <u>be</u> told.

8. The court ruled that the truth of evolutionary theory was not relevant, since Tennessee law <u>forbade</u> teaching it.

9. Scopes, who admitted teaching evolutionary theory, <u>lost</u> the case.

10. The Tennessee law forbidding the teaching of evolution <u>was</u> not <u>overturned</u> until 1967.

Exercise 1.5   Adjectives and Adverbs

Identify the underlined word as an adjective or an adverb.

EXAMPLE:

> *adjective*
> ➤ Education experts in the United States are debating the pros and cons of <u>standardized</u> testing.

1. How <u>well</u> do American students compare with those in other industrialized nations?

2. A student who receives the <u>best</u> education the United States offers is likely to be very well prepared.

3. However, many students, especially those in <u>poorer</u> neighborhoods, get substandard training.

4. Education professionals agree that the U.S. <u>educational</u> system has problems.

5. <u>Unfortunately</u>, they cannot agree on what to do to solve this problem.

6. One <u>proposed</u> solution involves nationwide standards.

7. With nationwide standards, students across the country would be <u>responsible</u> for learning the same curriculum as all other students in the United States.

8. Students could prove they had met the standards by performing <u>satisfactorily</u> on a standardized test.

9. Supporters of <u>this</u> method claim that standards would force students to master knowledge before being promoted or graduating.

10. Some opponents argue that students learn <u>more</u> easily when teachers are able to use their own judgment about the curriculum.

Exercise 1.6   Conjunctions and Prepositions

Identify the underlined word or words as a form of a conjunction or a preposition.

EXAMPLE:

> *preposition*
> ➤ A new rapidly growing branch <u>of</u> physics is chaos theory.

1. <u>For</u> about the last fifty years, physicists have been analyzing chaos.

2. <u>In spite of</u> common perceptions, chaos may not be completely random.

3. The operations of some incompletely understood biological systems—brains, <u>for example</u>—may thrive in the gray area between order and chaos.

For help with this exercise, see handbook section 1d and 1e in Successful College Writing.

For help with this exercise, see handbook sections 1f and 1g in Successful College Writing.

4. Some physicists believe that apparently chaotic behavior may actually act <u>according to</u> patterns.

5. <u>If</u> chaos is somehow systematic, it is nevertheless tremendously complex.

6. Finding the patterns of chaotic behavior is sometimes possible, <u>although</u> identifying them is difficult.

7. One difficulty lies <u>in</u> determining the type of model appropriate for a given complex system.

8. Understanding these complex systems <u>not only</u> is interesting in theory, <u>but also</u> has potential practical uses.

9. One group of physicists has tried to understand the abstractions of chaos theory <u>and</u> make concrete gains from their knowledge.

10. <u>As</u> part of an attempt to predict its future behavior, they are studying the complex and chaotic system known as the stock market.

Identifying Sentence Parts

For help with this exercise, see handbook section 2a in *Successful College Writing*.

Exercise 2.1   Subjects and Predicates

Identify the underlined portion of each sentence as a simple subject, a simple predicate, a complete subject, or a complete predicate.

EXAMPLE:
simple subject
➤ <u>What</u> makes one violin sound different from another?

1. <u>The making of violins</u> is an art that has been practiced for centuries.

2. Modern technological <u>advances</u> have hardly touched violin makers, known as luthiers.

3. The greatest violin makers of all time <u>worked two to three hundred years ago in Italy</u>.

4. Modern luthiers <u>still do not know exactly how those great violin makers — notably Stradivarius and Amati — produced such perfect instruments</u>.

5. <u>Stradivarius violins, only about 150 of which are known to exist today</u>, can be worth over a million dollars each.

6. Stradivarius, who worked in Cremona, Italy, <u>invented</u> the proportions of the modern violin.

7. Some experts <u>believe</u> that the shape of his violins produces their exquisite tone.

8. Others argue that the precise shape could be reproduced by modern methods, yet nobody <u>has succeeded so far in duplicating the famous Stradivarius sound</u>.

9. Another <u>theory</u> is that the maple wood Stradivarius used, which came from ancient trees in short supply today, gives his violins their tone.

10. Chemists <u>are experimenting</u> with ways to treat newer wood that might give violins the elusive resonance of a Stradivarius.

Exercise 2.2   Objects and Complements

Identify each underlined word as a direct object, an indirect object, a subject complement, or an object complement.

EXAMPLE:

indirect object

➤ Can computers give adult <u>brains</u> new capacities for learning foreign languages?

1. Some kinds of learning get <u>easier</u> as people grow older.

2. But most adults find learning a foreign language extremely <u>difficult</u>.

3. At birth, babies' brains can distinguish every <u>sound</u> in every human language.

4. As they grow, children's brains become less <u>able</u> to recognize different sounds.

5. After the age of ten, most people cannot acquire a foreign <u>language</u> without an accent.

6. Adult brains reinforce familiar <u>sounds</u> when they hear unfamiliar ones.

7. This phenomenon actually makes adults less <u>likely</u> to distinguish unfamiliar sounds with increased exposure.

8. An experimental computer simulation may give <u>adults</u> new abilities to learn unfamiliar language sounds.

9. The computer offers <u>students</u> a chance to hear the unfamiliar sounds in an exaggerated way.

10. Perhaps someday adult learners will also be fluent, unaccented <u>speakers</u> of foreign languages.

For help with this exercise, see handbook section 2a in *Successful College Writing.*

For help with this exercise, see handbook section 2b in *Successful College Writing*.

Exercise 2.3 Phrases

Identify the underlined phrase in each sentence as a prepositional phrase, a verbal phrase, an appositive phrase, or an absolute phrase.

EXAMPLE:

verbal phrase

➤ The science <u>of analyzing human DNA</u> has become very precise in recent years.

1. DNA, <u>the genetic code</u>, is a unique marker that is different in every human being.

2. DNA analysis can be used <u>as a crime-fighting tool</u>.

3. Like fingerprints, DNA <u>left at a crime scene</u> can help to identify a wrongdoer.

4. Today, most people contemplating a crime know how <u>to avoid leaving fingerprints</u>.

5. But criminals, <u>their DNA contained in every cell of their bodies</u>, can hardly avoid leaving identifying markers behind.

6. Any clue — <u>a single hair, a trace of saliva</u> — can eventually convict a criminal.

7. <u>A suspect having left a used coffee cup during questioning</u>, a police officer may not even need another sample to link him or her to the crime.

8. The good news <u>for some people</u> charged with or convicted of a crime is that DNA can also prove someone not guilty.

9. Some convicted criminals, <u>steadfastly maintaining their innocence</u>, have undergone new, sophisticated DNA analysis after years of imprisonment.

10. Recently, two men, <u>prisoners on death row</u>, were released after DNA tests proved they could not have committed the murder for which they were convicted.

For help with this exercise, see handbook section 2c in *Successful College Writing*.

Exercise 2.4 Subordinate Clauses

Underline the subordinate clause or clauses in each of the following sentences.

EXAMPLE:

➤ Superstitions, <u>which are irrational beliefs in charms and omens</u>, still have a hold on modern life.

1. Many superstitions date from classical or medieval times, when belief in witchcraft was widespread.

2. Superstitions were a way for people to explain whatever threatened them.

3. Because cats were believed to be witches in disguise, the fear of a black cat crossing one's path came about.

4. Walking under ladders has also long been considered unlucky; this superstition may survive because it protects pedestrians from falling objects.

5. Some people attribute to the Christian story of the Last Supper, where thirteen people were present, the origins of the superstitious fear of the number thirteen.

6. Wherever it began, fear of the number thirteen, or triskaidekaphobia, is still prevalent enough for many tall modern buildings not to have a thirteenth floor.

7. Early Romans believed that sneezing was a sign of the plague, so they feared it.

8. The method they invented to protect a sneezer was to say, "God bless you."

9. In the United States today, it is common to say "God bless you"—or "Gesundheit," which is German for "health"—following a sneeze.

10. Superstitions from the past may seem silly today, but who knows what strange customs of the present will be ridiculed in the future?

Exercise 2.5   Sentence Types

Indicate whether each of the following sentences is a simple, a compound, a complex, or a compound-complex sentence.

EXAMPLE:

➤ While extremely muscular or very thin people are often portrayed as the American ideal, Americans are, on the average, heavier than ever. *complex*

1. Models and beauty contest winners in the United States have become much thinner in the last fifty years.

2. The weight that most people consider ideal for their height has also adjusted downward since the middle of the twentieth century.

3. The media have recently become more aware of the unhealthy effect that overly thin models can have on people and are making an effort to depict more moderately sized models.

4. More and better nutritional information is available today, and most Americans know the right way to eat.

5. Yet the number of people who actually eat right and have positive body image seems to have declined.

For help with this exercise, see handbook section 2d in *Successful College Writing*.

6. Since people know it is not healthy to over- or undereat, why are both obesity and anorexia still national problems?

7. Part of the reason for obesity may be this nation's overall good fortune and abundance.

8. Most people rarely go without their favorite foods, and American favorites tend to be high in fat and calories.

9. On the other hand, the media's old image of "perfect" bodies might still be to blame for eating disorders and unhealthy dieting.

10. Despite the media's efforts to foster a culture of positive body image and controlled eating in America, many people in this country have yet to embrace a healthy medium when it comes to weight, and they struggle with every meal.

Writing Correct Sentences

Exercise 3.1   Sentence Fragments

For help with this exercise, see handbook section 3 in *Successful College Writing*.

Correct any sentence fragments in the following sentences. Some sentences may be correct as written.

EXAMPLE:

➤ Among the many treasures at Yale's library, ~~T~~he Voynich manuscript stands out.

1. There are older and more valuable manuscripts. Than the Voynich.

2. However, there is none more mysterious. The Voynich still puzzling scholars many years after its discovery.

3. This manuscript was written in a code. So far unable to solve it.

4. Because the origins of the manuscript are unclear; the puzzle is doubly difficult.

5. No one knows. What country it came from.

6. Therefore, it very hard to determine the language the code represents. This makes decoding it even more troublesome.

7. Handwriting specialists can only guess at its age. It may date back to the Middle Ages.

8. The writing does not resemble. Any letters that can be traced to a known alphabet.

9. The manuscript which contains many beautiful illustrations. Of plants, people, and other seemingly unrelated images.

10. Because the Voynich manuscript is such an intriguing mystery. That some scholars might actually be disappointed to learn all of its secrets.

Exercise 4.1   Run-On Sentences and Comma Splices

Correct any run-on sentences and comma splices in the following sentences.

EXAMPLE:

For help with this exercise, see handbook section 4 in *Successful College Writing*.

➤ Before her death in 1980, Mae West had become an institution; she had been in show business for seven decades.

1. Mae West began as a child star the career of "Baby Mae" took off when she performed at a local Brooklyn theater's amateur night.

2. At the age of nineteen, West began performing on Broadway she shocked audiences in 1911.

3. The voluptuous West became known for her suggestive clothing, even more famous were her suggestive wisecracks.

4. Attending black jazz clubs had introduced her to a new dance movement she performed this "shimmy" on Broadway, and it became a trademark for her.

5. West was not satisfied for long with the theatrical roles she was offered writing her own plays was one way to find good parts.

6. In 1925, she wrote a play called *Sex,* no producer she contacted would bring it to the stage.

7. The following year, West produced the play herself, advertisements for *Sex* were banned.

8. Nevertheless, the show played for nine months until it was closed down by the Society for the Suppression of Vice, West was arrested and spent eight days in jail.

9. In the 1930s and 1940s, Mae West took her naughty humor to Hollywood, while there she made a series of hit films and often wrote her own screenplays.

10. West made her final films in the 1970s by that time Americans found her less scandalous, but her name was still a household word.

For help with this exercise, see handbook section 5 in *Successful College Writing.*

Exercise 5.1   Subject-Verb Agreement

Correct any errors in subject-verb agreement in the following sentences. Some sentences may be correct as written.

EXAMPLE:

➤ African American heritage and the end of slavery ~~is~~ *are* celebrated every year on June 19.

1. The festival called "Juneteenth," which people once recognized only in a few southern areas of the United States, are now much more widespread.

2. The events Juneteenth commemorates occurred after the end of the Civil War.

3. The surrender of the Confederate States were made official at Appomattox Courthouse on April 9, 1865.

4. From that day on, the Confederacy and the Union was again a single country.

5. Neither the northern states nor the southern states was now legally able to permit slave-owning, which had been officially outlawed in the United States several years earlier.

6. However, not all of the former slaves were aware they had been legally freed.

7. The story from those long-ago days go that in Texas, slave owners murdered the messengers bringing word of emancipation.

8. Not until June 19, 1865, were the news able to reach the last group of Texas slaves.

9. Therefore, festivities marking the end of slavery are held not on April 9 each year, the anniversary of the South's surrender, but on June 19.

10. Today, people celebrating Juneteenth attends concerts, films, and other cultural events.

For help with this exercise, see handbook section 6 in *Successful College Writing.*

Exercise 6.1   Verb Forms

Correct any errors in verb form in the following sentences.

EXAMPLE:

➤ In 1915, a group of artists ~~had~~ decided to turn their backs on the traditional art world.

1. The horrors of World War I were convincing some artists that European society had to change radically.

2. Their reaction at first consist of musical and performance events they called the Cabaret Voltaire.

3. Soon, however, the most influential members of the group begun to focus on visual art.

4. The name *Dada* was chosen at random by the artists.

5. They rejected older artistic traditions, including avant-garde ideas that recently became popular.

6. Instead, the Dadaists challenging the whole concept of art.

7. Before the Dada movement had ended in 1923, several of the artists had experimented with random arrangements of materials.

8. Sometimes they chose the material they use from items discarded by other people.

9. One artist, Marcel Duchamp, even sat up ordinary objects at art shows, claiming that the act of choosing the objects made them art.

10. Dada was a rebellion, not an attempt to build a new tradition, so no identifiable stylistic legacy of the movement remain today.

Exercise 7.1   Pronoun Reference

Correct any instances of vague or unclear pronoun reference in the following sentences.

EXAMPLE:

➤ Many Americans express tremendous cynicism about the U.S. government, ~~which~~ is *and this attitude* not good for the country.

1. In much political analysis, they say that public distrust of the U.S. government began with Watergate.

2. That scandal's continuing legacy may make it one of the most influential American events of the twentieth century.

3. Since the early 1970s, political scandals have rarely interested Americans; they often seem to have very little effect.

4. Journalists provided the American people with a lot of information about the Iran-Contra hearings, but they could not have cared less.

5. Most people were indifferent; could it have been the result of post–Watergate trauma?

For help with this exercise, see handbook sections 7a–7d in *Successful College Writing.*

6. If Americans expect politicians to be corrupt, it will not surprise or even interest them.

7. Ironically, the media's coverage of scandals seems to have made the public suspicious of them as well.

8. Cynicism about political and journalistic motives leads to apathy, and it can spread contagiously.

9. Many people are so apathetic that it makes them refuse to vote.

10. If people do not believe that they can make a difference in the political process, it makes the country less democratic.

Exercise 7.2   Pronoun-Antecedent Agreement

For help with this exercise, see handbook sections 7c–7g in *Successful College Writing.*

Correct any errors in pronoun-antecedent agreement in the following sentences. Some sentences may be correct as written.

EXAMPLE:

➤ Human ~~lives~~ *life* is important, and more lives could be protected if more were known about deadly storms.

1. Meteorology has made many advances in the past few decades, but they still cannot answer a number of questions about tornados.

2. Every tornado has their own unique characteristics.

3. The science of tornado watching has its own system, the Fujita scale, for measuring storms from weakest (F0) to strongest (F5).

4. An F4 tornado or an F5 tornado can destroy everything in their path.

5. Scientists cannot predict precisely how strong any tornado will be before they happen.

6. One reason why meteorologists find it difficult to predict tornados is its many possible causes.

7. Tornados can form due to wind flow patterns, or it might be caused by other factors such as temperature, moisture, instability, and lift.

8. Improved meteorological technology and the skill to interpret data have made their contributions to tornado prediction.

9. Either a few extra minutes of warning or more information about a storm's power would prove their effectiveness in saving lives.

10. People who live in a tornado zone should always know where his or her nearest safe area is.

Exercise 7.3   Pronoun Case

Correct any errors in pronoun case in the following sentences. Some sentences may be correct as written.

EXAMPLE:

For help with this exercise, see handbook sections 7h–7m in *Successful College Writing*.

➤ Much of American mythology concerns heroes ~~whom~~ *who* solved problems by using violence.

1. Us residents of the United States are considered by much of the rest of the world to be an unusually violent people.

2. Many researchers have debated they're theories about violent behavior in this country.

3. Did the popular myth of the "Wild West" influence we and our ancestors?

4. Other industrialized nations and us have very different policies concerning guns.

5. Guns played an important part in Western settlement, but other machines may have been more significant than they.

6. Violence and justice are so intertwined for many Americans that disagreements between other people and they can erupt into fights.

7. American entertainment is frequently violent, too, and some people worry that such violence affects us and our children.

8. There are defenders of violent films, TV shows, and video games whom claim that entertainment reflects our tastes rather than influencing them.

9. What makes us Americans so prone to violence?

10. Sometimes it seems that our worst enemies are us.

Exercise 8.1   Shifts

Correct any inappropriate shifts in the following sentences.

EXAMPLE:

For help with this exercise, see handbook sections 8a–8g in *Successful College Writing*.

➤ Some scholars have asked ~~did~~ *whether* African folk traditions influence *d* African American folklore.

1. West African villages have strong oral traditions in which the younger people are told stories by their parents and grandparents.

2. Way back before the Revolutionary War, slave traders forced ancestors of the people from those villages to come to the United States.

3. In their difficult new situation in this country, the Africans adapted their stories so that you could learn from them.

4. Although different stories had different messages, one kind of character comes up over and over again.

5. The character is cunning and clever; call him a "trickster."

6. The stories about Br'er Rabbit are good examples of folktales whose hero was a trickster.

7. Many of the other animals want to gobble up Br'er Rabbit, who has only his wits to protect him.

8. Yet in every story, Br'er Rabbit not only escapes but his enemies are made to appear foolish by him as well.

9. Trickster characters like Br'er Rabbit showed slaves who heard these stories that they, too, could triumph by using cleverness when foes surround them.

10. Today, folklorists are exploring how did early African Americans encourage each other by telling stories of tricksters outsmarting powerful enemies.

Exercise 8.2   **Mixed Constructions**

Correct any mixed constructions in the following sentences.

EXAMPLE:

➤ A common misconception is the ~~ability~~ to identify when someone is telling a lie.
         idea that it is easy

1. Most people think perceiving falsehoods are easy to spot.

2. They think that interpreting nonverbal signals shows when someone is lying.

3. The fact that these signals, such as avoiding eye contact or hesitating before answering a question, are habits of truthful people as well.

4. The reason liars are hard to identify is because no single trait always proves that a person is lying.

5. Truthful people who are afraid they will not be believed may act suspiciously is one problem with lie detection.

6. There are a few people are unusually good at identifying liars.

7. However, perhaps because these people are attuned to deceitful behavior may explain why they are not especially good at identifying truth-tellers.

8. Listening to a stranger's lies may be easier to detect than a loved one's.

For help with this exercise, see handbook sections 8h–8j in *Successful College Writing*.

9. The better someone knows and likes another person seems to make spotting lies more difficult.

10. Someone who finds it hard to believe that her friends would try to deceive her is an understandable human characteristic.

Exercise 9.1   Adjectives and Adverbs

Correct any errors in the use of adjectives or adverbs in the following sentences.

EXAMPLE:

➤ People think of beauty different in different cultures.
ly (inserted above "different")

1. Many people go to a lot of trouble to look attractively.

2. In the United States, no one thinks a woman wearing high heels is dressed strange.

3. Many Americans even go to real extreme lengths, such as having surgery, to be beautiful.

4. People can see the strangeness of beauty rituals clearer if the rituals are unfamiliar.

5. For example, in China in past centuries, beautiful women had to have the tiniest feet.

6. To achieve this goal, families bound their daughters' feet so tight that the feet could not grow.

7. Subcultures within the United States also have their own standards of beauty that may seem odder to people who are not part of the subculture.

8. For many young Americans, tattoos and body piercing are the trendier fashion statements of the day.

9. They might argue that such beautification was no unusualer than plucking out one's eyebrows.

10. Parents, however, often feel vastly relief if their children reach adulthood without tattoos.

Exercise 10.1   Misplaced and Dangling Modifiers

Correct any misplaced or dangling modifiers in the following sentences.

EXAMPLE:

➤ The sports world has changed to reflect the number of young athletes. ~~rapidly growing.~~
rapidly growing (inserted)

For help with this exercise, see handbook section 9 in *Successful College Writing*.

For help with this exercise, see handbook section 10 in *Successful College Writing*.

1. Recently, several sports have gained popularity that no one had heard of thirty years ago.

2. With a name that suggests their dangerous allure, members of Generation X are attracted to these athletic events.

3. These "Generation X" games often involve going to inaccessible places, which include snowboarding and sky-surfing.

4. Snow activities are especially popular that can be done on remote mountaintops.

5. Some of these sports have become so widely accepted that participants can now compete in the Olympics, such as freestyle skiing and snowboarding.

6. Gasping at the antics of snowboarders, mountain bikers, and other athletes, these daredevils prove that the sports world really has changed.

7. Only these "in-your-face" athletes are a small part of what is interesting about the changes taking place in sports today.

8. Occasionally, even fans of extreme sports know that the quest for adventure leads people into dangerous situations.

9. Environmentalists also point out unfortunately that in some remote wilderness areas, extreme sports are taking their toll on nature.

10. Probably, whether people love them or hate them, extreme sports will continue to inspire extreme reactions.

Correcting Punctuation Errors

For help with this exercise, see handbook section 11 in *Successful College Writing*.

Exercise 11.1   End Punctuation

Correct any errors in the use of end punctuation marks in the following sentences. Some sentences may be correct as written.

EXAMPLE:

➤ No one knows what kind of undiscovered life forms exist at the bottom of the ocean?.
                                                                          ^

1. In some places, the ocean is more than seven miles deep!

2. Enormous pressure and complete darkness in the depths make it difficult for humans to discover what is down there?

3. When deep-sea fishing boats haul up their nets, they sometimes find creatures never before seen or prehistoric life forms that were believed to be extinct.

4. The sheer size of the ocean depths indicates that there may be many more species down there than are found on land!

5. Could there be millions of unknown species living in the deepest ocean trenches?

6. Scientists wonder what the implications of new species might be for human beings.

7. Is it also possible that the actions of humans are affecting life at the bottom of the sea.

8. Biologists who have recently measured the food supply on the ocean floor might be moved to exclaim, "It seems to be dwindling?"

9. Most of the food that reaches the bottom comes from near the surface, where there is light?

10. Warmer surface temperatures may be reducing the food supply at the bottom, and who has more influence on global warming than human beings.

Exercise 12.1   Adding Commas

Add or omit commas as necessary in the following sentences. Some sentences may be correct as written.

EXAMPLE:

➤ Horse racing, which has been a spectator sport for centuries, still delights fans.

1. Breeders have long prized their swiftest, most graceful horses, and raced them.

2. Horse racing in the United States generally means either thoroughbred racing or harness racing.

3. Harness racehorses pull small lightweight vehicles, handled by a driver.

4. Harness racing falls into the two categories of trotting, and pacing.

5. The most famous event in harness racing the Hambletonian, is a mile-long trotting race.

6. Harness racing may be known mainly to enthusiasts but even people who appreciate very little about horse racing are familiar with thoroughbred racing.

7. Thoroughbred racehorses, unlike harness racehorses, carry a rider.

8. The best-known events in thoroughbred racing, the Kentucky Derby, the Preakness Stakes, and the Belmont Stakes, are the three races, that make up the Triple Crown.

For help with this exercise, see handbook section 12 in *Successful College Writing.*

9. All of the Triple Crown races which vary in length are for three-year-old horses.

10. In the twentieth century only eleven horses won thoroughbred racing's Triple Crown.

For help with this exercise, see handbook section 12 in *Successful College Writing*.

Exercise 12.2   Working with Commas

Add or omit commas as necessary in the following sentences. Some sentences may be correct as written.

EXAMPLE:

➤   There are many theories/ about the kinds of police work that are the most effective/ at reducing crime.

1. Several years ago, many police departments ignored minor violations of the law, and concentrated on bigger crime problems.

2. Today, however, the "broken window" theory, is widely accepted.

3. According to this popular theory allowing broken windows to remain, unrepaired, leads to a loss of hope in a community.

4. Frequently, buildings that look neglected make neighbors feel that no one cares what goes on in the area.

5. Similarly, if petty crimes are ignored in a neighborhood people there may feel that larger crimes are acceptable as well.

6. Community policing is one result of the new emphasis on stopping "victimless" crimes such as loitering and panhandling.

7. But, can a police officer, walking a beat, really be more effective than a patrol car?

8. Some experts believe that police should be required to live in the communities, that they serve.

9. Police who live elsewhere may not understand the needs of the community, and they will certainly know less about the people living in the community.

10. Different methods of community policing may work in different areas but the goal should always be to keep communications open between the public and the police.

For help with this exercise, see handbook section 13 in *Successful College Writing*.

Exercise 13.1   Semicolons

Correct any errors in the use of semicolons in the following sentences. Some sentences may be correct as written.

EXAMPLE:

➤ The anti-Communist hysteria of the Cold War era marks one of the lowest points in American history⨯, when fear led to persecution of some citizens.

1. Many Americans think of the years after World War II as a golden era; a time before modern complexities made life more difficult.

2. Even without considering the quality of life at that time for women and minorities; an idyllic view of the mid-twentieth century ignores other issues.

3. The late 1940s and 1950s marked the height of the Cold War era; many Americans were frightened about what might happen in the future.

4. The Soviet Union, an ally of the United States during World War II, took control of the governments of neighboring countries, China, after a civil war, fell under Communist rule, and the Korean conflict, in which Americans were involved, seemed to prove that Communists wanted to take over as much land as possible.

5. Americans reacted to Communist activities elsewhere in the world, and part of their reaction included fear of communism at home.

6. Senator Joseph McCarthy may have shared this fear, he certainly capitalized on it to advance his political career.

7. In 1950, McCarthy announced that he had a list of Communists; who held positions in the U.S. State Department.

8. At about the same time, the House Un-American Activities Committee began investigating Hollywood; many stars were asked to testify about suspected Communists in the film industry.

9. Eventually, more than 150 film workers, including; performers, directors, and writers, were blacklisted by the Hollywood studios.

10. For the first half of the 1950s, anti-Communist leaders were very powerful in the United States; however, by 1955 McCarthy was in disgrace; and in 1957 the courts determined that membership in the Communist Party should no longer be a criminal offense in this country.

Exercise 14.1   Colons

Correct any errors in the use of colons in the following sentences. Some sentences may be correct as written.

For help with this exercise, see handbook section 14 in *Successful College Writing*.

EXAMPLE:

➤ Near the end of the expedition, Scott and his men were̷ cold, hungry, and exhausted.

1. In 1910, Robert Falcon Scott led his second expedition to Antarctica with two objectives to collect scientific data and to be the first humans at the South Pole.

2. The years before World War I were a heady time for: exploration of the frozen Antarctic continent.

3. The story of Scott's difficult journey continues to fascinate armchair adventurers: even though the expedition was, in many ways, a failure.

4. After arriving in Antarctica, Scott's scientists began their work, they collected specimens, surveyed the land, and recorded twelve volumes of data.

5. In 1911, Scott learned that the Norwegian explorer Roald Amundsen had decided to try to reach the South Pole as well.

6. Scott stuck to his original timetable for the South Pole journey, he did not want to engage in a race.

7. Scott and his men set out for the South Pole in the Antarctic summer of 1911: which is the winter season in the Northern Hemisphere.

8. In January 1912, Scott and the four companions who had traveled to the Pole with him were disappointed to learn that Amundsen's men had arrived a month earlier.

9. As they traveled back to their base camp, death took all five men Scott, Titus Oates, Edgar Evans, Henry Bowers, and Edward Wilson.

10. *Scott's Last Expedition: The Journals* records the explorer's last diary entry: "I do not think we can hope for any better things now. We shall stick it out to the end, but we are getting weaker, of course, and the end cannot be far. It seems a pity, but I do not think I can write more."

Exercise 15.1   Quotation Marks

Correct any errors in the use of quotation marks in the following sentences.

EXAMPLE:

➤ Is Hamlet contemplating suicide when he says, "To be, or not to be, that is the question?"?

For help with this exercise, see handbook section 15 in *Successful College Writing*.

1. The film producer shouted excitedly, "Everyone loves Shakespeare because he used so many familiar quotations"!

2. "When we make movies based on Shakespeare plays", he added "we don't have to pay royalties to the writer."

3. Films based on Shakespeare plays try to reveal the relevance of his work to a "modern" audience.

4. Although Shakespeare lived four hundred years ago, his work is currently "in demand" in Hollywood.

5. "West Side Story," "10 Things I Hate About You," and "She's the Man" are just a few of Hollywood's interpretations of Shakespeare's plays.

6. The producer commented, "When I hear that a new film will be based on Shakespeare, I wonder, like Juliet, "What's in a name?" "

7. If the name Shakespeare were not involved, would filmmakers be as interested in the material?

8. Shakespeare's plays are frequently performed in theaters, too, and several young playwrights recently wrote works based on his "sonnets."

9. Hamlet, perhaps Shakespeare's most famous character, laments Alas, poor Yorick! I knew him, Horatio, a fellow of infinite jest, of most excellent fancy.

10. Othello, one of Shakespeare's most complex characters, laments that he "loved not wisely, but too well".

Exercise 16.1 Ellipsis Marks

Shorten each quotation below by replacing the underlined portions with ellipsis marks, if appropriate. In some cases, an omission may be inappropriate.

EXAMPLE:

➤ "Don't tell me to get ready to die. ~~I know not what shall be.~~ The only preparation I can make is by fulfilling my present duties" (Emerson 365).

1. "A writer who keeps her audience in mind cannot fail to be effective."

2. "We hold these truths to be self-evident: that all men are created equal, that they are endowed by their creator with certain inalienable rights, that among these are life, liberty, and the pursuit of happiness."

For help with this exercise, see handbook section 16 in *Successful College Writing.*

3. "<u>Even though he himself owned slaves,</u> Thomas Jefferson wanted the Declaration of Independence to say that all men were 'created independent.'"

4. Elizabeth Cady Stanton's "Declaration of Sentiments" announces, "<u>In entering upon the great work before us</u>, we anticipate no small amount of misconception, misrepresentation, and ridicule, <u>but we shall use every instrumentality within our power to effect our object</u>."

5. "Stanton's 'Declaration of Sentiments' was based <u>quite consciously</u> on the language Jefferson had used in the Declaration of Independence."

6. "<u>It may seem strange that</u> any men should dare to ask a just God's assistance in wringing their bread from the sweat of other men's faces; but let us judge not that we be not judged," Lincoln said in his second inaugural address.

7. "Allusions to the language of familiar literature, <u>such as the Bible or the Declaration of Independence</u>, can lend authority to a text that uses them well."

8. Lincoln went on, "Fondly do we hope — <u>fervently do we pray</u> — that this mighty scourge of war may speedily pass away."

9. Martin Luther King Jr. expressed the wish that his children would be judged "<u>not by the color of their skin, but</u> by the content of their character."

10. "Repetition of structure can be an effective rhetorical device. <u>This is true whether the work is intended for an audience of readers or listeners.</u>"

For help with this exercise, see handbook section 17 in *Successful College Writing.*

Exercise 17.1   Apostrophes

Correct any errors in the use of apostrophes in the following sentences. Some sentences may be correct as written.

EXAMPLE:

➤ Some explorer's̸ ideas about the ruins in Mashonaland were incorrect.

1. African chief's stories led a German explorer to the stone ruins in Mashonaland, now in Zimbabwe, in 1871.

2. The explorer, who's name was Karl Mauch, tried to find out who had built the once-great city.

3. The tribes nearby could not answer Mauches' question, but they knew gold had been found there.

4. The African's called the site *Zimbabwe*.

5. Mauch became convinced that the city was Ophir, the source of the gold brought back to King Solomon's Israel around 1000 B.C.E.

6. He thought perhaps the cities' builder was the Queen of Sheba.

7. An archeologists' findings later demonstrated that the city was about six hundred years old and that it had been built by African natives.

8. The Shona tribe probably built the first walls on the site, but it's more complex structures were added later by the Rozwi tribe.

9. The Rozwi probably erected the temple, which was inhabited by Rozwi ruler-priests until their empire's end in the 1830's.

10. The legends about the origins of the city persisted for a long time, perhaps because of white South Africans and Europeans' resistance to the idea that black Africans had built the impressive structures.

Exercise 18.1   Parentheses and Brackets

Correct any errors in the use of parentheses or brackets in the following sentences.

EXAMPLE:

➤ The film poster announced, "The monster takes its revenge⸮ [sic]."

1. Bad movies, (some of which are quite enjoyable to watch), often have a cult following.

2. Some films routinely make every critic's list of worst films (Usually, these movies are so bad they are funny.).

3. A few filmmakers [like Ed Wood] and movie companies [like American International Pictures] have acquired fame among fans of bad movies.

4. Roger Corman's American International Pictures [AIP] churned out innumerable inexpensive, quickly made films.

5. One Corman film, *Little Shop of Horrors,* (1960) was filmed in less than three days.

6. But the director Edward D. Wood Jr. [1924–1978] has a special place in the world of bad movies.

7. Wood gained new fame with Tim Burton's film biography, *Ed Wood,* (1994).

For help with this exercise, see handbook section 18 in *Successful College Writing*.

8. Like Corman's movies, Wood's were made very quickly, but Wood, (unlike Corman), thought he was making great films.

9. Wood's "masterpiece," *Plan 9 from Outer Space,* (Bela Lugosi's last film) is a science fiction and horror film with bad acting, dreadful writing, and laughable special effects.

10. Wood said that "*Plan 9* (was his) pride and joy."

For help with this exercise, see handbook section 19 in *Successful College Writing*.

Exercise 19.1   Dashes

In the following sentences, add a dash or pair of dashes where they might be effective, and correct any errors in the use of dashes and other punctuation.

EXAMPLE:

➤ A backyard bird count takes place ⧸ at the end of every year.

1. Songbirds are a part of our national heritage, each state has its own official bird.

2. Some states have official birds — unique to the region.

3. The nene — Hawaii's state bird, is a goose found only on those islands.

4. In Salt Lake City, a statue of a seagull — which is Utah's state bird — honors the birds that ate a huge swarm of locusts — without the birds, most crops would have been eaten by the insects.

5. Other states share popular state birds, the cardinal, the meadowlark, and the mockingbird are all official birds in at least five states.

6. When Americans think of spring — they often think of songbirds chirping in the trees.

7. For many years the Audubon Society, an organization devoted to nature study — has studied populations of songbirds.

8. Birdwatchers — mainly trained volunteers count birds in small local areas during the year-end holiday season.

9. The numbers of some songbirds — though fortunately not all have declined alarmingly.

10. Although most people appreciate the sights and sounds of songbirds — they may not realize how modern human habits interfere with many birds' lives.

Managing Mechanics and Spelling

Exercise 20.1   Capitalization

Correct any errors in capitalization in the following sentences.

EXAMPLE:

For help with this exercise, see handbook section 20 in *Successful College Writing.*

➤   Some historians believe that the T̲wentieth C̲entury will be remembered as America's century.

1. At the turn of a new century and a new Millennium, many people reflected on historical changes that had taken place in the previous hundred years.

2. In the late 1990s, Americans began making lists reflecting their choices of the greatest Events, Literature, people, and Films of the century.

3. Most Americans would agree that the two World Wars shaped the twentieth century and this country's role in it.

4. List makers might, however, dispute the importance of *Ulysses* or *Gone with the wind.*

5. Between the beginning and the end of the twentieth century, the United States changed from a minor player in global politics into the single undisputed World Power.

6. Technology also advanced dramatically in the century of television, the *apollo* space missions, and personal computers.

7. Of course, technology was sometimes used for evil purposes, as the holocaust and nuclear weapons proved.

8. Some people would even argue that a significant feature of the century was an increasing concern for the environment—In the United States, in Europe, and in parts of the Former Soviet Union, among other places.

9. The trend toward urbanization saw people moving from rural areas to cities, with the result in this country that the great plains grew emptier while the Coasts' population increased.

10. Only historical distance will reveal whether the twentieth century was "The best of times" or "The worst of times."

For help with this exercise, see handbook section 21 in *Successful College Writing*.

Exercise 21.1   Abbreviations

Correct any errors in the use of abbreviations in the following sentences.

EXAMPLE:

➤   Humanitarian ~~orgs.~~ provide relief in disaster areas worldwide.
                 organizations

1. When disasters strike, victims count on international organizations like the Red Cross, Doctors without Borders, etc.

2. A Dr.'s help is often the most desperately needed form of aid.

3. People often offer canned goods and blankets, while major corps. receive tax benefits for donations of drugs and other medical supplies.

4. When Hurricane Mitch devastated Honduras, many U.S. cits. were quick to help.

5. An R.N. who is willing to travel to the disaster area can provide needed services.

6. For several years, volunteer doctors have tried to alleviate the AIDS crisis in Afr.

7. In some situations, e.g. during outbreaks of deadly diseases or in war-torn areas, medical personnel risk their own lives.

8. Doctors from the Atlanta, Ga.-based Centers for Disease Control travel the globe to isolate and study dangerous viruses.

9. The CDC doctors do not provide medical assistance in war zones, but other orgs. do.

10. In the aftermath of bloody fighting, a U.N. peacekeeping force may arrive to find intl. doctors already at work.

For help with this exercise, see handbook section 22 in *Successful College Writing*.

Exercise 22.1   Numbers

Correct any errors in the use of numbers in the following sentences.

EXAMPLE:

➤   The Beatles had more number *1* hits than any other group in pop history.
                                   one

1. John Lennon, Paul McCartney, George Harrison, and Ringo Starr were 4 young men from Liverpool, England, who formed what would become the most popular rock band of all time.

2. On January twenty-five, 1964, the Beatles' first hit entered the U.S. charts.

3. The song "I Want to Hold Your Hand" spent seven weeks at number one and 14 weeks in the top 40.

4. Almost immediately, the Beatles began to attract 1000s of screaming fans everywhere they went.

5. Throughout the nineteen-sixties, the Beatles were the world's most popular group.

6. During the eight years of the Beatles' reign on the charts, they had more than forty three-minute pop hits.

7. By the 2nd half of the decade, the Beatles had stopped touring.

8. They performed live together for the last time on the roof of Three Savile Row, the headquarters of their doomed record company, Apple.

9. 150 employees worked for Apple, which eventually went bankrupt.

10. By no means did each Beatle earn twenty-five percent of the group's profits, for Lennon and McCartney wrote more than ninety percent of the songs.

Exercise 23.1   Italics and Underlining

Correct any errors in the use of italics in the following sentences.

EXAMPLE:

➤ Information overload, a condition that makes people feel overwhelmed in the face of almost unlimited information, affects many Americans.

1. Americans today get their information from CNN, the New York Times, electronic sources, and thousands of other places.

2. Once, choices were limited: to find out about raising a child, for example, parents consulted Dr. Spock's book "Baby and Child Care."

3. Now, magazines like Parenting compete with the new edition of *Dr. Spock* and dozens of other titles.

4. Obscure information is more accessible than ever, so a fan of the song *Telstar* can find *The Joe Meek Story*, a full-length biography of its producer.

5. A student wanting to learn about the dead language called Old English could consult Web sites like the one maintained by *Georgetown University*.

6. It may no longer be possible for a single person to know all about, for example, *biology*.

For help with this exercise, see handbook section 23 in *Successful College Writing.*

7. Once, the term Renaissance man or Renaissance woman referred to a person well educated and talented in many subjects.

8. Leonardo da Vinci, the original Renaissance man, not only painted the "Mona Lisa" but also wrote botanical treatises and devised remarkable engineering plans.

9. Today, we do not expect the builder of the ocean liner Queen Elizabeth II to know other subjects.

10. A lifetime of study may lie behind a single article in the New England Journal of Medicine.

Exercise 24.1   Hyphens

For help with this exercise, see handbook section 24 in *Successful College Writing*.

Correct any errors in the use of hyphens in the following sentences.

EXAMPLE:

➤ Buying lottery/tickets is an extremely inefficient way to gain additional income.

1. Does buying lottery tickets and entering sweepstakes make a person selfemployed?

2. The odds of winning a major lottery prize are often over a million-to-one.

3. Yet many people, including desperately-poor ones who cannot afford the tickets, buy large numbers of them when the jackpot is high and the odds are worst.

4. A sensible approach to such sky high odds would be not to enter the lottery at all.

5. Sweepstakes are well-known to anyone with a mailbox.

6. Unlike lotteries, apparently-free sweepstakes do not require any cash investment other than the price of a stamp.

7. Yet many sweepstakes imply that buying a magazine-subscription or a product improves the chances of winning.

8. Some sweepstakes companies have been accused of trying to dupe customers who do not read the fine-print.

9. Some elderly people have thrown away their great grandchildren's inheritance, buying hundreds of products they don't need from sweepstakes advertisers.

10. The idea of getting rich with minimal work or investment is so strikingly-attractive that many people put logic aside and come up with the money.

Exercise 25.1   Spelling

Correct any spelling errors in the following paragraph.

EXAMPLE:

For help with this exercise, see handbook section 25 in *Successful College Writing*.

➤ It sometimes ~~seams~~ *seems* as if every business ~~dicision~~ *decision* today has to go through a focus group.

Focus groups consist of people selected to express there opinions about products rangeing from sneakers and gum to movies. Some times people who are supposed to be experts on a subject are selected. When companys test a new product, they choose people who might realisticly be expected to by it. If marketers are tring out a new soft drink, for example, they might ask teen agers for their advise. A company makeing a luxury car would be more inclined to seek the veiws of upper-middle-class buyers. On other ocasions, a focus group is picked at randem. To find out how much consumors like a new TV show, a network might ask shoppers at a mall to watch an episode and discuss it with other participents. The network could than learn, not only what viewers like and dislike about the show, but also which groups are most likly to watch it. This information helps the network determine what changes to make in the show and what sponsers to approach. Of course, sense many people perfer the familiar, focus groups sometimes insure that tryed and true formulas ocurr again and again at the expense of new ideas.

Avoiding ESL Troublespots

Exercise 26.1   Nouns and Articles

Correct any errors in the use of nouns or articles in the following sentences.

EXAMPLE:

For help with this exercise, see handbook section 26 in *Successful College Writing*.

➤ ~~National~~ *The national* parks of the United States remind visitors of the great natural ~~beauties~~ *beauty* of this country.

1. The first American land set aside for a national public park was Yellowstone National Park, which was established in 1872 by a President Ulysses S. Grant.

2. Yellowstone National Park has not only the beautiful scenery but also the strange results of ancient volcanoes.

3. Underground lava left from the millions of years ago heats cold ground-water.

4. This heating results in hot springs, geysers, and the boiling muds.

5. Sequoia National Park, second national park established in the United States, is the home of many giant sequoia trees.

6. To the north of the Sequoia National Park is the third oldest national park, Yosemite National Park.

7. Like Sequoia National Park, Yosemite National Park offers the area of incredible beauty.

8. A waterfalls are found in some of our nation's oldest parks, such as Yosemite National Park and Niagara Reservation State Park.

9. Many other national parks have unusual natural formations; Denali National Park, for example, contains a highest mountain in North America.

10. A visitor who takes the time to see America's national parks will have a experience he or she will never forget.

For help with this exercise, see handbook section 26 in Successful College Writing.

Exercise 26.2   Count and Noncount Nouns

In each sentence, circle the correct count or noncount noun in parentheses.

EXAMPLE:

➤ Arielle got her (nail, (nails)) manicured for the wedding.

1. I plan to serve (shrimp, shrimps) at our party tomorrow night.

2. When you go to the store later, please pick up two pints of (cream, creams).

3. Please make the three (bed, beds) upstairs before you leave.

4. Did someone dust the (furniture, furnitures) in the living room?

5. The (smoke, smokes) from Paulie's cigar made me cough.

6. Please put the (book, books) back on the shelves where they belong.

7. I will sweep up the (sand, sands) in the front hall.

8. Tell Daniel that he must put all of his (tool, tools) back in the garage.

9. I don't want any of his (equipment, equipments) lying around when the guests arrive.

10. Let's check yesterday's and today's (mail, mails) to see who is coming to the party.

For help with this exercise, see handbook section 27 in Successful College Writing.

Exercise 27.1   Verbs

Correct any errors in the use of the underlined verbs in the following sentences. Some sentences may be correct as written.

EXAMPLE:

➤ Carlos Santana ~~have~~ some American radio hits with English lyrics and some with Spanish lyrics.
has had

1. As a young boy in Mexico, Carlos Santana learned <u>playing</u> the clarinet and violin.

2. From his early years, Carlos Santana never stopped <u>to play</u> instruments.

3. When Santana was fourteen, he <u>taked</u> up the guitar.

4. The Santana family <u>was moving</u> to San Francisco in 1962, when Carlos was fifteen.

5. By 1967, Santana <u>has formed</u> a band.

6. The Santana Blues Band <u>begun</u> to make a name in San Francisco clubs.

7. San Francisco in the late 1960s <u>had been</u> a center for new musical talent, and Santana's band attracted attention.

8. The promoters of the 1969 Woodstock Music Festival asked the band, now called Santana, <u>playing</u> at their three-day outdoor concert.

9. Carlos Santana, who <u>just turned</u> twenty-two, led his band through a long composition called "Soul Sacrifice."

10. The crowds <u>were</u> delighted, and Santana <u>became</u> a star.

Exercise 27.2   Infinitives and Gerunds

For each of the following sentences, fill in the blank with the appropriate infinitive or gerund formed from the verb in parentheses.

For help with this exercise, see handbook section 27 in *Successful College Writing.*

EXAMPLE:

➤ It is easy to understand foreign students' _____*being*_____ [be] confused about grades in American university classes.

1. Most U.S. professors prefer their students _____ [work] independently, but professors do offer help to students who need it.

2. University policies forbid _____ [share] answers to a test.

3. However, instructors often encourage their students _____ [collaborate] in teams on projects other than tests and papers.

4. Universities consider _____ [plagiarize] written work as grounds for expulsion.

5. Dishonest students may jeopardize their relationship with other students who resent their _____ [cheat].

6. Instructors expect students _____ [do] the work for a class even if the work is not graded.

7. Some teachers believe that not grading an assignment enables students
_____ [judge] their own work.

8. If students want to improve their grades, professors often support students'
_____ [work] with a tutor.

9. But most professors don't appreciate their students' _____ [ask] about
grades on a test or paper in the middle of class.

10. Students who want class time to discuss grades risk _____ [anger] their
professors.

For help with
this exercise, see
handbook
section 27 in
*Successful College
Writing.*

Exercise 27.3   Modal Verbs

In the exercise below, circle the correct modal auxiliary.

EXAMPLE:

➤ (May/Would) you help me complete the assignment?

1. It doesn't rain very often in Arizona, but today it looks like it (can/might).
2. I know I (will/ought to) call my aunt on her birthday, but I always find an excuse.
3. Sarah (should/must) study for her English exam, but she is happier spending time
with her friends.
4. John (can/would) be the best person to represent our class.
5. Since the close presidential election of 2016, many people now believe they
(could/should) vote in every election.
6. All students (will/must) bring two pencils, a notebook, and a dictionary to class
every day.
7. (Would/May) you show me the way to the post office?
8. I (could/should) not ask for more than my health, my family, and my job.
9. Do you think they (could/can) come back tomorrow to finish the painting job?
10. A dog (should/might) be a helpful companion for your disabled father.

For help with
this exercise, see
handbook
section 28 in
*Successful College
Writing.*

Exercise 28.1   The Prepositions *in*, *on*, and *at*

Fill in each blank with the correct preposition: *in, on,* or *at.*

EXAMPLE:

➤ Putting fresh vegetables __*in*__ a salad makes a tremendous difference.

1. For many people, a feature of modern life is eating food that comes _____ cans or boxes.

2. _____ dinnertime, the convenience of frozen and canned food is undeniable, but there is a trade-off.

3. Many Americans have grown dissatisfied with the convenience foods available _____ the supermarket.

4. Frequently, shoppers are willing to look harder for foods grown _____ local farms.

5. Both farmers and city dwellers benefit when agricultural products are available _____ urban areas.

6. Farmers get extra money _____ their pockets, and city people get delicious vegetables.

7. Why should rural dwellers be the only ones to enjoy an ear of sweet corn _____ a July day?

8. Farm products grown nearby also retain more vitamins than foods that have traveled long distances _____ a truck or train.

9. Decades ago, when most Americans sat _____ the dinner table, the foods they ate were likely to come from local growers.

10. _____ the United States today, regional foods and local produce are making a healthy comeback.

Exercise 29.1   Adjectives

Correct any errors in the use of adjectives in the following sentences. Some sentences may be correct as written.

EXAMPLE:

> ~~Brightly colored,~~ fluffy quilts are great to have in the autumn and winter ~~cold~~ weather.
> *F   , brightly colored   cold*

1. The three first quilts that I made were not very intricate.

2. My fourth quilt's pattern, however, comprised 2,000 two-inch squares of multicolored fabric.

3. I found inspiration for the pattern in a short magazine article about memory quilts.

4. The article said that the most best memory quilts don't have fabric new in them.

For help with this exercise, see handbook section 29 in *Successful College Writing.*

5. To make the squares for my memory quilt, I cut up my old son's shirts and boxer shorts.

6. He has many drawers full of clothing that he has outgrown.

7. Assembling a memory quilt from these items was an opportunity good for me to make space in his bureau and to practice my sewing.

8. It was also an opportunity good for me to preserve his memories childhood.

9. My son considers it a treasured heirloom.

10. He thought the wonderful quilt was an idea, and he now wants me to make one bigger.

For help with this exercise, see handbook section 30 in *Successful College Writing*.

Exercise 30.1   Common Sentence Problems

Correct any common sentence problems in the following sentences.

EXAMPLE:

➤ Contagious diseases have frightened throughout history. people around the world.
                                          people around the world

1. Many people once believed that the twentieth century would produce medical miracles would bring an end to infectious diseases.

2. Medical research had not made at the end of the twentieth century this wish a reality.

3. Vaccines removed from the list of childhood diseases some terrible illnesses, such as polio.

4. One dangerous disease completely disappeared in the twentieth century was smallpox.

5. However, a few laboratories can still provide to trusted researchers access to samples of the virus.

6. Ordinary people forgot about smallpox their fears, but other diseases soon took its place.

7. The AIDS epidemic struck in the 1980s many previously healthy young people.

8. AIDS proved that medical science could declare total victory never over disease.

9. In the same decade, other terrifying new viruses that their existence was until recently unknown, such as Ebola, raced through local populations.

10. Medicine today can reveal much more about diseases than people knew during medieval plagues, but not always can this knowledge save the lives of sick people.

Exercise 30.2   Forming Negative Sentences

Rewrite each sentence in the space provided so that it correctly expresses a negative statement.

EXAMPLE:

➤   The president will veto the tax bill.

The president will not veto the tax bill.

1. Speed limits are a good idea.

2. Hector knows the baseball scores.

3. He is a baseball fan.

4. Olga understands the importance of math class.

5. Medical careers are where math skills make the most difference.

6. Conversation is acceptable in the library.

7. Morning is the hardest time for Julia to concentrate.

8. Young hunters can shoot safely.

9. Marco always worries about the health of his relatives in Brazil.

10. The high school may build a new gymnasium.

For help with this exercise, see handbook section 30 in *Successful College Writing*.

Answers to Exercises

Exercise P.1   Possible Answers (page 190)

1. Given that America is not the only nation with a tradition of rich food, Americans are right to wonder why obesity is not as big a problem in other countries as it is here in America.

2. Studies show that many children who are patients in hospitals enjoy visits from trained pet therapists.

3. Though I didn't finish the race, running in the Boston Marathon taught me a lot about determination and friendship.

4. Effective

5. Because the convenience of the Internet allows people to browse more profiles faster, online dating has become popular as a more efficient way of meeting people.

6. Effective

7. Keeping up with the intimate details of movie stars' lives has become more important to some American teenagers than knowing the crucial details of American history.

8. One of the places where we can still find harmful stereotypes of African Americans, Native Americans, and Arabs is in Disney movies.

9. Like many other supposedly public places, national parks now charge fees that are far too high for the average visitor.

10. Effective

Exercise P.2   Possible Answers (page 191)

1. Most ordinary Americans, however, like their government, need to borrow money in order to survive economically.

2. Modern technology, however, has made it possible for many Americans to avoid the exercise that was once a part of daily life in this country.

3. Therefore, parents who want to give their child a head start should begin to play classical music for the child even before the baby's birth.

Exercise P.3   Answers (page 193)

1. (5) Interestingly, the word *bagatelle* can also refer to a short poem or piece of music.

2. (4) According to folklore, when observers see one of these "shooting stars," they should make a wish. (5) Vaporized matter from burned-out meteors adds about ten tons to the mass of the earth every day.

3. (3) Running a family farm has never been easy. (7) The expense of new harvesting machines, called combines, and the need to get the harvest in as quickly as possible are major reasons farmers hire custom cutters rather than doing the work themselves.

Exercise P.4   Answers (page 194)

1.   One alternative to drugs for treating depression is the controversial Eye Movement Desensitization and Reprocessing or EMDR. This treatment is particularly useful for people who are depressed as a result of a traumatic event. ~~Prozac is also useful for treating depression. For those who don't respond to Prozac, doctors often recommend Zoloft.~~ In an EMDR session, the therapist makes hand motions or flashes a light in front of the patient's face while he or she talks about an upsetting experience. ~~People who have experienced trauma often need a lot of support.~~ Many people have

found this nontraditional therapy to be very helpful in processing their experiences, though no one knows for sure why EMDR works. _____*not unified*_____

2.   The advertisements that now appear before the movie are not effective because they only make moviegoers irritable. ~~Coke is one of the most frequently advertised products and one of the most recognized American brands. People often drink Coke or other soft drinks when they go to the movies.~~ Ads take away from the otherwise enjoyable experience of seeing a movie in the theater. These days, you have to sit through ten minutes of commercials before the previews start. ~~Advertisers also use product placement as a way to increase their product's visibility.~~ By the time the movie begins, you may already have been in your seat for half an hour. Because of this inconvenience, people may decide that it's worthwhile to wait for the DVD and skip the ads. Movie-theater owners would be wise to remember their paying audience and reconsider this partnership with advertisers. _____*not unified*_____

3.   unified

4.   One of America's most well-known and important court cases is the Scopes "Monkey Trial." ~~Students should learn their country's history at an early age. Knowing the past can help us predict the future.~~ In 1925, John Scopes, a high school biology teacher, was charged with violating state law by teaching the theory of evolution to his students. He believed he was teaching an important scientific theory, but others believed that evolution contradicted the story of creation told in the Bible. The trial became famous because so many people had such strong feelings on both sides. It has also remained relevant because we haven't come to a definitive conclusion about which ideas students should or should not learn in school. ~~There are many old conflicts that remain unresolved. For instance, people have been arguing for decades over whether or not abortion should be legal.~~ _____*not unified*_____

5.   More animal shelters should adopt a "no kill" policy. Controlling the stray animal population by euthanizing is not the best solution. Killing unwanted pets solves the problem of overpopulation only temporarily, and it creates a bigger problem because it teaches people that animals are disposable. ~~Many people don't consider snakes, iguanas, and other reptiles as pets. When I was seven, I adopted a snake from our local shelter, and he turned out to be a wonderful pet.~~ We need to learn to be kinder and more responsible when it comes to animals. We need to have pets fixed and accept them even when they have special needs. ~~We need to accept humans with special needs as well.~~ Many of the animals in shelters are there because they were neglected or mistreated. If we change our own behavior, fewer animals will end up abused and unwanted. _____*not unified*_____

6.   Buying a house is not always a good investment. People who sell their houses after owning them for only a couple of years often lose money. ~~Spending money on a computer is not always a good investment either. Computers lose their value very quickly. Unless the buyer uses the computer for work, money spent on a computer is money lost.~~ People who don't buy enough insurance for their homes can lose money if there is a fire, flood, or other disaster. Houses also require a lot of maintenance. When people sell their houses, often they find it difficult to make back the money they spent fixing up the house. Sometimes people are better off investing their money in something that does not cost so much. _____*not unified*_____

7. unified

8. Hilary Swank is a positive role model for young actresses. ~~Beyoncé Knowles is a good role model for future dancers and singers. Many girls look up to their mothers as well.~~ Unlike many successful women in the movie industry, Swank is not afraid to challenge herself when choosing roles. In both *Boys Don't Cry* and *Million Dollar Baby,* Swank focuses not on looking pretty but on inhabiting her characters and their difficult lives. Her determination and willingness to take these risks may come in part from her background. She was not born into a rich or privileged family and, like some of the characters she plays, she has had to work very hard to achieve her goals. ~~Many famous people have rough starts. Beyoncé Knowles did not come from a rich family.~~ It's important for young girls to see a successful movie star who has dedication, integrity, and a real love of acting. _____ *not unified* _____

Exercise P.5   Possible Revisions (page 198)

1. A family gathering is supposed to fill us with a joyful sense of belonging, but it may not. Getting together for a family event, such as Thanksgiving dinner, can produce anxiety, anger, or depression just as often as it results in a warm, satisfied glow. People who are thrown together because they are related — by blood or by marriage — don't necessarily understand or like each other especially well. When relatives and in-laws get together, there are bound to be members of the group who don't get along. In my family, for example, my brother Philip and my aunt Julia are likely to get into an argument about some topic. Because family members are supposed to love each other, Philip and Julia usually try to talk with each other politely, never going into much depth or discussing dangerous topics such as politics, but the strain of trying to be nice can make them tense. And if they both have a few beers, the two of them don't even really try to chat any longer; they just glare at one another from their respective corners of the long dining-room table. Finally, Philip makes a sarcastic remark, Julia spits back a furious reply, and the rest of us feel embarrassed.

2. A movie can't be good unless all of the pieces — from the directing and screenwriting to the casting and music — come together successfully. I recently saw *Titanic* and thought that the concept and special effects were great, but the script was padded with laughable lines and two completely unnecessary gunfights. The script isn't always the problem; in *She's Gotta Have It,* for example, there was some fine writing, but the lead actress, Tracy Camilla Johns, never let the audience forget she was only playing a role. In contrast, Sean Penn and Christopher Walken were convincing as father and son in *At Close Range,* but the events in that movie happened so slowly that I wondered what the director, James Foley, was thinking. Even if everything else is on target, overbearing music can ruin a good scene, as in parts of *Saving Private Ryan,* where composer John Williams doesn't seem to trust the audience to know what to feel. With so many variables, it's a wonder that any good movies exist. They do, of course; *Rushmore* and *Big Night* are just two examples of recent films whose witty scripts, fine acting, crisp pace, and mood-enhancing music made audiences feel that everything about them was right.

3. Children should have a dog or cat as soon as they are old enough to play gently with it and avoid hurting it. Feeding and cleaning up after a pet is a good experience for any child. If parents are firm with their children and don't do their animal-care chores for them, the children will learn how to behave responsibly; it's

hard to ignore or forget a beloved dog waiting for his little owner to feed and walk him. Additionally, having a pet can teach children about loving and protecting a creature weaker than themselves; any child who has ever held a contented, purring cat will find it very hard to be cruel to any animal. Responsibility and empathy are valuable lessons for children to learn and can help them grow into humane, decent adults. Finally, having a dog or cat can be a reward in itself — the animal returns affection and can actually make a child's life happier. At times, such as when parents or friends have disappointed a child, the family dog or cat will be a steadfast companion. Most adults who had a pet in childhood have wonderful memories of a much-loved Fido or Fluffy.

Exercise P.6   Answers (page 198)

1. underdeveloped
2. underdeveloped
3. well developed
4. underdeveloped
5. well developed
6. underdeveloped
7. underdeveloped
8. underdeveloped

Exercise P.7   Possible Revisions (page 202)

1.   The French may still have the international reputation of being the people most interested in gourmet food, **but** Americans are quickly gaining **gastronomical ground. Once**, "American food" meant fast foods like hamburgers and hot dogs, **and in fact**, people around the world still associate these foods with American culture. **That perception is not entirely accurate now**: U.S. food lovers may seek out the best burgers, fries, and barbecue foods, **but** they also want to sample foods from ethnic cultures within the United States and **from** other countries. **Today**, people want the best of what American produce has to offer and will go far to find fresh, local ingredients that are expertly prepared.

2.   Modern conceptions of timekeeping owe a lot to the ancient Babylonians. **They** gave people today the twelve-month year, the twenty-four-hour day, the sixty-minute hour, and the sixty-second minute. The number *twelve* was significant to the **Babylonian culture because the people** noticed that there were usually twelve full moons in a year. **Therefore**, the Babylonian calendar contained twelve months of thirty days each. **Because** five days were left over each year, every six years they had to add an extra month to the year. **Continuing to emphasize the mystical number** *twelve*, **the Babylonians** divided the day and night into twelve hours each. **In addition to** *twelve,* the number *sixty* was important to **this culture because it** can be evenly divided by many integers — two, three, four, five, six, ten, twelve, fifteen, twenty, and thirty. **Consequently, Babylonian time** divided each hour into sixty minutes and each minute into sixty seconds. **Later**, the Romans changed the length of some Babylonian months from thirty to thirty-one or twenty-eight days, **but** the Babylonians' other time measurements survive to this day.

3.   The Restoration period in England, which began with the return of the monarchy in 1660, was marked by the kind of public behavior on the part of aristocrats and courtiers that would still provoke a shocked reaction today. **The Restoration king**, Charles II, served as the model of moral—or immoral—behavior for members of his court. **Charles had** no children by his wife, **but** he had a large number of children by his several mistresses. **Following the king's example**, young male courtiers boasted of numerous love affairs. **To please these aristocrats**, court poets and dramatists composed bawdy, amoral literary works. Many **of these works** contained words and suggestions that even modern newspapers would not print. **During the Restoration**, the public loved to attend performances of plays **even though** simply being seen at a theater could give a person a questionable reputation. The clergy and other representatives of moral authority protested the literary, theatrical, and personal misbehavior of the aristocrats. **Eventually**, bawdiness became less fashionable, **and** a much more conservative age followed the Restoration.

Exercise P.8   Answers (page 203)

Title	**More Than Just a Place to Sleep**
Introduction	*Thesis:* Though it requires some preparation and adaptability, staying at a traditional Japanese hotel, or *ryokan,* is an enjoyable and worthwhile way for a Western visitor to learn about Japanese culture.
Body Paragraph 1	Finding a *ryokan*

- locate Web sites that list *ryokans* (6)
- determine your price range
- decide how formal or informal a *ryokan* you'd like (2)
- make advance reservations

Body Paragraph 2   Apparel etiquette in a *ryokan*

- take off your shoes when you enter the *ryokan* and put on slippers
- take off the slippers when walking on the tatami mats (3)
- wear *geta* (wooden clogs) if you stroll around the *ryokan* grounds
- wear your *yukata* (robe provided by the *ryokan*) when in the *ryokan* (4)
- *yukatas* should be worn left side over right; right side over left is for funerals (7)
- wear a *tanzen* (outer robe) over your *yukata* if you get cold

Body Paragraph 3   Japanese bath etiquette

- Japanese often bathe before dinner
- in changing room, put *yukata* in basket provided
- wash yourself in the bathing area using shower or basin before entering the public bath (9)

- do not drain the water from the tub when finished
- dry yourself thoroughly before returning to the changing room (8)

Body Paragraph 4   Engaging with your host or hosts
- learn a few key phrases in Japanese
- ask about the building and garden
- ask about the best sights to see in their town (5)

Body Paragraph 5   A day in the life of a different culture
- be willing to try unusual breakfast foods, like cold squid and miso soup (1)
- enjoy the serenity of life without television
- try meditating
- adjust to the firmness of a futon mattress (10)

Conclusion   While staying in a familiar Western-style hotel might feel easier, after a night or two in a *ryokan,* you'll find yourself more mindful of Japanese culture and traditions, and remarkably refreshed.

Exercise E.1   Possible Answers (page 205)

1. American parents choose carefully when naming their children.
2. Comparing popular names of today and of the past shows how much our ideas about naming children have changed.
3. Girls' names have changed the most.
4. Forty years ago, most baby girls received traditional names rather than unusual ones.
5. Some of the older names gradually became less popular, and newer names, like Jennifer, now a perennial favorite, took their place.
6. Today, parents often give their daughters names that were once considered masculine, like Sidney or Taylor.
7. Some parents try to make their daughters' names seem unusual by spelling a traditional name in a nontraditional way.
8. Boys' names, however, have not changed as noticeably.
9. For decades the most popular boys' name has been Michael.
10. Perhaps, as the results of a recent poll suggest, parents think having an unusual name helps girls and harms boys.

Exercise E.2   Possible Answers (page 206)

1. Nicotine, which is an addictive drug, is an ingredient in cigarettes.
2. No smoker sets out to become addicted to cigarettes, but most people have difficulty stopping once they start smoking.
3. Movies can affect young people profoundly; they often portray smokers as glamorous and sexy.

4. Many thirty-year-old people who do not smoke are unlikely to begin smoking.

5. The tobacco companies need new customers, and they are more apt to find such customers among the younger generations.

6. When some teenagers take up smoking, they don't consider the possible consequences.

7. The Joe Camel cartoon advertisements were controversial because cartoons often appeal to children.

8. The Joe Camel advertising campaign was withdrawn, and new restrictions have been placed on tobacco ads.

9. Smoking can be unsightly and unhealthy, but it is legal.

10. The number of lawsuits against tobacco companies has risen recently; families have argued that tobacco companies are to blame for the deaths of their loved ones.

Exercise E.3   Possible Answers (page 207)

1. In the nineteenth century, criminal tendencies were mistakenly thought to be related to physical traits.

2. Phrenologists, who studied bumps on the skull, mapped the human head for anti-social protrusions.

3. They hoped that they could identify potential criminals before crimes occurred.

4. Carefully recording their findings, other researchers, followers of a pseudoscience called craniometry, measured the proportions of the human head.

5. Using measurements of skull circumference, craniometrists inferred conclusions about brain size and intelligence as well as criminality.

6. From the beginning, these scientists' studies were fatally flawed because they found what they expected to find.

7. Since these "sciences" fell out of favor in the mid-twentieth century, researchers have been focusing on psychology as a means of understanding criminal actions.

8. The debate over which influence is stronger, heredity or environment, continues among social scientists.

9. One of the key controversies among scientists, the issue may never be resolved to everyone's satisfaction.

10. In scientific inquiry, however, important questions generate useful research as well as theories that are later discredited.

Exercise E.4   Answers (page 208)

1. The United States uses large amounts of energy, **depends** heavily on oil, and imports much of that oil.

2. Burning oil for energy pollutes the air, causes global warming, destroys an irreplaceable commodity, and **wastes** resources.

3. During the 1970s, an embargo made oil expensive and **difficult** to get.

4. The oil crisis led to a wider interest in alternative energy sources that would be renewable, environmentally sound, and **less expensive** than oil.

5. Some new homes used solar heating, although it was expensive to install and still relatively untested.

6. Many Americans expected electric cars to be perfected and widely available by the end of the twentieth century.

7. Instead, the embargo ended, the cost of oil dropped, and gasoline prices **declined**.

8. At the same time, money to invent alternative energy technologies, to develop new products, and **to market** the products dried up.

9. Scientists and **environmentalists** who study the environment hope that there will be plentiful renewable energy sources someday.

10. It would be better to have alternative energy possibilities soon than **to wait** for the world's oil reserves to run dry.

Exercise E.5   **Possible Answers** (page 209)

1. Annual "Fashion Week" events in American and European cities draw big crowds.

2. Photographers, journalists, models, and celebrities attend shows by new and established designers.

3. Many people in the audience show off their model-thin bodies and photogenic faces.

4. Often, *haute couture* shows with their expensive, trend-setting fashions entice the largest numbers of eager spectators.

5. Designers do not expect ordinary people to wear *haute couture* garments.

6. Designers frequently consider their *haute couture* creations to be works of art rather than mere outfits.

7. Only runway models can wear such clothing in public.

8. Other people attract ridicule in *haute couture* clothes.

9. Dressers can drape clothes more easily on models who have very thin bodies.

10. The spectacle impresses some people more than the clothes do.

Exercise E.6   **Possible Answers** (page 209)

Americans have recently been **forced to accept** the fact that anorexia nervosa, a disease of self-starvation, is becoming more widespread. Anorexia sufferers are overwhelmingly made up of teenage girls and young women. Most of them are white and come from middle-class or upper-class families. They are also usually **intelligent**. They seem to other people to have **nearly** every advantage. Their families and **friends** ordinarily have a **difficult** time comprehending why they will not eat. Because anorexia is a psychological disorder, the sufferers themselves may not **understand** what caused the onset of their illness. Anorexics have a **distorted** body image. They often believe they are **extremely** overweight unless they are dangerously **thin**. The disease is notoriously difficult to treat, even if the patient tries to **cooperate with** her doctors.

Exercise E.7 Possible Answers (page 210)

1. Every year, almost all college-bound high school juniors take one or more college admissions tests.
2. A high test score can help a student gain admission to a prestigious college.
3. Test-preparation courses, which give students practice exams to measure their progress, are becoming popular.
4. These courses can cost hundreds of dollars.
5. Educators disagree about whether test-preparation courses actually help students prepare for the exam and for college work.
6. Many students who take a standardized test before and after a test-preparation course show at least some improvement in their scores after the course.
7. The amount of improvement may be only a few percentage points.
8. Opponents of the courses argue that by taking them, wealthy students can, in effect, buy a better score.
9. Others say that the scores of students who take test-preparation courses are not significantly higher than the scores of students who don't.
10. Many worried parents continue to pay for test preparation, reasoning that it can't hurt their children's chances.

Exercise E.8 Possible Answers (page 210)

1. For generations, women were considered to be spun-glass angels too fragile for sports.
2. Many people thought that women would die like a butterfly in a whirlwind if they were too physically active.
3. Even though these mistaken beliefs were widespread, women athletes have moved forward, hurdling over all obstacles.
4. Individual women athletes, like the track and golf star Babe Didrikson Zaharias, had to be as strong as a well-toned muscle.
5. During World War II, a women's baseball league drew spectators like bees to a field of poppies when a shortage of male players depleted men's teams.
6. The end of the war drained the blood from the women's league.
7. The American women's movement of the 1970s was the beginning of a new season for women in sports.
8. A "battle of the sexes" took place in tennis during that decade, when Billie Jean King, a star female player, made Bobby Riggs, an avowed "male chauvinist" who had challenged her, look as weak as a newborn baby's grip.
9. In the following decades, some individual women became sports heroes, like Florence Griffith Joyner, who could run like a cheetah.
10. Finally, in the 1990s, the popularity of women's basketball and soccer spread like the "wave" in a packed stadium.

Exercise E.9   Possible Answers (page 211)

1. The treatment of mental illness has troubled societies throughout history.
2. A thousand years ago, observers thought mental disturbance proved that the sufferer was possessed by demons.
3. Many mentally ill people died in the course of treatment for demonic possession.
4. Belief in demonic possession eventually decreased in much of the world.
5. Instead, doctors and others classified mental illness as a kind of disease.
6. Sufferers were frequently confined and, often, forgotten.
7. Officials decided that mentally ill people were antisocial, not sick.
8. Most healthy people rarely considered the mentally ill.
9. In the nineteenth century, a reformer, Dorothea Dix, investigated the treatment of the mentally ill in Massachusetts.
10. Her report shocked people so much that Massachusetts, and soon other states, legislated humane treatment for sufferers of mental illness.

Exercise 1.1   Answers (page 212)

1. verb
2. noun
3. verb
4. noun
5. pronoun
6. verb
7. noun
8. pronoun
9. verb
10. noun

Exercise 1.2   Answers (page 212)

1. Parents in the early twentieth century **were** warned that detective magazines could warp children's minds.
2. Pulp fiction about crime did indeed **become** rather lurid.
3. Correct
4. Many scholars have **given** Edgar Allan Poe credit for being the first author to write detective fiction in English.
5. Correct
6. Correct
7. Correct
8. Arthur Conan Doyle, the creator of Holmes and Watson, **was** amazed at the popularity of his fictional characters.

9. Correct

10. While not all detective stories are worthy of serious study, the best ones are **considered** by scholars to be very rewarding.

Exercise 1.3   Answers (page 213)

1. simple past
2. past progressive
3. present perfect
4. past perfect
5. simple present
6. simple future
7. past perfect
8. past perfect progressive
9. future progressive
10. simple future

Exercise 1.4   Answers (page 214)

1. subjunctive
2. indicative
3. indicative
4. subjunctive
5. imperative
6. indicative
7. subjunctive
8. indicative
9. indicative
10. indicative

Exercise 1.5   Answers (page 215)

1. adverb
2. adjective
3. adjective
4. adjective
5. adverb
6. adjective
7. adjective
8. adverb
9. adjective
10. adverb

Exercise 1.6   Answers (page 215)

1. preposition
2. preposition
3. conjunction
4. preposition
5. conjunction
6. conjunction
7. preposition
8. conjunction
9. conjunction
10. preposition

Exercise 2.1   Answers (page 216)

1. complete subject
2. simple subject
3. complete predicate
4. complete predicate
5. complete subject
6. simple predicate
7. simple predicate
8. complete predicate
9. simple subject
10. simple predicate

Exercise 2.2   Answers (page 217)

1. subject complement
2. object complement
3. direct object
4. subject complement
5. direct object
6. direct object
7. object complement
8. indirect object
9. indirect object
10. subject complement

Exercise 2.3   Answers (page 218)

1. appositive phrase
2. prepositional phrase

3. verbal phrase

4. verbal phrase

5. absolute phrase

6. appositive phrase

7. absolute phrase

8. prepositional phrase

9. verbal phrase

10. appositive phrase

Exercise 2.4   Answers (page 218)

1. Many superstitions date from classical or medieval times, <u>when belief in witchcraft was widespread</u>.

2. Superstitions were a way for people to explain <u>whatever threatened them</u>.

3. <u>Because cats were believed to be witches in disguise</u>, the fear of a black cat crossing one's path came about.

4. Walking under ladders has also long been considered unlucky; this superstition may survive <u>because it protects pedestrians from falling objects</u>.

5. Some people attribute to the Christian story of the Last Supper, <u>where thirteen people were present</u>, the origins of the superstitious fear of the number thirteen.

6. <u>Wherever it began</u>, fear of the number thirteen, or triskaidekaphobia, is still prevalent enough for many tall modern buildings not to have a thirteenth floor.

7. Early Romans believed <u>that sneezing was a sign of the plague</u>, so they feared it.

8. The method <u>they invented</u> to protect a sneezer was to say, "God bless you."

9. In the United States today, it is common to say "God bless you" — or "Gesundheit," <u>which is German for "health"</u> — following a sneeze.

10. Superstitions from the past may seem silly today, but <u>who knows what strange customs of the present will be ridiculed in the future?</u>

Exercise 2.5   Answers (page 219)

1. simple

2. complex

3. simple

4. compound

5. complex

6. complex

7. simple

8. compound

9. simple

10. compound-complex

Exercise 3.1   Possible Answers (page 220)

1. There are older and more valuable manuscripts than the Voynich.

2. However, there is none more mysterious. The Voynich is still puzzling scholars many years after its discovery.

3. This manuscript was written in a code. So far, no one has been able to solve it.

4. Because the origins of the manuscript are unclear, the puzzle is doubly difficult.

5. No one knows what country it came from.

6. Therefore, it is very hard to determine the language the code represents. This makes decoding it even more troublesome.

7. Correct

8. The writing does not resemble any letters that can be traced to a known alphabet.

9. The manuscript contains many beautiful illustrations. It depicts plants, people, and other seemingly unrelated images.

10. The Voynich manuscript is such an intriguing mystery that some scholars might actually be disappointed to learn all of its secrets.

Exercise 4.1   Possible Answers (page 221)

1. Mae West began as a child star. The career of "Baby Mae" took off when she performed at a local Brooklyn theater's amateur night.

2. At the age of nineteen, West began performing on Broadway; she shocked audiences in 1911.

3. The voluptuous West became known for her suggestive clothing and even more famous for her suggestive wisecracks.

4. Attending black jazz clubs had introduced her to a new dance movement. She performed this "shimmy" on Broadway, and it became a trademark for her.

5. West was not satisfied for long with the theatrical roles she was offered; writing her own plays was one way to find good parts.

6. In 1925, she wrote a play called *Sex,* but no producer she contacted would bring it to the stage.

7. The following year, when West produced the play herself, advertisements for *Sex* were banned.

8. Nevertheless, the show played for nine months until it was closed down by the Society for the Suppression of Vice. West was arrested and spent eight days in jail.

9. In the 1930s and 1940s, Mae West took her naughty humor to Hollywood. While there she made a series of hit films and often wrote her own screenplays.

10. West made her final films in the 1970s. By that time Americans found her less scandalous, but her name was still a household word.

Exercise 5.1   Answers (page 222)

1. The festival called "Juneteenth," which people once recognized only in a few southern areas of the United States, **is** now much more widespread.
2. Correct
3. The surrender of the Confederate States **was** made official at Appomattox Courthouse on April 9, 1865.
4. From that day on, the Confederacy and the Union **were** again a single country.
5. Neither the northern states nor the southern states **were** now legally able to permit slave-owning, which had been officially outlawed in the United States several years earlier.
6. Correct
7. The story from those long-ago days **goes** that in Texas, slave owners murdered the messengers bringing word of emancipation.
8. Not until June 19, 1865, **was** the news able to reach the last group of Texas slaves.
9. Correct
10. Today, people celebrating Juneteenth **attend** concerts, films, and other cultural events.

Exercise 6.1   Answers (page 222)

1. The horrors of World War I **convinced** some artists that European society had to change radically.
2. Their reaction at first **consisted** of musical and performance events they called the Cabaret Voltaire.
3. Soon, however, the most influential members of the group **began** to focus on visual art.
4. **The artists chose** the name *Dada* at random.
5. They rejected older artistic traditions, including avant-garde ideas that **had** recently **become** popular.
6. Instead, the Dadaists **challenged** the whole concept of art.
7. Before the Dada movement **ended** in 1923, several of the artists had experimented with random arrangements of materials.
8. Sometimes they chose the material they **used** from items discarded by other people.
9. One artist, Marcel Duchamp, even **set** up ordinary objects at art shows, claiming that the act of choosing the objects made them art.
10. Dada was a rebellion, not an attempt to build a new tradition, so no identifiable stylistic legacy of the movement **remains** today.

Exercise 7.1   Possible Answers (page 223)

1. Many political analysts say that public distrust of the U.S. government began with Watergate.

2. That scandal's continuing legacy may make Watergate one of the most influential American events of the twentieth century.

3. Since the early 1970s, political scandals have rarely interested Americans; the scandals often seem to have very little effect.

4. Journalists provided the American people with a lot of information about the Iran-Contra hearings, but the public could not have cared less.

5. Could the indifference of most people have been the result of post–Watergate trauma?

6. If Americans expect politicians to be corrupt, government scandals will not surprise or even interest the public.

7. Ironically, the media's coverage of scandals seems to have made the public suspicious of journalists as well.

8. Cynicism about political and journalistic motives, which can spread contagiously, leads to apathy.

9. Many people are so apathetic that they refuse to vote.

10. If people do not believe that they can make a difference in the political process, the country becomes less democratic.

Exercise 7.2   Answers (page 224)

1. Meteorology has made many advances in the past few decades, but **it** still cannot answer a number of questions about tornados.

2. Every tornado has **its** own unique characteristics.

3. Correct

4. An F4 tornado or an F5 tornado can destroy everything in **its** path.

5. Scientists cannot predict precisely how strong any tornado will be before **it** happens.

6. One reason why meteorologists find it difficult to predict tornados is **their** many possible causes.

7. Tornados can form due to wind flow patterns, or **they** might be caused by other factors such as temperature, moisture, instability, and lift.

8. Correct

9. Either a few extra minutes of warning or more information about a storm's power would prove **its** effectiveness in saving lives.

10. People who live in a tornado zone should always know where **their** nearest safe area is.

Exercise 7.3   Answers (page 225)

1. **We** residents of the United States are considered by much of the rest of the world to be an unusually violent people.

2. Many researchers have debated **their** theories about violent behavior in this country.

3. Did the popular myth of the "Wild West" influence **us** and our ancestors?

4. Other industrialized nations and **we** have very different policies concerning guns.

5. Correct

6. Violence and justice are so intertwined for many Americans that disagreements between other people and **them** can erupt into fights.

7. Correct

8. There are defenders of violent films, TV shows, and video games **who** claim that entertainment reflects our tastes rather than influencing them.

9. Correct

10. Sometimes it seems that our worst enemies are **we**.

Exercise 8.1   Possible Answers (page 225)

1. West African villages have strong oral traditions in which parents and grandparents tell the younger people stories.

2. Before the Revolutionary War, slave traders forced ancestors of the people from those villages to come to the United States.

3. In their difficult new situation in this country, the Africans adapted their stories so that people could learn from them.

4. Although different stories had different messages, one kind of character came up over and over again.

5. The character is cunning and clever; he is a "trickster."

6. The stories about Br'er Rabbit are good examples of folktales whose hero is a trickster.

7. Many of the other animals want to eat Br'er Rabbit, who has only his wits to protect him.

8. Yet in every story, Br'er Rabbit not only escapes but he makes his enemies appear foolish as well.

9. Trickster characters like Br'er Rabbit showed slaves who heard these stories that they, too, could triumph by using cleverness when foes surrounded them.

10. Today, folklorists are exploring how early African Americans encouraged each other by telling stories of tricksters outsmarting powerful enemies.

Exercise 8.2   Possible Answers (page 226)

1. Most people think falsehoods are easy to spot.

2. They think that nonverbal signals show when someone is lying.

3. These signals, such as avoiding eye contact or hesitating before answering a question, are habits of truthful people as well.

4. Liars are hard to identify because no single trait always proves that a person is lying.

5. One problem with lie detection is that truthful people who are afraid they will not be believed may act suspiciously.

6. A few people are unusually good at identifying liars.

7. However, perhaps because these people are attuned to deceitful behavior, they are not especially good at identifying truth-tellers.

8. A stranger's lies may be easier to detect than a loved one's.

9. The better someone knows and likes another person, the more difficult it seems to be to spot his or her lies.

10. Finding it hard to believe that one's friends would try to deceive one is an understandable human characteristic.

Exercise 9.1   Possible Answers (page 227)

1. Many people go to a lot of trouble to look **attractive**.

2. In the United States, no one thinks a woman wearing high heels is dressed **strangely**.

3. Many Americans even go to **really** extreme lengths, such as having surgery, to be beautiful.

4. People can see the strangeness of beauty rituals **more clearly** if the rituals are unfamiliar.

5. For example, in China in past centuries, beautiful women had to have **tiny** feet.

6. To achieve this goal, families bound their daughters' feet so **tightly** that the feet could not grow.

7. Subcultures within the United States also have their own standards of beauty that may seem **odd** to people who are not part of the subculture.

8. For many young Americans, tattoos and body piercing are the **trendiest** fashion statements of the day.

9. They might argue that such beautification is no **more unusual** than plucking out one's eyebrows.

10. Parents, however, often feel **vast** relief if their children reach adulthood without tattoos.

Exercise 10.1   Possible Answers (page 227)

1. Recently, several sports that no one had heard of thirty years ago have gained popularity.

2. With a name that suggests their dangerous allure, extreme sports are attracting members of Generation X.

3. These "Generation X" games, which include snowboarding and sky-surfing, often involve going to inaccessible places.

4. Snow activities that can be done on remote mountaintops are especially popular.

5. Some of these sports, such as freestyle skiing and snowboarding, have become so widely accepted that participants can now compete in the Olympics.

6. Gasping at the antics of snowboarders, mountain bikers, and other athletes, fans can see that the sports world really has changed.

7. These "in-your-face" athletes are only a small part of what is interesting about the changes taking place in sports today.

8. Even fans of extreme sports know that the quest for adventure occasionally leads people into dangerous situations.

9. Environmentalists also point out that in some remote wilderness areas, extreme sports are unfortunately taking their toll on nature.

10. Whether people love them or hate them, extreme sports will probably continue to inspire extreme reactions.

Exercise 11.1   Answers (page 228)

1. In some places, the ocean is more than seven miles deep.

2. Enormous pressure and complete darkness in the depths make it difficult for humans to discover what is down there.

3. Correct

4. The sheer size of the ocean depths indicates that there may be many more species down there than are found on land.

5. Correct

6. Correct

7. Is it also possible that the actions of humans are affecting life at the bottom of the sea?

8. Biologists who have recently measured the food supply on the ocean floor might be moved to exclaim, "It seems to be dwindling!"

9. Most of the food that reaches the bottom comes from near the surface, where there is light.

10. Warmer surface temperatures may be reducing the food supply at the bottom, and who has more influence on global warming than human beings?

Exercise 12.1   Answers (page 229)

1. Breeders have long prized their swiftest, most graceful horses and raced them.

2. Correct

3. Harness racehorses pull small, lightweight vehicles handled by a driver.

4. Harness racing falls into the two categories of trotting and pacing.

5. The most famous event in harness racing, the Hambletonian, is a mile-long trotting race.

6. Harness racing may be known mainly to enthusiasts, but even people who appreciate very little about horse racing are familiar with thoroughbred racing.

7. Correct

8. The best-known events in thoroughbred racing, the Kentucky Derby, the Preakness Stakes, and the Belmont Stakes, are the three races that make up the Triple Crown.

9. All of the Triple Crown races, which vary in length, are for three-year-old horses.

10. In the twentieth century, only eleven horses won thoroughbred racing's Triple Crown.

Exercise 12.2   Answers (page 230)

1. Several years ago, many police departments ignored minor violations of the law and concentrated on bigger crime problems.

2. Today, however, the "broken window" theory is widely accepted.

3. According to this popular theory, allowing broken windows to remain unrepaired leads to a loss of hope in a community.

4. Correct

5. Similarly, if petty crimes are ignored in a neighborhood, people there may feel that larger crimes are acceptable as well.

6. Correct

7. But can a police officer walking a beat really be more effective than a patrol car?

8. Some experts believe that police should be required to live in the communities that they serve.

9. Correct

10. Different methods of community policing may work in different areas, but the goal should always be to keep communications open between the public and the police.

Exercise 13.1   Answers (page 230)

1. Many Americans think of the years after World War II as a golden era, a time before modern complexities made life more difficult.

2. Even without considering the quality of life at that time for women and minorities, an idyllic view of the mid-twentieth century ignores other issues.

3. Correct

4. The Soviet Union, an ally of the United States during World War II, took control of the governments of neighboring countries; China, after a civil war, fell under Communist rule; and the Korean conflict, in which Americans were involved, seemed to prove that Communists wanted to take over as much land as possible.

5. Correct

6. Senator Joseph McCarthy may have shared this fear; he certainly capitalized on it to advance his political career.

7. In 1950, McCarthy announced that he had a list of Communists who held positions in the U.S. State Department.

8. Correct

9. Eventually, more than 150 film workers, including performers, directors, and writers, were blacklisted by the Hollywood studios.

10. For the first half of the 1950s, anti-Communist leaders were very powerful in the United States; however, by 1955 McCarthy was in disgrace, and in 1957 the courts determined that membership in the Communist Party should no longer be a criminal offense in this country.

Exercise 14.1   Answers (page 231)

1. In 1910, Robert Falcon Scott led his second expedition to Antarctica with two objectives: to collect scientific data and to be the first humans at the South Pole.

2. The years before World War I were a heady time for exploration of the frozen Antarctic continent.

3. The story of Scott's difficult journey continues to fascinate armchair adventurers even though the expedition was, in many ways, a failure.

4. After arriving in Antarctica, Scott's scientists began their work: they collected specimens, surveyed the land, and recorded twelve volumes of data.

5. Correct

6. Scott stuck to his original timetable for the South Pole journey: he did not want to engage in a race.

7. Scott and his men set out for the South Pole in the Antarctic summer of 1911, which is the winter season in the Northern Hemisphere.

8. Correct

9. As they traveled back to their base camp, death took all five men: Scott, Titus Oates, Edgar Evans, Henry Bowers, and Edward Wilson.

10. Correct

Exercise 15.1   Answers (page 232)

1. The film producer shouted excitedly, "Everyone loves Shakespeare because he used so many familiar quotations!"

2. "When we make movies based on Shakespeare plays," he added, "we don't have to pay royalties to the writer."

3. Films based on Shakespeare plays try to reveal the relevance of his work to a modern audience.

4. Although Shakespeare lived four hundred years ago, his work is currently in demand in Hollywood.

5. *West Side Story, 10 Things I Hate About You,* and *She's the Man* are just a few of Hollywood's interpretations of Shakespeare's plays.

6. The producer commented, "When I hear that a new film will be based on Shakespeare, I wonder, like Juliet, 'What's in a name?'"

7. If the name "Shakespeare" were not involved, would filmmakers be as interested in the material?

8. Shakespeare's plays are frequently performed in theaters, too, and several young playwrights recently wrote works based on his sonnets.

9. Hamlet, perhaps Shakespeare's most famous character, laments "Alas, poor Yorick! I knew him, Horatio, a fellow of infinite jest, of most excellent fancy."

10. Othello, one of Shakespeare's most complex characters, laments that he "loved not wisely, but too well."

Exercise 16.1   Answers (page 233)

1. Correct
2. "[A]ll men are . . . endowed by their creator with certain inalienable rights, . . . among these are life, liberty, and the pursuit of happiness."
3. ". . . Thomas Jefferson wanted the Declaration of Independence to say that all men were 'created independent.'"
4. Elizabeth Cady Stanton's "Declaration of Sentiments" announces, "[W]e anticipate no small amount of misconception, misrepresentation, and ridicule. . . ."
5. "Stanton's 'Declaration of Sentiments' was based . . . on the language Jefferson had used in the Declaration of Independence."
6. Correct
7. "Allusions to the language of familiar literature . . . can lend authority to a text that uses them well."
8. Lincoln went on, "Fondly do we hope . . . that this mighty scourge of war may speedily pass away."
9. Martin Luther King Jr. expressed the wish that his children would be judged "by the content of their character."
10. "Repetition of structure can be an effective rhetorical device."

Exercise 17.1   Answers (page 234)

1. African **chiefs**' stories led a German explorer to the stone ruins in Mashonaland, now in Zimbabwe, in 1871.
2. The explorer, **whose** name was Karl Mauch, tried to find out who had built the once great city.
3. The tribes nearby could not answer **Mauch's** question, but they knew gold had been found there.
4. The **Africans** called the site *Zimbabwe*.
5. Correct
6. He thought perhaps the **city's** builder was the Queen of Sheba.
7. An **archeologist's** findings later demonstrated that the city was about six hundred years old and that it had been built by African natives.
8. The Shona tribe probably built the first walls on the site, but **its** more complex structures were added later by the Rozwi tribe.
9. The Rozwi probably erected the temple, which was inhabited by Rozwi ruler-priests until their empire's end in the **1830s**.
10. The legends about the origins of the city persisted for a long time, perhaps because of white South **Africans**' and Europeans' resistance to the idea that black Africans had built the impressive structures.

Exercise 18.1   Answers (page 235)

1. Bad movies (some of which are quite enjoyable to watch) often have a cult following.
2. Some films routinely make every critic's list of worst films (usually, these movies are so bad they are funny).
3. A few filmmakers (like Ed Wood) and movie companies (like American International Pictures) have acquired fame among fans of bad movies.
4. Roger Corman's American International Pictures (AIP) churned out innumerable inexpensive, quickly made films.
5. One Corman film, *Little Shop of Horrors* (1960), was filmed in less than three days.
6. But the director Edward D. Wood Jr. (1924–1978) has a special place in the world of bad movies.
7. Wood gained new fame with Tim Burton's film biography, *Ed Wood* (1994).
8. Like Corman's movies, Wood's were made very quickly, but Wood (unlike Corman) thought he was making great films.
9. Wood's "masterpiece," *Plan 9 from Outer Space* (Bela Lugosi's last film), is a science fiction and horror film with bad acting, dreadful writing, and laughable special effects.
10. Wood said that "*Plan 9* [was his] pride and joy."

Exercise 19.1   Possible Answers (page 236)

1. Songbirds are a part of our national heritage—each state has its own official bird.
2. Some states have official birds unique to the region.
3. The nene—Hawaii's state bird—is a goose found only on those islands.
4. In Salt Lake City, a statue of a seagull, which is Utah's state bird, honors the birds that ate a huge swarm of locusts—without the birds, most crops would have been eaten by the insects.
5. Other states share popular state birds—the cardinal, the meadowlark, and the mockingbird are all official birds in at least five states.
6. When Americans think of spring, they often think of songbirds chirping in the trees.
7. For many years, the Audubon Society—an organization devoted to nature study—has studied populations of songbirds.
8. Birdwatchers—mainly trained volunteers—count birds in small local areas during the year-end holiday season.
9. The numbers of some songbirds—though fortunately not all—have declined alarmingly.
10. Although most people appreciate the sights and sounds of songbirds, they may not realize how modern human habits interfere with many birds' lives.

Exercise 20.1   Answers (page 237)

1. At the turn of a new century and a new **millennium**, many people reflected on historical changes that had taken place in the previous hundred years.

2. In the late 1990s, Americans began making lists reflecting their choices of the greatest **events**, **literature**, people, and **films** of the century.

3. Most Americans would agree that the two **world wars** shaped the twentieth century and this country's role in it.

4. List makers might, however, dispute the importance of *Ulysses* or *Gone with the Wind*.

5. Between the beginning and the end of the twentieth century, the United States changed from a minor player in global politics into the single undisputed **world power**.

6. Technology also advanced dramatically in the century of television, the *Apollo* space missions, and personal computers.

7. Of course, technology was sometimes used for evil purposes, as the **Holocaust** and nuclear weapons proved.

8. Some people would even argue that a significant development of the century was an increasing concern for the environment — in the United States, in Europe, and in parts of the **former** Soviet Union, among other places.

9. The trend toward urbanization saw people moving from rural areas to cities, with the result in this country that the **Great Plains** grew emptier while the **coasts'** population increased.

10. Only historical distance will reveal whether the twentieth century was "**the** best of times" or "**the** worst of times."

Exercise 21.1   Answers (page 238)

1. When disasters strike, victims count on international organizations like the Red Cross and Doctors without Borders.

2. A **doctor's** help is often the most desperately needed form of aid.

3. People often offer canned goods and blankets, while major **corporations** receive tax benefits for donations of drugs and other medical supplies.

4. When Hurricane Mitch devastated Honduras, many U.S. **citizens** were quick to help.

5. A **registered nurse** who is willing to travel to the disaster area can provide needed services.

6. For several years, volunteer doctors have tried to alleviate the AIDS crisis in **Africa**.

7. In some situations, **such as** during outbreaks of deadly diseases or in war-torn areas, medical personnel risk their own lives.

8. Doctors from the Centers for Disease Control **(CDC) in Atlanta, Georgia**, travel the globe to isolate and study dangerous viruses.

9. The CDC doctors do not provide medical assistance in war zones, but other **organizations** do.

10. In the aftermath of bloody fighting, a U.N. peacekeeping force may arrive to find **international** doctors already at work.

Exercise 22.1   **Answers** (page 238)

1. John Lennon, Paul McCartney, George Harrison, and Ringo Starr were **four** young men from Liverpool, England, who formed what would become the most popular rock band of all time.

2. On January **25**, 1964, the Beatles' first hit entered the U.S. charts.

3. The song "I Want to Hold Your Hand" spent seven weeks at number one and **fourteen** weeks in the top **forty**.

4. Almost immediately, the Beatles began to attract **thousands** of screaming fans everywhere they went.

5. Throughout the **1960s**, the Beatles were the world's most popular group.

6. During the eight years of the Beatles' reign on the charts, they had more than forty **3**-minute pop hits.

7. By the **second** half of the decade, the Beatles had stopped touring.

8. They performed live together for the last time on the roof of **3** Savile Row, the headquarters of their doomed record company, Apple.

9. **One hundred fifty** employees worked for Apple, which eventually went bankrupt.

10. By no means did each Beatle earn **25** percent of the group's profits, for Lennon and McCartney wrote more than **90** percent of the songs.

Exercise 23.1   **Answers** (page 239)

1. Americans today get their information from CNN, the *New York Times,* electronic sources, and thousands of other places.

2. Once, choices were limited: to find out about raising a child, for example, parents consulted Dr. Spock's book *Baby and Child Care.*

3. Now, magazines like *Parenting* compete with the new edition of Dr. Spock and dozens of other titles.

4. Obscure information is more accessible than ever, so a fan of the song "Telstar" can find *The Joe Meek Story,* a full-length biography of its producer.

5. A student wanting to learn about the dead language called Old English could consult Web sites like the one maintained by Georgetown University.

6. It may no longer be possible for a single person to know all about, for example, biology.

7. Once, the term *Renaissance man* or *Renaissance woman* referred to a person well educated and talented in many subjects.

8. Leonardo da Vinci, the original Renaissance man, not only painted the *Mona Lisa* but also wrote botanical treatises and devised remarkable engineering plans.

9. Today, we do not expect the builder of the ocean liner *Queen Elizabeth II* to know other subjects.

10. A lifetime of study may lie behind a single article in the *New England Journal of Medicine*.

Exercise 24.1   Answers (page 240)

1. Does buying lottery tickets and entering sweepstakes make a person self-employed?

2. The odds of winning a major lottery prize are often over a million to one.

3. Yet many people, including desperately poor ones who cannot afford the tickets, buy large numbers of them when the jackpot is high and the odds are worst.

4. A sensible approach to such sky-high odds would be not to enter the lottery at all.

5. Sweepstakes are well known to anyone with a mailbox.

6. Unlike lotteries, apparently free sweepstakes do not require any cash investment other than the price of a stamp.

7. Yet many sweepstakes imply that buying a magazine subscription or a product improves the chances of winning.

8. Some sweepstakes companies have been accused of trying to dupe customers who do not read the fine print.

9. Some elderly people have thrown away their great-grandchildren's inheritance, buying hundreds of products they don't need from sweepstakes advertisers.

10. The idea of getting rich with minimal work or investment is so strikingly attractive that many people put logic aside and come up with the money.

Exercise 25.1   Answers (page 241)

Focus groups consist of people selected to express **their** opinions about products **ranging** from sneakers and gum to movies. **Sometimes** people who are supposed to be experts on a subject are selected. When **companies** test a new product, they choose people who might **realistically** be expected to **buy** it. If marketers are **trying** out a new soft drink, for example, they might ask **teenagers** for their **advice**. A company **making** a **luxury** car would be more inclined to seek the **views** of upper-middle-class buyers. On other **occasions**, a focus group is picked at **random**. To find out how much **consumers** like a new TV show, a network might ask shoppers at a mall to watch an episode and discuss it with other **participants**. The network could **then** learn, not only what viewers like and dislike about the show, but also which groups are most **likely** to watch it. This information helps the network determine what changes to make in the show and what **sponsors** to approach. Of course, **since** many people **prefer** the familiar, focus groups sometimes **ensure** that **tried** and true formulas **occur** again and again at the expense of new ideas.

Exercise 26.1   Answers (page 241)

1. The first American land set aside for a national public park was Yellowstone National Park, which was established in 1872 by President Ulysses S. Grant.

2. Yellowstone National Park has not only beautiful scenery but also the strange results of ancient volcanoes.

3. Underground lava left from millions of years ago heats cold groundwater.

4. This heating results in hot springs, geysers, and boiling **mud**.

5. Sequoia National Park, **the** second national park established in the United States, is the home of many giant sequoia trees.

6. To the north of Sequoia National Park is the third oldest national park, Yosemite National Park.

7. Like Sequoia National Park, Yosemite National Park offers **an** area of incredible beauty.

8. **Waterfalls** are found in some of our nation's oldest parks, such as Yosemite National Park and Niagara Reservation State Park.

9. Many other national parks have unusual natural formations; Denali National Park, for example, contains **the** highest mountain in North America.

10. A visitor who takes the time to see America's national parks will have **an** experience he or she will never forget.

Exercise 26.2   Answers (page 242)

1. shrimp
2. cream
3. beds
4. furniture
5. smoke
6. books
7. sand
8. tools
9. equipment
10. mail

Exercise 27.1   Answers (page 242)

1. to play
2. playing
3. took
4. moved
5. had formed
6. began
7. was
8. to play
9. had just turned
10. correct

Exercise 27.2   Answers (page 243)

1. to work
2. sharing
3. to collaborate
4. plagiarizing
5. cheating
6. to do
7. to judge
8. working
9. asking
10. angering

Exercise 27.3   Answers (page 244)

1. might
2. ought to
3. should
4. would
5. should
6. must
7. would
8. could
9. can
10. might

Exercise 28.1   Answers (page 244)

1. in
2. At
3. at
4. on
5. in
6. in
7. on
8. on
9. at
10. In

Exercise 29.1   Answers (page 245)

1. The first three quilts that I made were not very intricate.
2. Correct

3. Correct

4. The article said that the best memory quilts don't have new fabric in them.

5. To make the squares for my memory quilt, I cut up my son's old shirts and boxer shorts.

6. Correct

7. Assembling a memory quilt from these items was a good opportunity for me to make space in his bureau and to practice my sewing.

8. It was also a good opportunity for me to preserve his childhood memories.

9. Correct

10. He thought the quilt was a wonderful idea, and he now wants me to make a bigger one.

Exercise 30.1   Possible Answers (page 246)

1. Many people once believed that the twentieth century would produce medical miracles that would bring an end to infectious diseases.

2. At the end of the twentieth century, medical research had not made this wish a reality.

3. Vaccines removed some terrible illnesses, such as polio, from the list of childhood diseases.

4. One dangerous disease that completely disappeared in the twentieth century was smallpox.

5. However, a few laboratories can still provide access to samples of the virus to trusted researchers.

6. Ordinary people forgot their fears about smallpox, but other diseases soon took its place.

7. The AIDS epidemic struck many previously healthy young people in the 1980s.

8. AIDS proved that medical science could never declare total victory over disease.

9. In the same decade, other terrifying new viruses whose existence was until recently unknown, such as Ebola, raced through local populations.

10. Medicine today can reveal much more about diseases than people knew during medieval plagues, but this knowledge cannot always save the lives of sick people.

Exercise 30.2   Answers (page 247)

1. Speed limits are not a good idea.

2. Hector does not know the baseball scores.

3. He is not a baseball fan.

4. Olga does not understand the importance of math class.

5. Medical careers are not where math skills make the most difference.

6. Conversation is not acceptable in the library.

7. Morning is not the hardest time for Julia to concentrate.

8. Young hunters cannot shoot safely.

9. Marco never worries about the health of his relatives in Brazil.

10. The high school may not build a new gymnasium.

16

Writing Self-Assessment

The two assessment tests that follow will help you and your instructor determine aspects of your writing that you need to improve. The first test (pp. 277–78) assesses your ability to develop and support ideas about a topic and express them clearly and correctly in an essay. The second test (pp. 278–84) measures your ability to recognize and correct errors in grammar, punctuation, and mechanics.

Writing Essays

Choose *either* Essay Assignment A or Essay Assignment B for this writing assessment test. Although the essay assignments are from courses in interpersonal communications and sociology, you do not need any background in these subject areas to write either essay. For whichever option you choose, then, draw from your personal experience for ideas for the essay. Be sure your essay is about the topic you choose and that it states, develops, and supports one main point about your topic. When you have finished drafting your essay, be sure to revise, edit, and proofread it. Your instructor will evaluate your final essay and identify any writing skills that need improvement. With your instructor's feedback, you will then be able to use the Action Plan Checklist (pp. 285–86) to find help with those skills that need improvement.

Essay Assignment A

Suppose you are taking a course in interpersonal communications and have been assigned a two-page essay on one of the following topics. Choose a topic, develop a thesis statement, and support your thesis with evidence.

1. Describe a communication breakdown you have observed or experienced, telling what happened, why it happened, and what could have been done to prevent it.
2. Pretend that you are preparing for a job interview. Describe the communication and leadership skills you would bring to the position of assistant manager at a department store.

3. Recall a conflict, disagreement, or argument you have had with someone. What feelings and emotions did you and the other person express? Explain how you communicated those feelings to each other and how the conflict was (or was not) resolved.

4. Explain how you can tell when a person doesn't mean what he or she says, using people you know as examples.

Essay Assignment B

Suppose you are taking a sociology course and have been assigned a two-page essay on *one* of the following topics. Choose a topic, develop a thesis statement, and support your thesis with evidence.

1. Describe one important function of the family in American life. Explain why it is important and what is expected of family members. Use your own family as an example.

2. Explain one important function of dating in the United States. Support your ideas with your own dating experiences.

3. Examine one major function of the wedding ceremony. Why is this function important? Use weddings that you have attended or been involved in as evidence to support your thesis.

Recognizing and Correcting Sentence Errors

Most of the following sentences contain errors; some are correct as written. Look in the <u>underlined</u> part of each sentence for errors in usage, punctuation, grammar, capitalization, or sentence construction. Then choose the one revision that corrects the sentence error(s). If the original sentence contains no errors, select "d. no change." Circle the letter of the item you choose as your answer.

1. <u>Lonnie and Robert should put his ideas together</u> and come up with a plan of action for the class project.
   a. Lonnie and Robert should put his idea together
   b. Lonnie and Robert should put her ideas together
   c. Lonnie and Robert should put their ideas together
   d. no change

2. The school district newsletter informs <u>all parents of beneficial programs for you and your children</u>.
   a. all parents of beneficial programs for your children.
   b. each parent about beneficial programs for you and your children.
   c. you of all beneficial programs for you and your children.
   d. no change

3. Margaret earned an A <u>on her term paper, consequently, she</u> was excused from taking the final exam.
   a. on her term paper; consequently, she
   b. on her term paper, consequently; she
   c. on her term paper consequently, she
   d. no change

4. Some students choose courses <u>without studying degree requirements these students often make</u> unwise choices.
   a. without studying degree requirements, these students often make
   b. without studying degree requirements. These students often make
   c. without studying degree requirements; so these students often make
   d. no change

5. Twenty-five band members <u>picked up their instruments from their chairs which were tuned and began to play</u>.
   a. picked up their tuned instruments from their chairs and began to play.
   b. picked up their instruments from their chairs tuned and began to play.
   c. picked up and began to play their instruments from their chairs which were tuned.
   d. no change

6. I am sure I <u>did good on my midterm exam</u> because it seemed easy to me.
   a. did awful good on my midterm exam
   b. did real good on my midterm exam
   c. did well on my midterm exam
   d. no change

7. In many American families, the financial decisions are made jointly by <u>husband and wife, the wife</u> makes most of the routine household decisions.
   a. husband and wife, in contrast the wife
   b. husband and wife the wife
   c. husband and wife. The wife
   d. no change

8. Professor Simmons <u>pace while he lectures</u>.
   a. pacing while he lectures.
   b. pace while he lecture.
   c. paces while he lectures.
   d. no change

9. When Tara set <u>the cup on the glass-topped table, it broke</u>.
   a. her cup on the glass-topped table, she broke it.
   b. the cup on the table with a glass top; it broke.
   c. it on the glass-topped table, the cup broke.
   d. no change

10. <u>Swimming to shore, my arms got tired.</u>
    a. My arms got tired swimming to shore.
    b. When I was swimming to shore, my arms got tired.
    c. My arms, swimming to shore, got tired.
    d. no change

11. Thousands of fans waited <u>to get into the stadium. Swarmed around the parking lot</u> like angry bees until security opened the gates.
    a. to get into the stadium. Swarming around the parking lot
    b. to get into the stadium; swarmed around the parking lot
    c. to get into the stadium. They swarmed around the parking lot
    d. no change

12. <u>After I left the college library I went</u> to the computer lab.
    a. After I left the college library, I went
    b. After leaving the college library I went
    c. After I left the college library; I went
    d. no change

13. <u>To be honest is better than dishonesty.</u>
    a. Being honest is better than dishonesty.
    b. To be honest is better than being dishonest.
    c. It is better to be honest than dishonest.
    d. no change

14. The amount of time <u>students spend researching a topic depends on his familiarity</u> with the topic.
    a. students spend researching a topic depends on his or her familiarity
    b. students spend researching a topic depends on their familiarity
    c. a student spends researching a topic depends on their familiarity
    d. no change

15. After Carlos completed <u>his term paper, he seems</u> less tense.
    a. his term paper, he seemed
    b. his term paper, he will seem
    c. his term paper, he is seeming
    d. no change

16. <u>When Maria tried to sign up for those courses in the fall, but they were full.</u>
    a. When Maria tried to sign up for those courses in the fall; however, they were full.
    b. Although Maria tried to sign up for those courses in the fall, but they were full.
    c. Maria tried to sign up for those courses in the fall, but they were full.
    d. no change

17. A course in nutrition <u>may be useful; it may help you make</u> wise food choices.
    a.   may be useful, it may help you make
    b.   may be useful it may help you make
    c.   may be useful; because it may help you make
    d.   no change

18. According to the reporter, <u>many pets are run over by automobiles roaming around untended</u>.
    a.   many pets are run over roaming around untended by automobiles.
    b.   many pets roaming around untended are run over by automobiles.
    c.   many pets who are run over by automobiles roaming around untended.
    d.   no change

19. You need to take <u>life more serious if you hope to do well</u> in school.
    a.   life more serious if you hope to do good
    b.   life more seriously if you hope to do well
    c.   life seriouser if you hope to do well
    d.   no change

20. Leon has already taken <u>three social sciences courses, Introduction to Psychology,</u> Sociology 201, and Anthropology 103.
    a.   three social sciences courses; Introduction to Psychology,
    b.   three social sciences courses: Introduction to Psychology,
    c.   three social sciences courses. Introduction to Psychology,
    d.   no change

21. <u>There's several people who can</u> advise you about the engineering program.
    a.   There are several people who can
    b.   There is several people who can
    c.   There's two people who can
    d.   no change

22. <u>In Chapter 6 of your book it describes</u> the causes of mental illness.
    a.   In Chapter 6 of your book, they describe
    b.   Chapter 6 of your book describes
    c.   In Chapter 6 of the book, it describes
    d.   no change

23. <u>Flood damage was visible crossing the river.</u>
    a.   Flood damage was visible, crossing the river.
    b.   Crossing the river, the flood damage was visible.
    c.   Flood damage was visible as we crossed the river.
    d.   no change

24. She had to leave the <u>van in the driveway. The heavy, wet snow halfway up</u> the garage door.
    a.   van in the driveway. The heavy, wet snow had piled halfway up
    b.   van in the driveway. Because of the heavy, wet snow halfway up
    c.   van in the driveway; the heavy, wet snow halfway up
    d.   no change

25. Mail <u>carriers who have been bitten by dogs are</u> wary of them.
    a.   carriers, who have been bitten by dogs, are
    b.   carriers who have been bitten, by dogs, are
    c.   carriers who, having been bitten by dogs, are
    d.   no change

26. Alfonso <u>need to practice</u> his clarinet every day.
    a.   needing to practice
    b.   needes to practice
    c.   needs to practice
    d.   no change

27. <u>Everyone should be sure to bring their notebook</u> to class on Wednesday.
    a.   Everyone should be sure to bring their notebooks
    b.   Everyone should be sure to bring his or her notebook
    c.   Everyone should be sure to bring his notebook
    d.   no change

28. <u>The television program ended Janelle read a book</u> to her son.
    a.   When the television program ended, Janelle read a book
    b.   The television program ended and Janelle read a book
    c.   The television program ended, Janelle read a book
    d.   no change

29. Georgia <u>replied "The way to a man's heart is through his stomach."</u>
    a.   replied "The way to a man's heart is through his stomach".
    b.   replied; "The way to a man's heart is through his stomach."
    c.   replied, "The way to a man's heart is through his stomach."
    d.   no change

30. The <u>plan to travel to three cities in two days seem</u> overly ambitious.
    a.   plan to travel to three cities in two days are
    b.   plan to travel to three cities in two days seems
    c.   plan to travel to three cities in two days do seem
    d.   no change

31. <u>You discover that your concentration improves</u> with practice, so now I can study more in less time.
    a. I discovered that my concentration improves
    b. You discover that concentration improves
    c. You discovered that your concentration improves
    d. no change

32. I couldn't watch the <u>rest of the football game. Because there was no chance that we could win</u> now. We were behind by three touchdowns.
    a. rest of the football game and there was no chance that we could win
    b. rest of the football game because there was no chance that we could win
    c. rest of the football game; because there was no chance that we could win
    d. no change

33. <u>"Shopping" Barbara explained "is</u> a form of relaxation for me."
    a. "Shopping" Barbara explained, "is
    b. "Shopping," Barbara explained "is
    c. "Shopping," Barbara explained, "is
    d. no change

34. <u>A balanced diet, exercising regularly, and to get enough sleep</u> are essential to good health.
    a. Eating a balanced diet, exercising regularly, and to get enough sleep
    b. A balanced diet, regular exercise, and enough sleep
    c. To eat a balanced diet, exercising regularly, and to get enough sleep
    d. no change

35. <u>The use of air bags was designed</u> to increase driver and passenger safety.
    a. Air bags were designed
    b. The use of air bags were designed
    c. Increased use of air bags was designed
    d. no change

36. The <u>articles and the book contains</u> the information I need.
    a. book and the articles contains
    b. articles and the book contain
    c. articles and the book has contained
    d. no change

37. Top firms are always <u>looking for skilled managers. People who can adapt</u> to changing times and rise to new challenges.
    a. looking for skilled managers; people who can adapt
    b. looking for skilled managers. People, who can adapt
    c. looking for skilled managers who can adapt
    d. no change

38. <u>Individuals and community groups can assist students in financial need, and</u> help them secure a good education.
    a.   Individuals and community groups, can assist students in financial need and
    b.   Individuals, and community groups can assist students in financial need, and
    c.   Individuals and community groups can assist students in financial need and
    d.   no change

39. <u>Someone left their briefcase</u> under the table.
    a.   Everyone left their briefcase
    b.   Someone left their briefcases
    c.   Someone left his or her briefcase
    d.   no change

40. Mustard is a versatile <u>seasoning and it can be</u> used to enhance the flavor of many dishes.
    a.   seasoning; and it can be
    b.   seasoning, and it can be
    c.   seasoning, therefore it can be
    d.   no change

41. We <u>spent our most happiest days</u> in the little cottage on the lake.
    a.   spent our happiest days
    b.   spent our more happiest days
    c.   spent our more happy days
    d.   no change

42. Swimming is an <u>excellent form of exercise, it produces</u> a good aerobic workout.
    a.   excellent form of exercise it produces
    b.   excellent form of exercise and it produces
    c.   excellent form of exercise because it produces
    d.   no change

For a guide to scoring your assessment, turn to p. 286.

Action Plan Checklist

The Action Plan Checklist below will help you find the appropriate resources for improving the writing skills that you and your instructor have identified as problem areas.

Resources

- **Part 7: Handbook: Writing Problems and How to Correct Them.** The Handbook section of *Successful College Writing* contains a systematic review of the rules that correspond to most of the topics listed under "Sentence Skills" in the Action Plan Checklist, as well as exercises to help you understand and apply the rules. If your instructor selected as your course text *Successful College Writing*, Brief Seventh Edition, which omits the handbook, you can find this material in the LaunchPad for *Successful College Writing*, Seventh Edition (**launchpadworks.com**).

- **LearningCurve and Additional Exercises for *Successful College Writing*.** The exercises in this book and in LearningCurve (accessible from **launchpadworks .com**) offer you practice in applying the principles presented in Part 7. This workbook contains additional exercises for all the topics listed in the Action Plan Checklist as well as other topics you may wish to review. LearningCurve and this workbook are designed so that you can check your answers immediately after completing an exercise. As you work through each exercise, be sure to take the time to discover why you answered any items incorrectly and, if you are still uncertain, to check with a classmate or your instructor.

Directions: Place a check mark next to each skill that you or your instructor identified as a problem area.

Skills That Need Improvement		Resources That Will Help You	
Paragraph Skills	✔	*Text/Handbook**	*Workbook*
Details–Relevant		Ch. 6	Exercise P.3
Details–Specific		Ch. 6	Exercise P.5
Topic Sentences		Ch. 6	Exercise P.1
Topic Sentences		Ch. 6	Exercise P.2
Sentence Skills			
Adjective and Adverb Usage		H9	Exercise 9.1
Capitalization		H20	Exercise 20.1
Colon Usage		H14	Exercise 14.1
Comma Splices		H4	Exercise 4.1
Comma Usage		H12	Exercises 12.1, 12.2
Dangling Modifiers		H10	Exercise 10.1
Sentence Fragments		H3	Exercise 3.1
Misplaced Modifiers		H10	Exercise 10.1
Mixed Constructions		H8	Exercise 8.2
Parallelism		Ch. 9	Exercise E.4
Pronoun-Antecedent Agreement		H7	Exercise 7.2
Pronoun Reference		H7	Exercise 7.1
Punctuation of Quotations		H15	Exercise 15.1
Run-On Sentences		H4	Exercise 4.1
Semicolon Usage		H13	Exercise 13.1
Shifts		H8	Exercise 8.1
Subject-Verb Agreement		H5	Exercise 5.1
Spelling		H25	Exercise 25.1
Verb Forms		H6	Exercise 6.1

*Handbook sections are preceded by the letter *H* in this chart.

Working through Your Action Plan

Once you have filled in the check marks in your Action Plan Checklist, use the following suggestions to achieve maximum success in improving your writing skills.

1. Begin by reading the appropriate section(s) in Chapters 6 and 9 and in Part 7 and studying the examples. You may have to read the material several times to grasp it fully.

2. Test your understanding of a particular rule or explanation by looking away from the text and writing the rule or principle in your own words in your journal. If you cannot do so, you do not fully understand the rule. Try discussing it with a classmate and your instructor and recording what you learn from them in your own words. When you can explain the principle or rule in your own words, you are more apt to understand and remember the material.

3. Once you are confident that you understand a rule or explanation for a sentence skill or problem, complete the corresponding exercise in the Handbook, the workbook, or online.

4. Set a deadline by which you will understand the rules and complete the exercises for all of your problem areas. Try to complete everything within the next two to three weeks. The sooner you understand this essential material, the sooner you will be fully prepared to write clear, effective essays.

Scoring and Interpreting Your Grammar Assessment

Score your assessment by using the answer key that follows. Each question assesses your ability to recognize and correct a particular sentence problem. In the answer key, circle the number of each item you answered incorrectly.

Answer Key: Error Correction Self-Assessment

Answer	Sentence Skill or Problem
1. c	Pronoun-Antecedent Agreement
2. c	Shift in Person
3. a	Comma Splice
4. b	Run-On Sentence
5. a	Misplaced Modifier
6. c	Adverb and Adjective Usage
7. c	Comma Splice
8. c	Subject-Verb Agreement
9. c	Pronoun Reference
10. b	Dangling Modifier
11. c	Sentence Fragment
12. a	Comma Usage
13. c	Parallelism
14. b	Pronoun-Antecedent Agreement
15. a	Shift in Tense

16. c	Mixed Construction
17. d	Semicolon Usage
18. b	Misplaced Modifier
19. b	Adverb and Adjective Usage
20. b	Colon Usage
21. a	Subject-Verb Agreement
22. b	Pronoun Reference
23. c	Dangling Modifier
24. a	Sentence Fragment
25. d	Comma Usage
26. c	Verb Form
27. b	Pronoun-Antecedent Agreement
28. a	Run-On Sentence
29. c	Punctuation of Quotation
30. b	Subject-Verb Agreement
31. a	Shift in Point of View
32. b	Sentence Fragment
33. c	Comma Usage
34. b	Parallelism
35. a	Mixed Construction
36. b	Subject-Verb Agreement
37. c	Sentence Fragment
38. c	Comma Usage
39. c	Pronoun-Antecedent Agreement
40. b	Comma Usage
41. a	Adverb and Adjective Usage
42. c	Comma Splice